IMAGES
of America

HISTORIC BETHABARA PARK

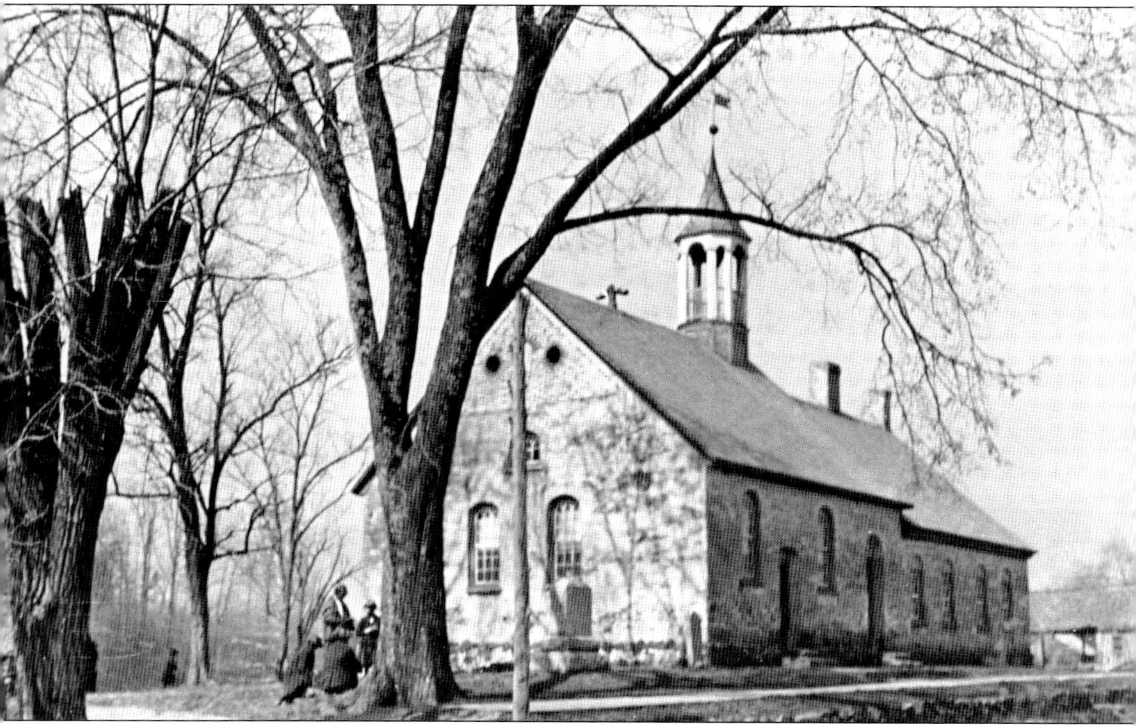

This image of the Bethabara *Gemeinhaus* was taken sometime after the 1903 sesquicentennial celebration. A group stands near the plaque dedicated to the original settlers, which was unveiled during the festivities on that special day. (Courtesy of Salem Academy and College Archives.)

ON THE COVER: On April 17, 1938, Bethabara Moravian Church held an Easter service at 3:00 p.m. Calvary Moravian Church's band led the procession to God's Acre, the oldest Moravian cemetery in North Carolina. (Courtesy of the Forsyth County Public Library Photograph Collection, Winston-Salem, North Carolina.)

IMAGES
of America

HISTORIC BETHABARA PARK

Diana Bahnson Overbey

ARCADIA PUBLISHING

ISBN 978-1-4671-6282-1

Published by Arcadia Publishing
Charleston, South Carolina

Printed in the United States of America

Library of Congress Control Number: 2025935727

For all general information, please contact Arcadia Publishing:
Telephone 843-853-2070
Fax 843-853-0044
E-mail sales@arcadiapublishing.com

Visit us on the Internet at www.arcadiapublishing.com

For my family, who instilled in me the importance of history and the people who came before us

CONTENTS

ACKNOWLEDGMENTS

First and foremost, I would like to thank the people who held onto photographs of Bethabara and recognized their importance. They shared these images with others who were able to preserve them so that people like me could study and better understand the history of this special place. For their foresight I am grateful.

Many others gave their time to help me find these images. Thank you to Nicole Crabbe, librarian of the Museum of Early Southern Decorative Arts at Old Salem, who went out of her way to scour their collection for any image related to Bethabara. Thank you to Tom McCullough, assistant archivist at the Moravian Archives in Bethlehem, Pennsylvania, for all his help obtaining early drawings and maps of Bethabara. Olaf Nippe of the Moravian Archives in Herrnhut, Germany, and Meaghan O'Riordan of the Moravian Archives, Southern Province, also assisted with images to illustrate the beginnings of Bethabara. Thank you to Cade Carlson, the photograph collection librarian of the Forsyth County Public Library, for many of the wonderful 19th- and 20th-century images. Donna Rothrock, library archivist of Salem College, also helped with later images. This book would not have been possible without all of your help, and I am very thankful for it.

Thank you also to Caroline Vickerson, senior content editor at Arcadia Publishing, for all of her support and guidance through this process. I very much needed and appreciated both. Thank you most of all to my husband, Jon; my family; and the staff and crew at Historic Bethabara Park for all of your support. It means the world to me.

INTRODUCTION

In the fall of 1753, fifteen unmarried men ranging in age from 28 to 42 began their trek down the Great Wagon Road from Bethlehem, Pennsylvania, to the Piedmont of North Carolina. They were tasked with creating a foothold in the Wachovia tract, nearly 100,000 acres that had recently been purchased by the Moravian Church.

The Moravian Church, or Unitas Fratrum, is a Protestant denomination whose origin stretches back to 1457, sixty years before Martin Luther wrote his 95 Theses. Its founders lived mostly in Bohemia and Moravia, located in the present-day Czech Republic, and followed a Bohemian reformer and martyr named Jan Hus, who was burned at the stake for his beliefs in 1415. These Hussites, as they were called, attempted to simplify Christianity in hopes of making it more accessible and meaningful to their daily lives, stating that Christ was the head of the church (rather than the pope) and the only real source of religious truth was the Bible. Their religion spread, gaining 200,000 members by the early 16th century. This did not go unnoticed by the Roman Catholic Church, which began to persecute and kill Hussites. Survivors fled to more tolerant areas of Europe, and those who stayed within the Holy Roman Empire had to practice their religion in secret. This changed in 1722, when Count Nicholas Ludwig von Zinzendorf offered sanctuary on his estate in Saxony to Hussite refugees fleeing Moravia. They built the town of Herrnhut that same year and began to attract other refugees who were determined to bring their religious practices out of hiding. The renewal of the Unitas Fratrum began in earnest in 1727 with Count Zinzendorf taking a leadership role. The church's following grew steadily, and by the 1740s, its reach spanned from Europe to the Americas.

After a failed attempt to settle in Georgia, the Moravian Church found success in Pennsylvania, first with the town of Bethlehem in 1741, followed by the establishment of Nazareth and Lititz. The Moravians' industrious and peaceful nature impressed British statesman and Lord Proprietor John Carteret, 2nd Earl Granville, who offered to sell a large amount of his land in North Carolina to them. In 1752, Bishop August Gottlieb Spangenberg led a survey expedition into the western part of the colony, finally settling on an area in the Piedmont of North Carolina that was the drainage basin of Muddy Creek, a tributary to the Yadkin River. The 98,985-acre tract, which today comprises most of Forsyth County, was named Wachau in honor of Count Zinzendorf, whose ancestral estate bore the same name. It was later anglicized to Wachovia.

The first 15 men to journey to Bethabara were chosen by the Moravian Church because of their varied and useful skill sets, their firm faith, their age, and their unmarried status. Church leaders did not believe the Carolina frontier was safe for women and children at the time and selected men who were experienced but still young enough to engage in the hard labor of clearing and plowing fields as well as constructing houses and roads. While the tract of land was considered fairly isolated from other settlers, it was important that the men traveling to North Carolina were in strong standing with the church so that they were not tempted by outside influences that might cause their faith to waiver or disrupt the mission of building the new town.

When they arrived at their destination on November 17, 1753, the safe but exhausted men huddled inside an abandoned cabin left by Hans Wagner a year earlier and held the very first lovefeast in North Carolina. A Moravian tradition, the lovefeast is a religious singing service followed by simple food and drink shared in fellowship. The men were thankful for their safe journey and looked toward the work that lay ahead of them.

They named their settlement Bethabara, meaning "house of passage." It was meant as a temporary establishment until a site better suited for the *Gemein Ort*, or central trades town, could be scouted. This plan was delayed in part due to the outbreak of the French and Indian War, which lasted from 1754 until 1763. It disrupted the Moravians' ability to communicate with Europe and at times made it difficult to travel between Pennsylvania and North Carolina.

The Moravians in Bethabara wasted no time making the most of their new home. They busied themselves with building new structures and clearing land to create a garden and fields in which to grow crops. When travel was safe, more Moravians were sent from Pennsylvania to join them, including married couples and tradesmen such as Gottfried Aust, a potter whose work brought interested buyers from miles around, often selling out within the first hour the kiln was opened. Neighbors along the Yadkin River visited the town to purchase goods, and after a palisade fort was constructed around the town and the Bethabara mill during the French and Indian War, many came to seek refuge during times when danger intensified in the area.

By the late 1750s, Bethabara had grown so large that church leaders began to worry. Bethabara was originally intended to be a temporary settlement, and instead it had grown into a sizable town that might create competition with the future central trades town. Church leaders sent Bishop Spangenberg down to Bethabara to establish a second Moravian town and to select some of Bethabara's townspeople to move to it. He arrived during the Anglo-Cherokee War of 1759, when many of Bethabara's neighbors were being attacked along the Yadkin River. Spangenberg was afraid creating a town of only a small group of Moravians would leave it vulnerable to attack. Instead, he chose to allow some non-Moravian families who were in good standing with the Moravian Church to also live there and soon established the town of Bethania.

After the shadow of war lifted, the town of Bethabara saw more growth in the 1760s. Trappers brought furs to trade for shoes, pottery, nails, and other goods made in the town. Deerskins were all the rage in Europe, and the Moravians would take the tanned hides to the coast and sell them for profit. The town's proximity to the Great Wagon Road meant many travelers came to stay at the tavern, where alcohol made by Bethabara's distillery was sold.

In 1764, *Oeconomus* Frederic William Marshall visited Wachovia to begin the important task of seeking out the perfect place for the long-planned-for Gemein Ort. By February 1765, the site for the town of Salem was selected, and in 1766, the first tree was felled to begin construction.

In 1767, Bethabara received a visit from royal governor William Tryon, who was so impressed by the items made by the Moravians that when he left, he ordered a windmill, 478 pounds of candles, 150 pounds of butter, six beehives, and a new gun from them. Governor Tryon's wife was equally taken by the Moravians' love of music and enjoyed playing the organ while she was there and receiving a small concert by some of the girls in the town. Governor Tryon would return to Bethabara in 1771 in the aftermath of the Regulator Movement, camping outside the town after the Regulators' defeat. He informed the Moravians that it had been proposed that they burn Bethabara for possible Regulator ties, but Governor Tryon had put a stop to it because he had never found the Moravians to be disloyal in any way, and he was glad to see he had been correct. The Moravians were grateful and glad that Governor Tryon had visited them before during a more peaceful time to judge their true nature.

By 1772, Salem was completed, and the majority of tradesmen in Bethabara closed up shop and moved to the new town. Bethabara's time as the main commercial center in Wachovia drew to a close, and its population dropped precipitously, from 104 to 54, while Salem's congregation grew from 57 to 120. While Bethabara was diminished, it still operated a tavern, a distillery, a general store, and a pottery. The town remained near the Great Wagon Road and continued to be a place for travelers to stop.

When the American Revolution began, soldiers from both sides of the war frequented the tavern, at times trying to determine which side the pacifist Moravians were truly on. The aftermath of the October 1780 Battle of Kings Mountain, which took place near modern-day Blacksburg, South Carolina, had a profound effect on the town. After the battle, 240 British and Tory prisoners of war were brought to Bethabara, where they were kept in abysmal conditions for 19 days. During that time, the prisoners and their guards depleted the community's food stores. It was not only the lack of food that distressed the 69 Moravians then living in Bethabara. Militia in charge of the prisoners were constantly being changed out, causing influxes of even more soldiers. One Tory was almost hanged in the town, which terrified the peaceful Moravians. Rumors about soldiers' plans to loot their homes kept the townspeople in a state of alarm. Their homes were searched when soldiers went missing. When 140 Tories from South Carolina were finally released, they spent the night in the town and built many fires by which to cook and warm themselves. The Moravians could not hold their evening service as a result and noted how pitiful the prisoners looked. They left the following day, and in the *Records of the Moravians in North Carolina*, the town diarist recorded, "We thanked our dear Saviour, who has helped us through these trying times, and has protected us from all harm."

The American Revolution was winding down in 1782 when blue dyer Johannes Schaub Jr. built a brick home for his family, which later became the home of potters Gottlob Krause and John Butner. A new Gemeinhaus, or church and minister's living quarters, was constructed in 1788, and after a fire destroyed the distillery and lodgings for the distiller and his family, a new distiller's house was built in 1803.

In the 19th century, Bethabara became a rural community inhabited by a handful of families. Bethabara became known as Old Town, but the significance of the first Moravian settlement in North Carolina was never forgotten. In the 20th century, Edwin L. Stockton led efforts to restore the 1788 Gemeinhaus and to purchase land where the original town once stood. This land was then excavated by state archaeologist Stanley South. Because Bethabara had become farmland, much of the early town's artifacts were preserved, and South was able to piece together a picture of what life was like for the inhabitants of Bethabara in the 18th century. In 1966, Bethabara officially became a historic site.

While it was meant only as a temporary settlement, Bethabara became an important part of the Moravian story and of the story of North Carolina. It effectively established a Moravian foothold in the Piedmont, and with its success came the creation of the towns of Bethania, Salem, Friedberg, Friedland, and Hope. Its people endured the hardships of both the French and Indian War and the American Revolution. They endured despite these challenges due to their unwavering faith and sense of community. Their story continues today through the written and archaeological records they left behind and a historic site eager to share them.

One

A New Home in North Carolina
18th-Century Bethabara

On October 7, 1753, fifteen single men received a special blessing from the Moravian Church in Bethlehem, Pennsylvania, for the journey and work they were about to undertake. Originally from Germany, Norway, Holstein, New York, and Pennsylvania, these men were selected for their ability to contribute to the creation of the first Moravian settlement in North Carolina. Among them were a doctor, a minister, a business manager, shoemakers, a carpenter, a cooper, millwrights, and farmers. Not all the men would stay in North Carolina—some would help guide the men along the way and take notes about the new land to report back to Bethlehem.

Bethabara was established not far from the Great Wagon Road, and it did not take long for "strangers," or non-Moravians, to begin visiting the town. Many came from miles around to be cared for by the European-trained physician. Others used Bethabara as a place to stop and rest along their journey. So many strangers visited that the Moravians quickly built a sleeping hall so they no longer had to give up their living quarters to them. In addition to building new structures, the men cleared and plowed fields, created a garden, and looked for ways to make Bethabara economically viable.

The Moravians soon learned they needed their neighbors' help, too. After learning they were lackluster hunters, the men purchased meat and other foodstuffs from those nearby. The Moravians bought more than they sold but had the advantage of a communal economy, called the *Oeconomie*. Unlike other families trying to make a living in the Carolina backcountry, the Moravians had the coffers of the Moravian Church to fall back on. The Bethlehem congregation paid for the shortfall Bethabara experienced during its first few years.

Once other tradesmen arrived and a mill was built, Bethabara's economy became self-sufficient, and by 1768, over 18 businesses operated in the town. Women and children now made up a portion of the 136 inhabitants. Bethabara was finally a viable commercial center, but it would not last. Once Salem was built, the majority of tradesmen moved, and those left had to grapple with a new identity.

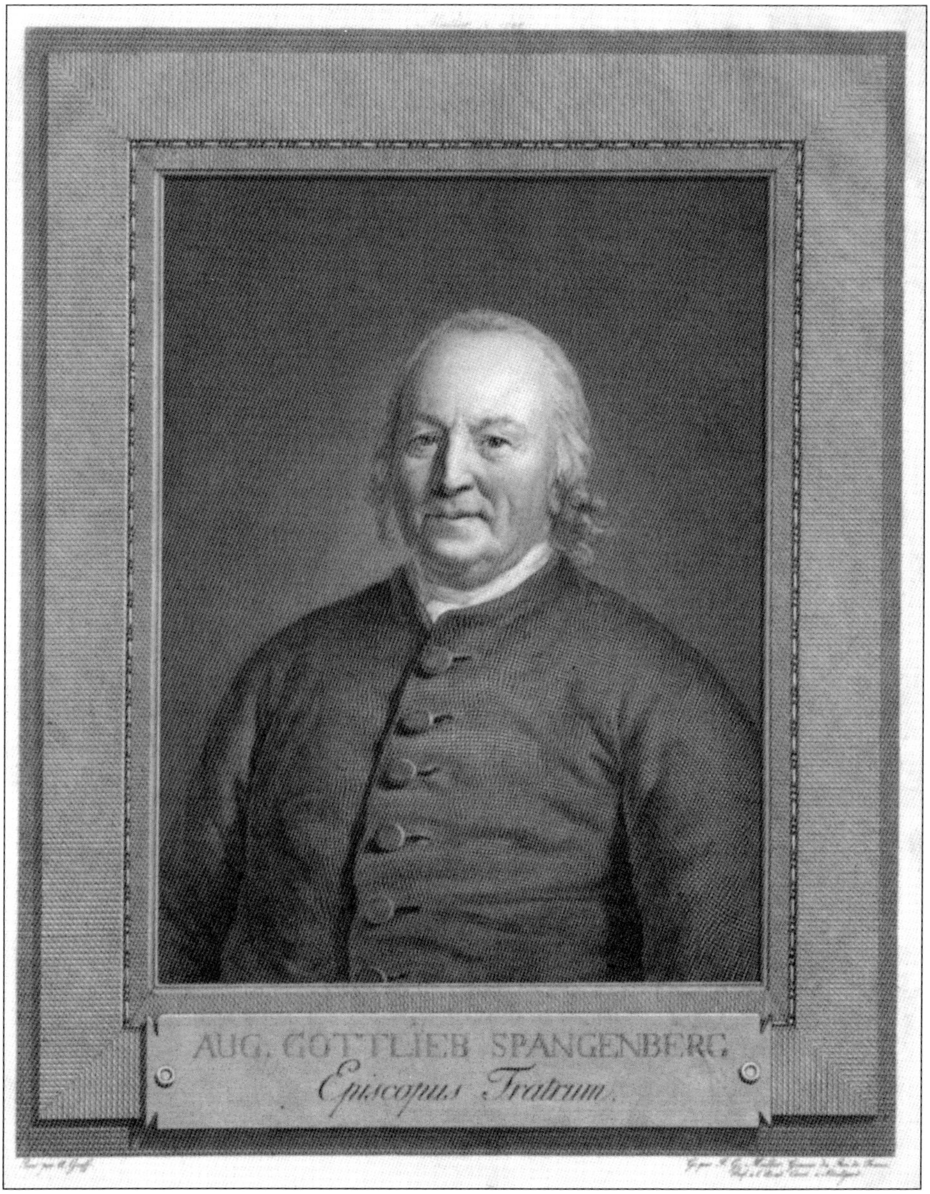

Bishop August Gottlieb Spangenberg (1704–1792) was born in Klettenberg, Saxony. He attended the University of Jena to study law, but after he converted to Pietism in 1722, he changed his focus to theology. While in Jena, Spangenberg met Count Nicholas von Zinzendorf and became interested in the theological values of the Moravian Church. In 1732, he became a theology professor at Halle, but he was soon expelled for his association with Zinzendorf and his ideas. He moved to Herrnhut, where he became the adjunct to Zinzendorf. As adjunct, Spangenberg traveled to the Americas, where he helped establish Moravian communities in Georgia and Pennsylvania. In 1752, Spangenberg led a surveying party through western North Carolina and selected the land to be purchased in the Piedmont, naming it Wachovia. Ten years later, he returned to Herrnhut, where he wrote what would become the accepted statement of Moravian beliefs along with a number of hymns. This 1788 copper engraving was made by Anton Graff (artist) and J.G. Muller (engraver). (Courtesy of the Moravian Archives, Bethlehem, Pennsylvania.)

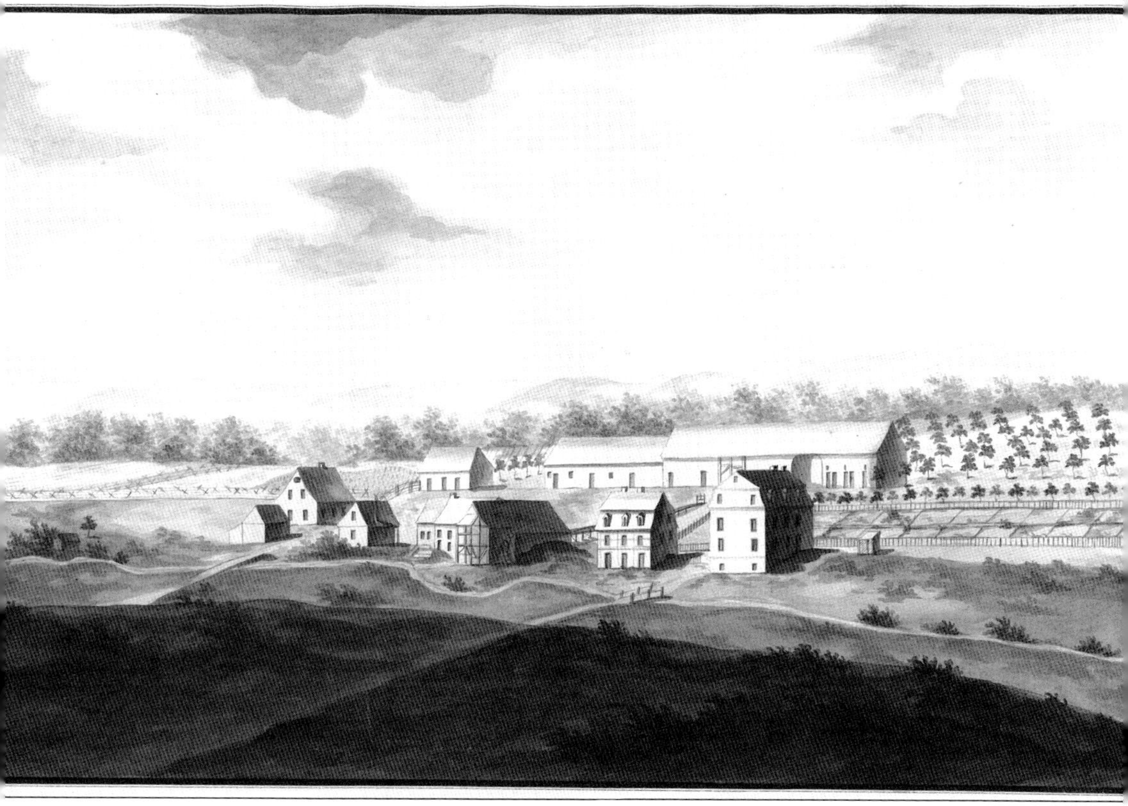

This ink drawing depicts the agricultural town of Christiansbrunn, Pennsylvania, around 1750. The majority of single men selected as the first Moravian settlers of Bethabara lived in this town. They were members of the Single Brothers' Choir, one of several choirs that made up Moravian society, which divided individuals by age and gender. Attention was paid to the men's professions as well as the strength of their faith in the Moravian Church. It was important that the skill sets of the men selected be well-suited to the Carolina backcountry. These men included Bernhard Adam Grube, a 37-year-old minister as well as an occasional cook and gardener; Jacob Loesch, a 31-year-old business manager; Hans Martin Kalberlahn, a 31-year-old trained physician; Erich Ingebretsen, a carpenter who was also a millwright; Henrich Feldhausen, a millwright who was also skilled in carpentry; Christopher Merkley, a baker and farmer; and Jacob Lung, a gardener who was also proficient at animal husbandry. (Courtesy of the Moravian Archives, Herrnhut, Germany.)

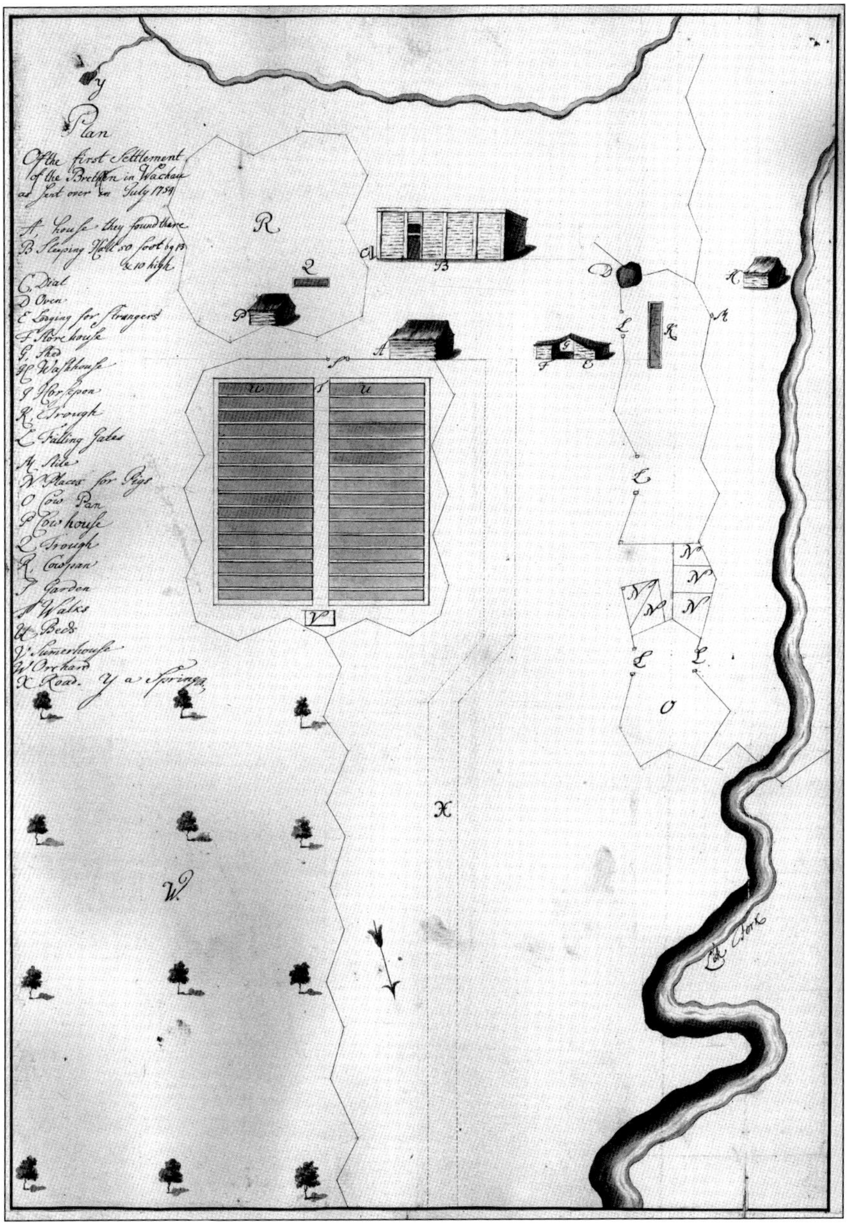

This map, entitled "Plan of the First Settlement in Wachau," has no identified author but is dated 1754 and was sent to Herrnhut. It includes the cabin once belonging to Hans Wagner (figure A), the larger sleeping quarters the Moravians constructed (figure B), lodging for non-Moravians, or "strangers" (figure E), "places for pigs" (figure N), a cow pen (figure O), and gardens (figure U). The Single Brothers began building a sleeping hall for themselves on January 8, 1754. While felling trees, Hans Petersen was struck unconscious, and Dr. Kalberlahn, himself with a scalded foot, hurried over to the scene and bled Petersen, who soon recovered consciousness. The other Brethren carried Petersen to the Wagner cabin, where Dr. Kalberlahn bandaged his head wound. As the *Records of the Moravians in North Carolina* notes, "We all pitied Br. Petersen, and Br. Kalberlahn again suffered great pain in his foot, so there were two patients in our little cabin." They held a short singing service, then took a much-needed rest. (Courtesy of the Moravian Archives, Herrnhut, Germany.)

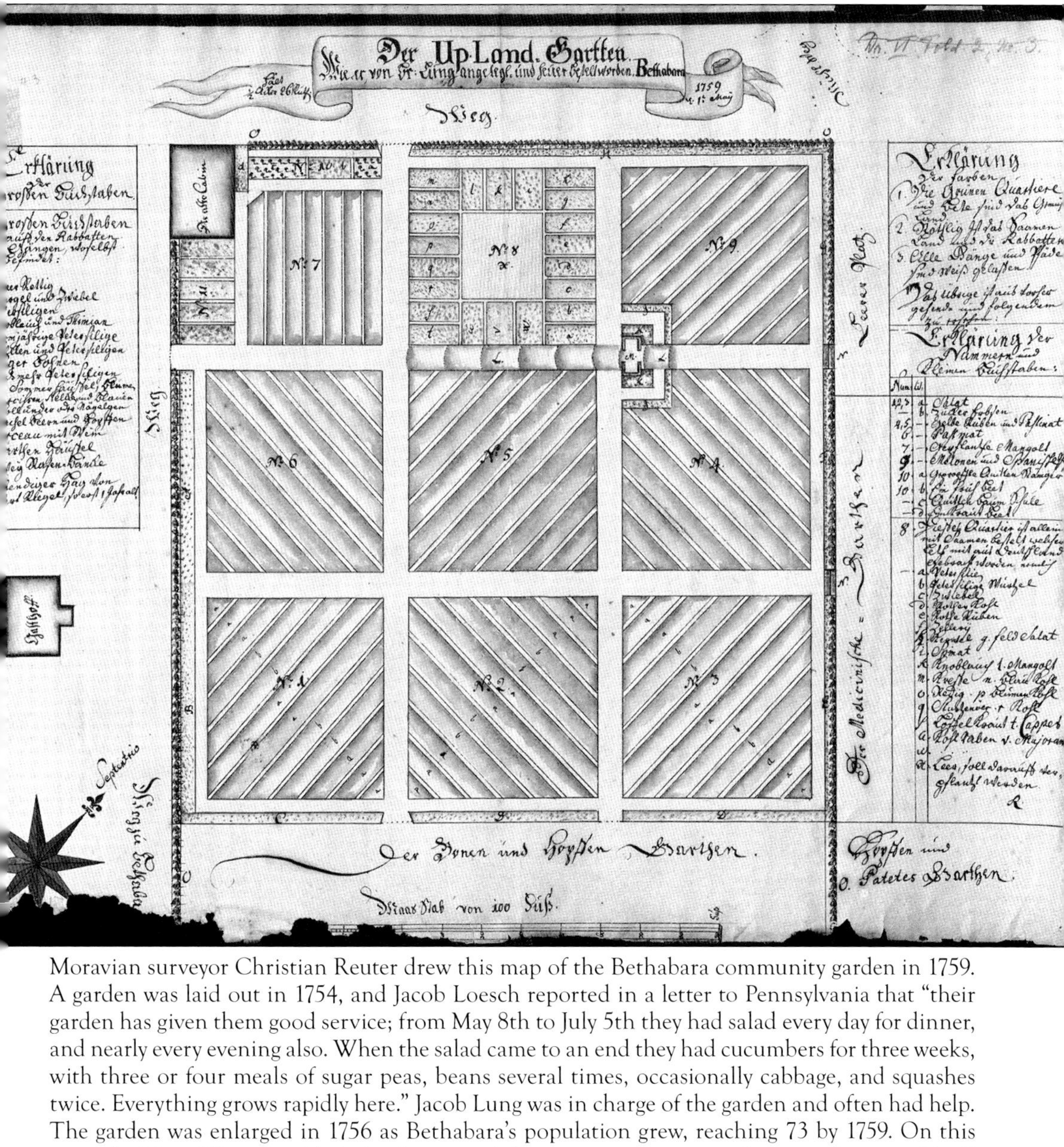

Moravian surveyor Christian Reuter drew this map of the Bethabara community garden in 1759. A garden was laid out in 1754, and Jacob Loesch reported in a letter to Pennsylvania that "their garden has given them good service; from May 8th to July 5th they had salad every day for dinner, and nearly every evening also. When the salad came to an end they had cucumbers for three weeks, with three or four meals of sugar peas, beans several times, occasionally cabbage, and squashes twice. Everything grows rapidly here." Jacob Lung was in charge of the garden and often had help. The garden was enlarged in 1756 as Bethabara's population grew, reaching 73 by 1759. On this map, the Hans Wagner cabin is in the upper left corner, and a grape arbor runs between No. 8 and No. 5. Bethabara had a communal economy known as the Oeconomie, and the food from the garden was shared among the townspeople until they began to have their own individual gardens. (Courtesy of the Moravian Archives, Bethlehem, Pennsylvania.)

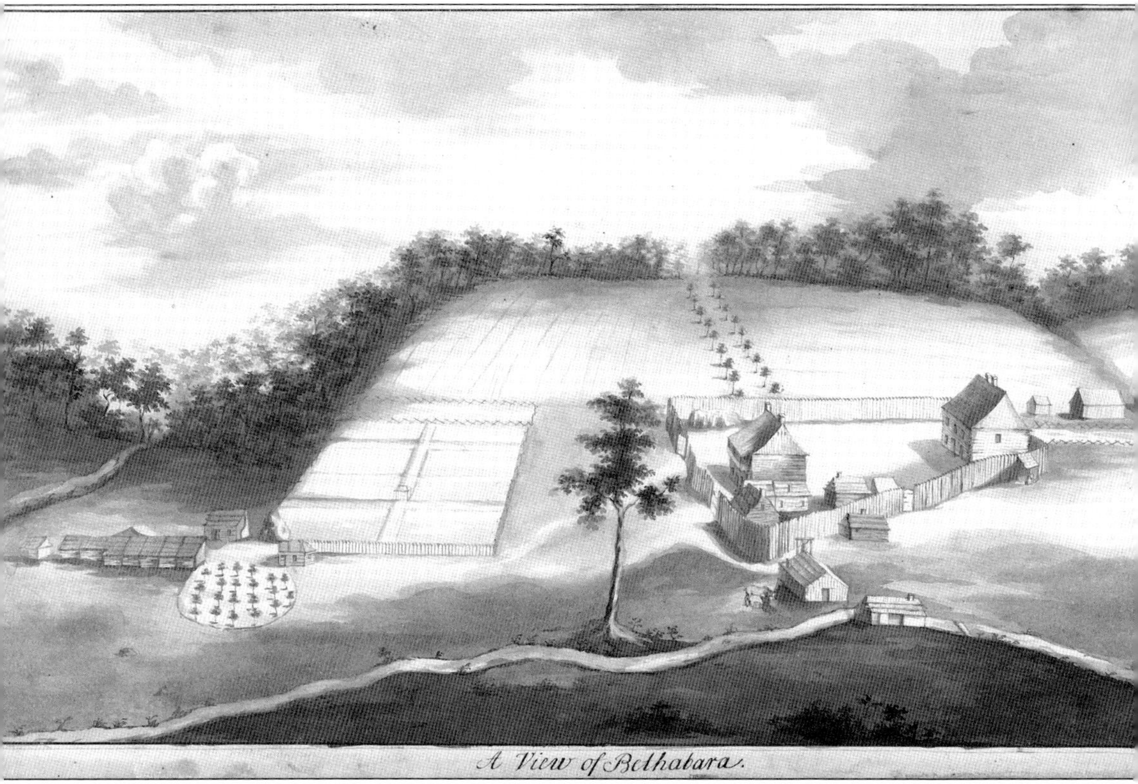

This drawing, entitled "A View of Bethabara," was made between 1756 and 1763 during the time the town was enclosed by a palisade fort. Inside the fort, the Gemeinhaus, or church, is located on the right, and the Single Brothers' House is on the left. The tree-lined path going up the hill behind the fort leads to God's Acre, the Moravian cemetery. To the left of the fort are the remains of the original 1754 village as well as the gardens. The Moravians in Bethabara decided to construct a palisade fort during the French and Indian War. As stated in the *Records of the Moravians in North Carolina* from the memorabilia of the year 1756, "It was decided to protect our houses with palisades, and make them safe before the enemy should invade our tract or attack us. . . . All who were not busy with the harvest went to work the same day, and by the 23rd the palisade was finished except the gates." The pacifist Moravians were never attacked. (Courtesy of the Moravian Archives, Herrnhut, Germany.)

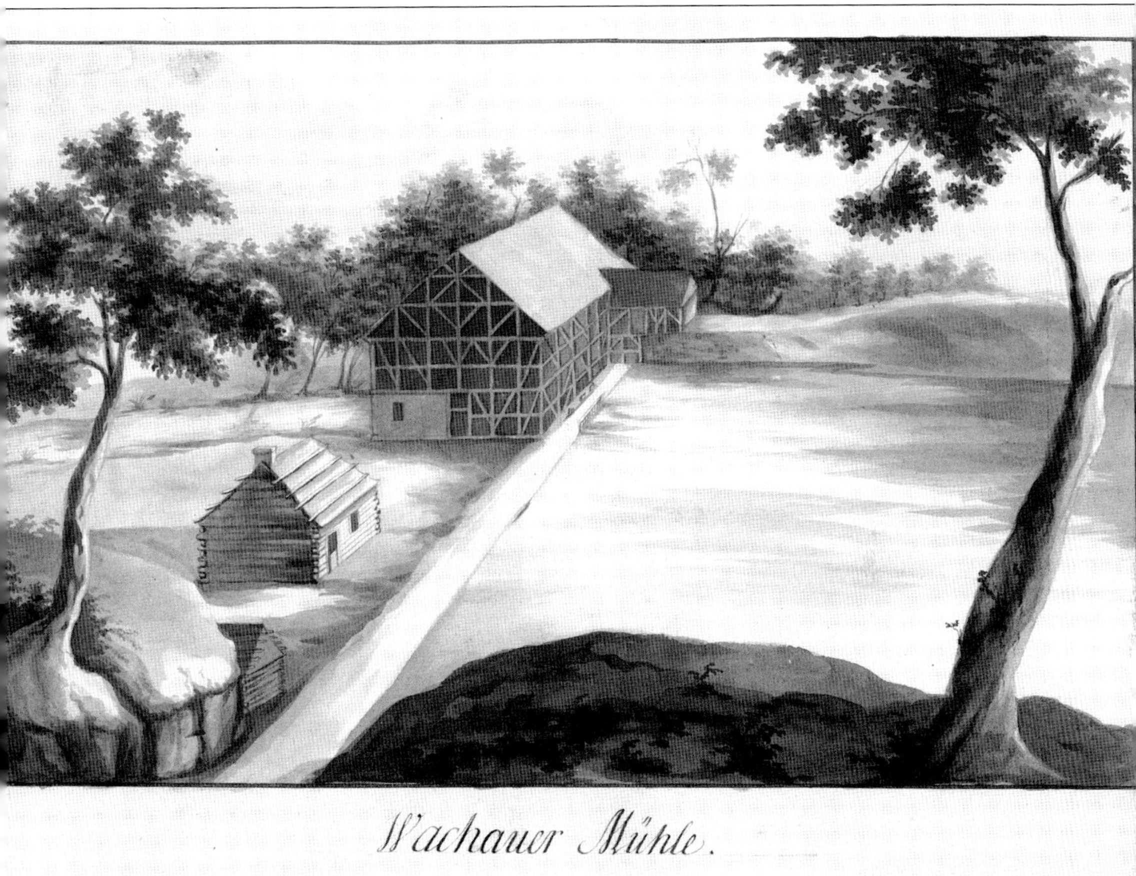

The c. 1760 drawing of "The Wachauer Mühle" features the Bethabara mill and millwright's house with a further description indicating the mill was located on the Johanna River in Wachovia and sat one mile west of Bethabara. As Bishop Spangenberg had envisioned when surveying the land, the streams running through Wachovia were good places for mills. The Bethabara mill was completed over the course of 1755. Stone for millstones was found 10 miles away, and a road was cut to the stone so that the men could chisel and shape them, completing their work in 12 days. It took 10 horses to bring the millstones to their final location. Once completed, the gristmill used the stones to grind corn and wheat as well as flint for glazing pottery. The building also contained a sawmill. Two days after the mill ground the first wheat for flour, the Moravians celebrated with a lovefeast, where they shared a simple meal of bread made with the flour ground at the mill. (Courtesy of the Moravian Archives, Herrnhut, Germany.)

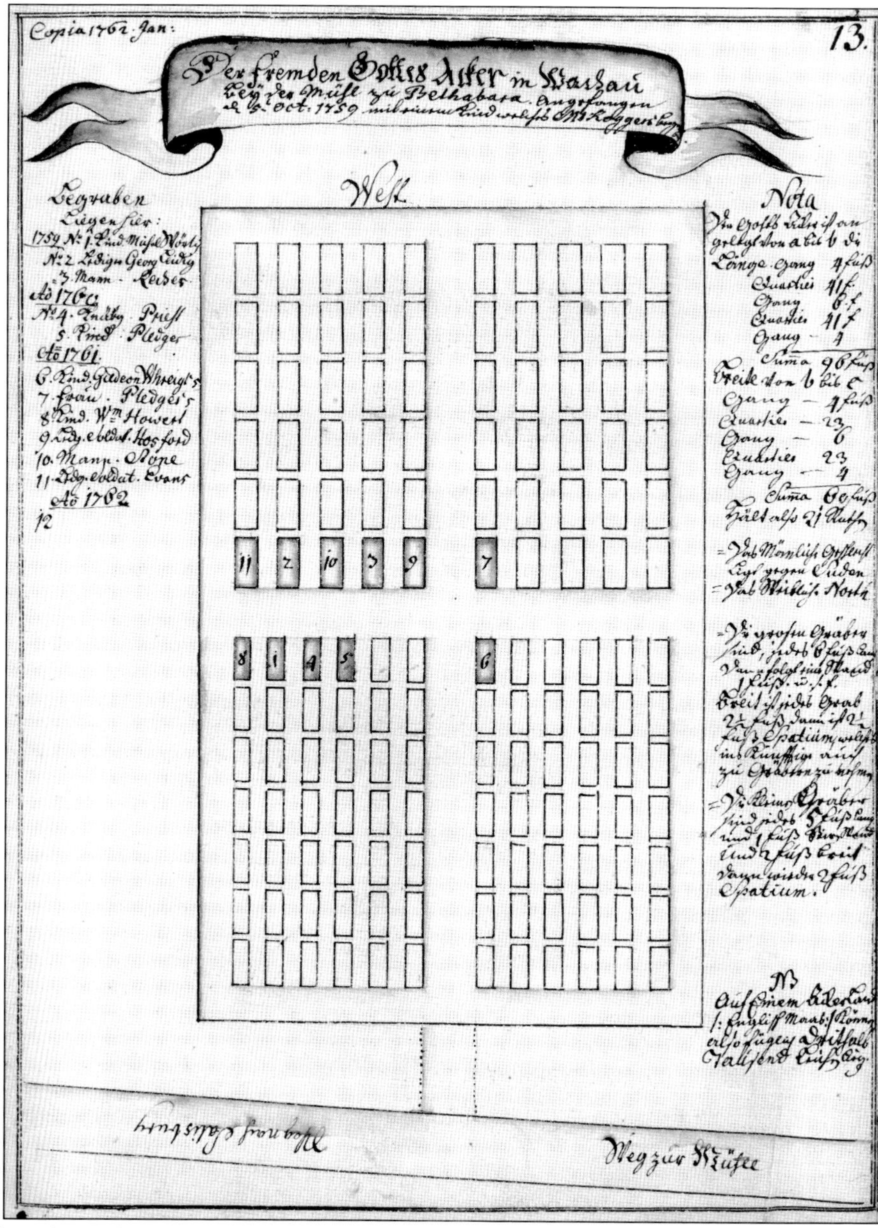

While Bethabara's settlers were mostly central European and spoke German, the town was founded in an English colony. English colonies were broken into parishes, and Bethabara became part of Dobbs Parish when it was created in 1755. Jacob Rogers, an English Moravian, became the parish's first appointed minister in 1758. The cemetery for strangers (non-Moravians), seen here, was laid out near Bethabara's mill and became the Dobbs Parish Cemetery. By 1759, a number of refugees from the Anglo-Cherokee War lived in 10 houses constructed around the palisaded mill. On October 5, 1759, the first person was buried in the stranger's cemetery. Rogers held the funeral service for the child, whose parents had come to the mill as refugees. The child was the first of 84 total interments dating from 1759 to 1825. While it was a cemetery for strangers, the Moravians still buried the dead as they did their own, in choirs. Individuals were buried according to gender as well as by age. This is why the numbers are not in order on the map. (Courtesy of Moravian Archives, Herrnhut, Germany.)

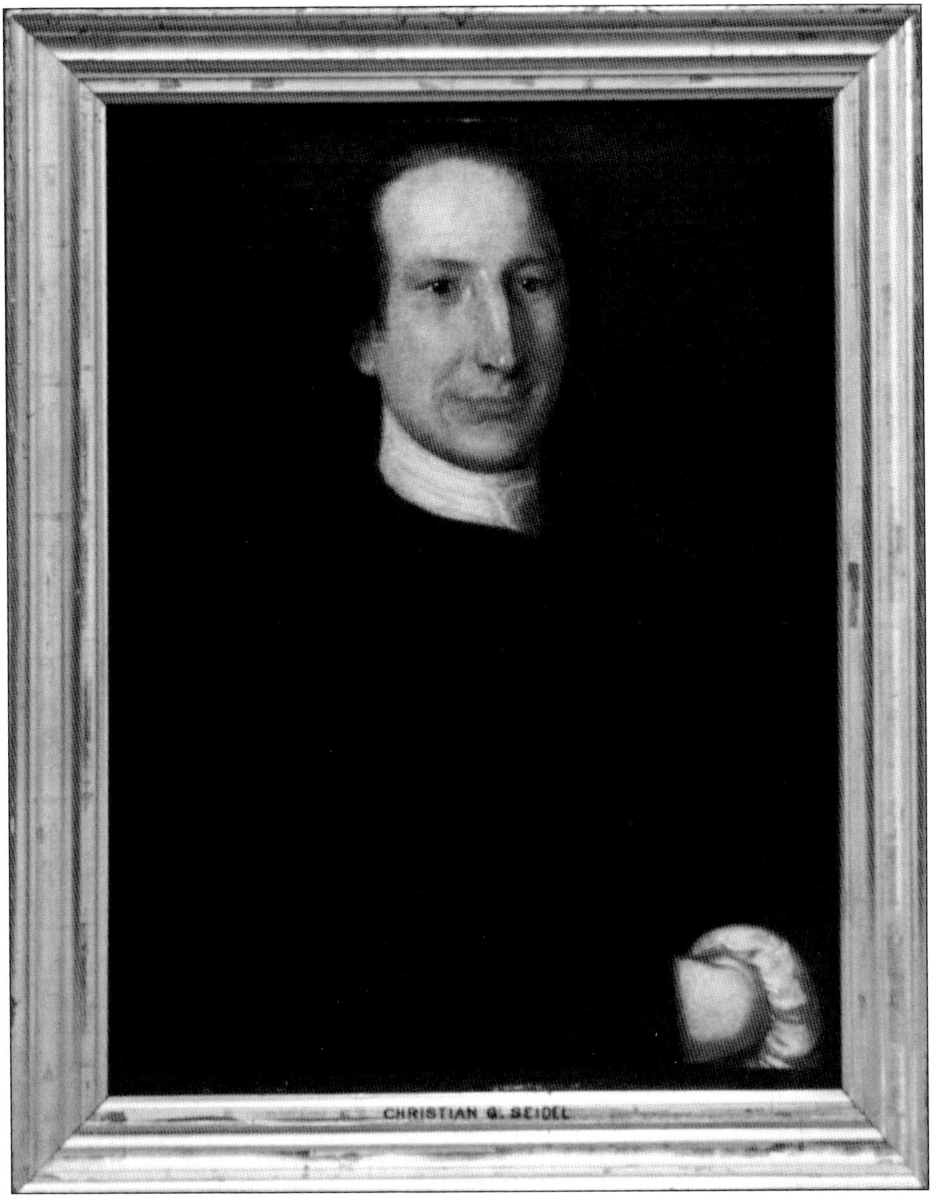

This is a portrait of Christian Seidel (1718–1759) made between 1756 and 1757. Seidel saw the first 15 settlers off with a prayer on October 8, 1753. In 1756, he came to Bethabara himself, where he held the role of minister. As part of his role, he baptized newborn Anna Maria Opiz, who died only six days after she was born and became the first Moravian buried in Bethabara's God's Acre. In 1758, Christian Seidel joined other single men on a trip to Bethlehem, Pennsylvania. While there, Seidel married Maria Catharina Binder. In May 1759, he and his wife, along with other newly married couples, traveled back to Bethabara. That summer, a disease believed to be typhus broke out inside the palisade fort. Maria Seidel succumbed to the illness and was buried on July 23. Christian Seidel followed her just three days later. The *Records of the Moravians in North Carolina* reported, "Last night at twelve o'clock it pleased Him to come for our dear Br. Christian Seidel, and to transplant him into the heavenly congregation." (Courtesy of the Moravian Archives, Bethlehem, Pennsylvania.)

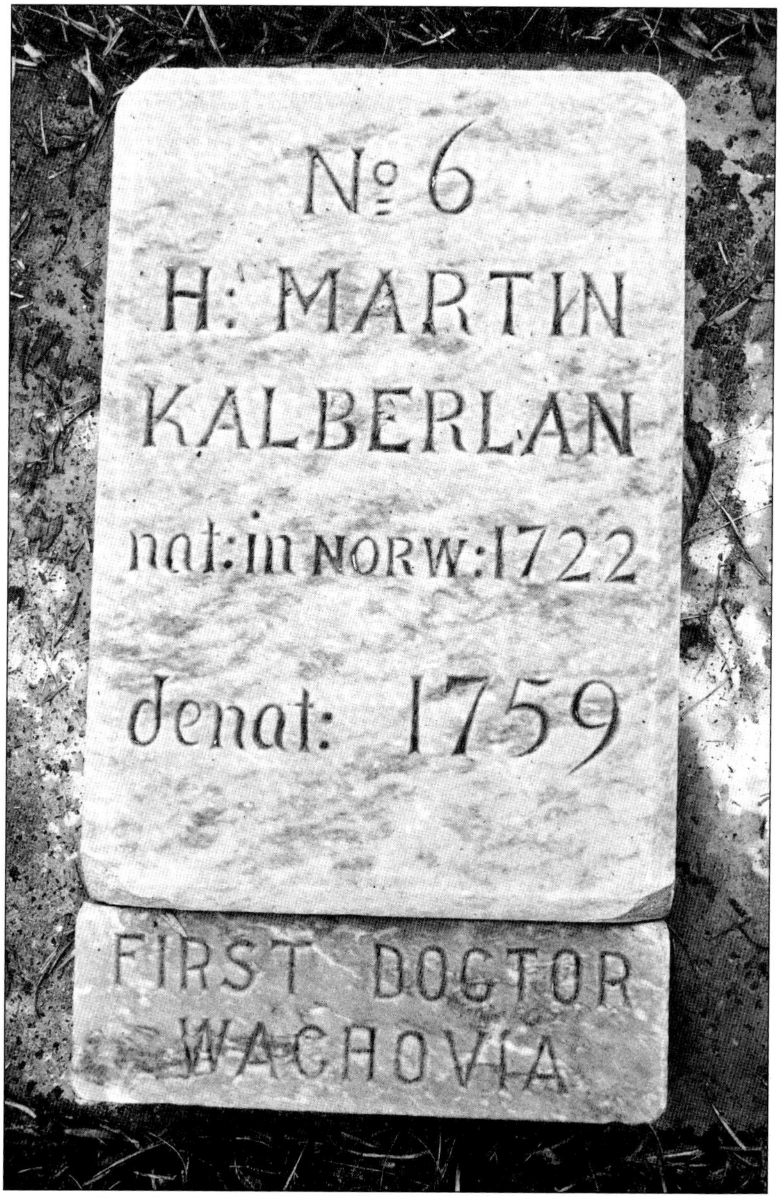

Dr. Hans Martin Kalberlahn (1722–1759) was born in Norway and became a physician's apprentice in 1743. He then traveled throughout Europe studying medical practices, picking up skills that would serve him well in the Carolina backcountry. He practiced medicine in the Moravian community of Herrnhaag until 1753, when he traveled to America to help establish Bethabara. Dr. Kalberlahn treated illnesses along with injuries sustained by the other men as the town was being built. As strangers visited the town, word spread about the medically trained physician. One man traveled 80 miles to see Dr. Kalberlahn, while another rode 60 miles to deliver a letter from his mother asking him for medical advice. Kalberlahn also paid house calls that took him throughout the backcountry but especially along the Yadkin River. His greatest challenge came in 1759, when a disease thought to be typhus broke out in the town. While treating the sick, he succumbed to the illness one day before his first wedding anniversary. He is buried next to Christian Seidel in God's Acre. (Courtesy of the Bethabara Collection.)

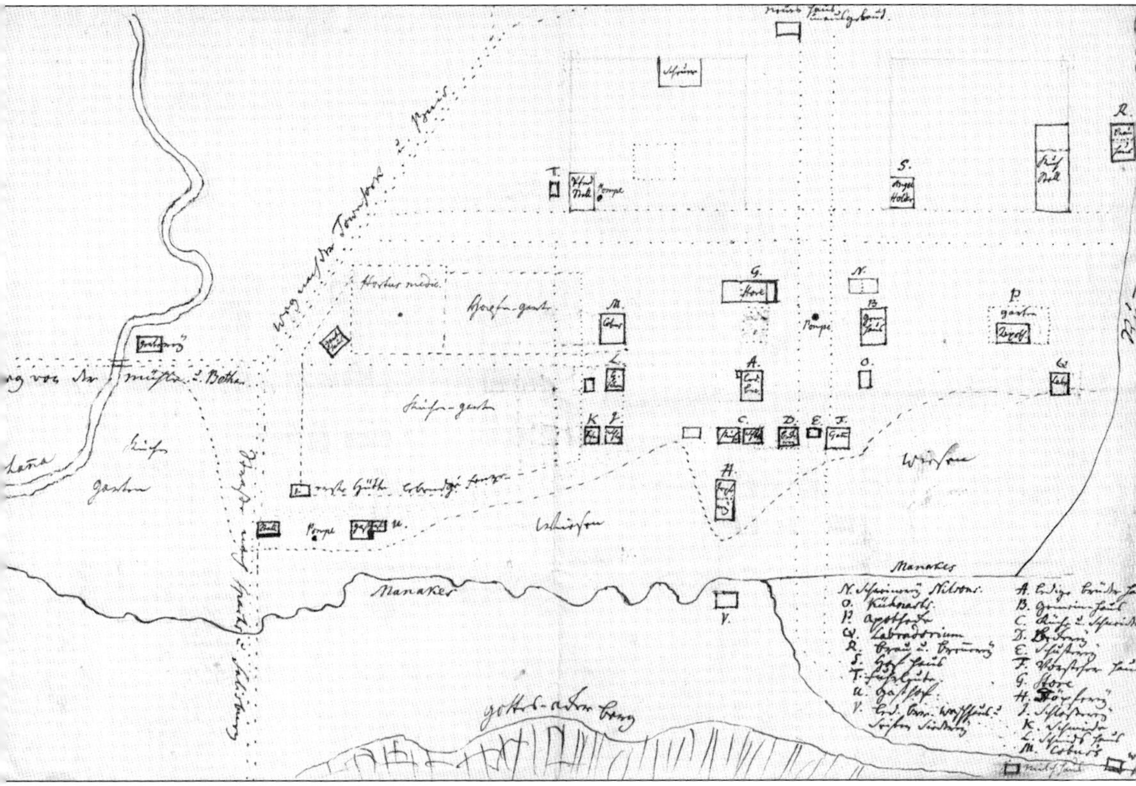

This c. 1763–1764 map of Bethabara was drawn by Johannes Ettwein, who came to Bethabara in 1758 to replace Christian Seidel as minister while he was in Pennsylvania and stayed after Seidel's passing. The map gives insight into the buildings that were in Bethabara as it began to grow following the end of the French and Indian War. On the far left of the map is Johanna Creek, which runs just to the left of the kitchen garden. The path to the mill consists of two dotted lines that cross the creek and run next to the tannery, which was placed on the edge of town due to the smell. The hops garden, medicinal garden, and community garden are the dotted rectangles to the right of the vertical dotted lines marking the road to Salisbury. To the middle right of the map are the Gemeinhaus (church, B), the Single Brothers' House (A), the kitchen and tailor's shop (C), the bakery (D), and the shoemaker's shop (E). The pottery is located below that line of buildings (H). (Courtesy of the Moravian Archives, Bethlehem, Pennsylvania.)

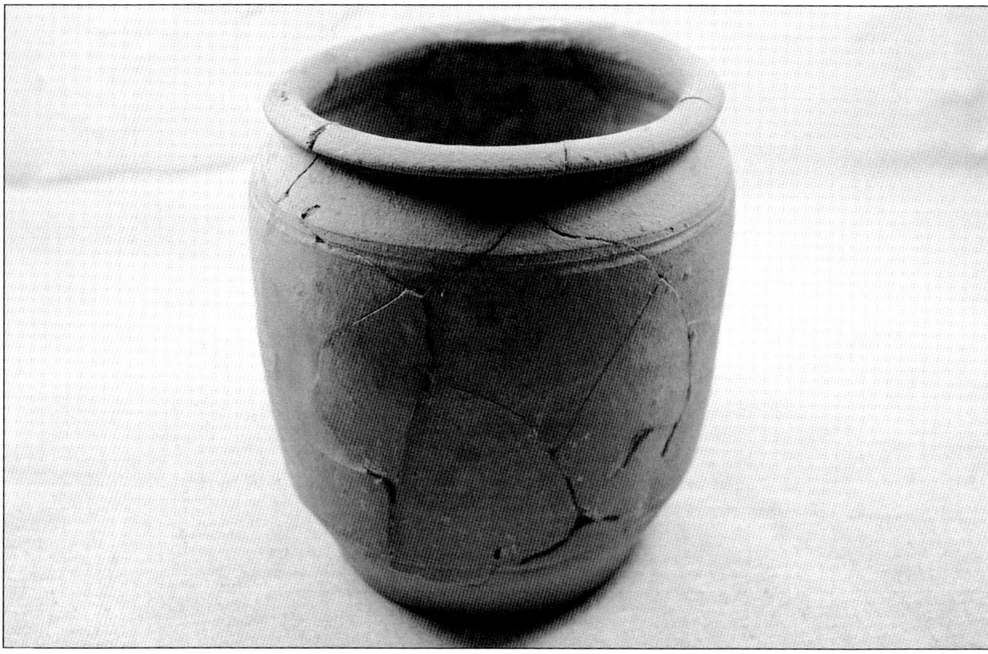

The apothecary jar above and chamber pot below are excellent examples of the utilitarian ware that master potter Gottfried Aust produced as the first potter in Bethabara. Born in Heidersdorf, Silesia, in 1722, he first learned the trade of linen weaver before he moved to Herrnhut, where he apprenticed as a potter. He came to Bethlehem, Pennsylvania, in 1754 before traveling to Bethabara in 1755. Pottery was much needed both by the townspeople and to sell to non-Moravians. His kiln was up and running by August 1756, and the *Records of the Moravians in North Carolina* note, "Br. Aust burned earthenware in his new kiln for the first time, and was pleased with it." His pottery would be used (and later found by archaeologists) throughout the town. (Both, courtesy of the Bethabara Collection.)

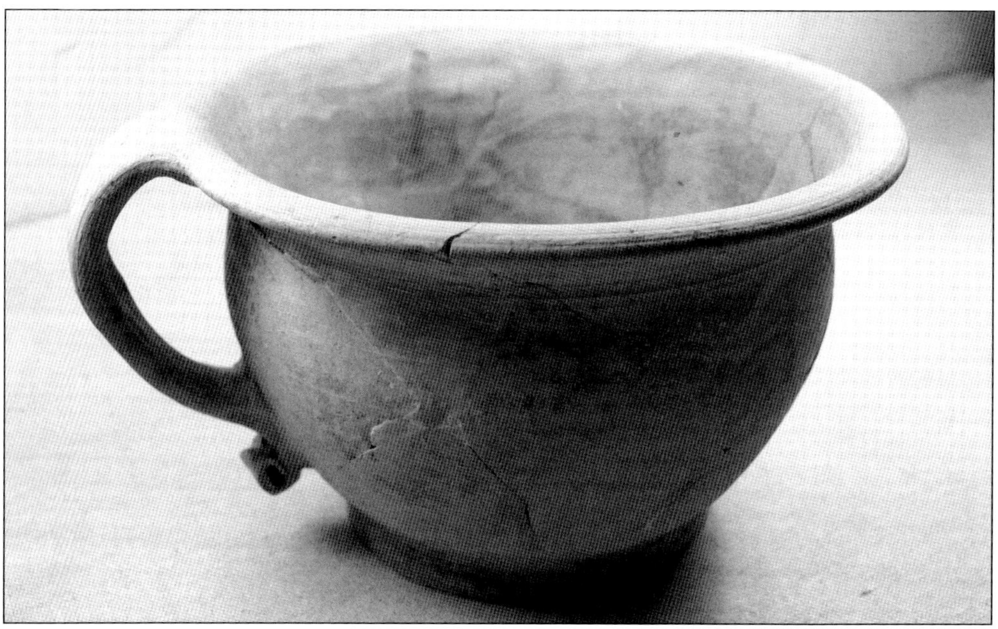

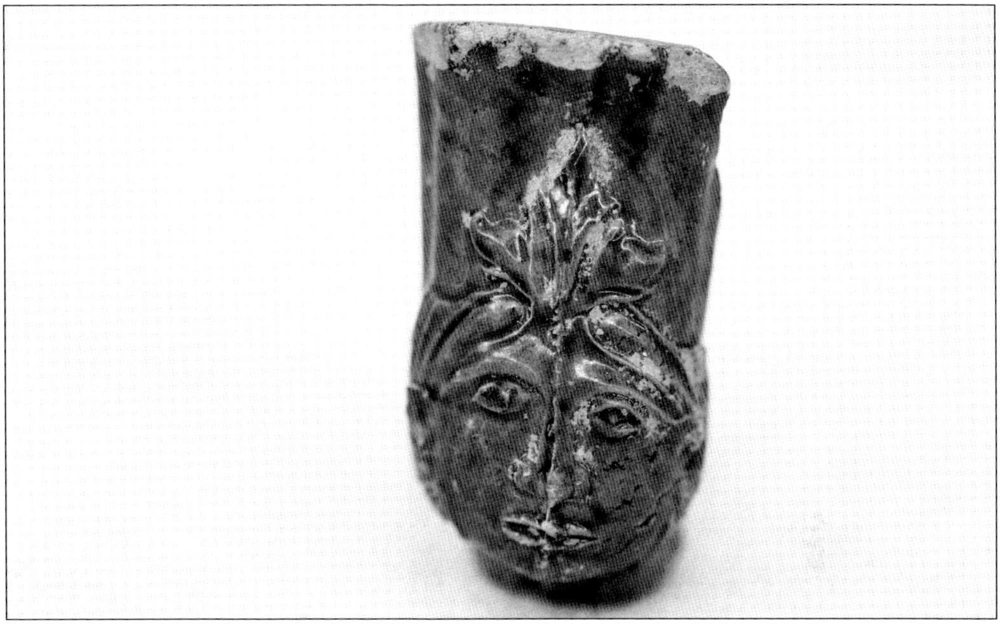

This clay pipe head was recovered during the Stanley South archaeological dig of 1963–1966 and is attributed to Gottfried Aust. This particular pipe head is of an anthropomorphic design and was a popular item among customers. These were made using a press, which Aust likely brought with him from Europe. These same pipe heads were made by later potters in Bethabara, showing their continued popularity. (Courtesy of the Bethabara Collection.)

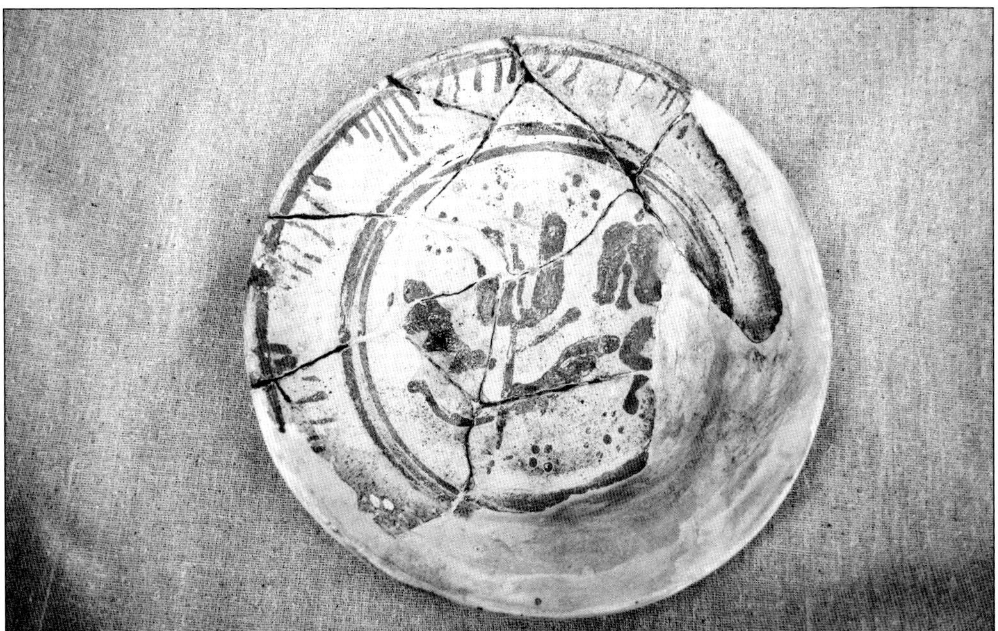

This slipware plate was uncovered during the Stanley South dig of 1963–1966. It, like the pipe head, was considered flawed and was tossed in a waster dump. This plate is attributed to Gottfried Aust, and the design is a common one of his featuring a flower. It was pieced back together by the archaeological team. (Courtesy of the Bethabara Collection.)

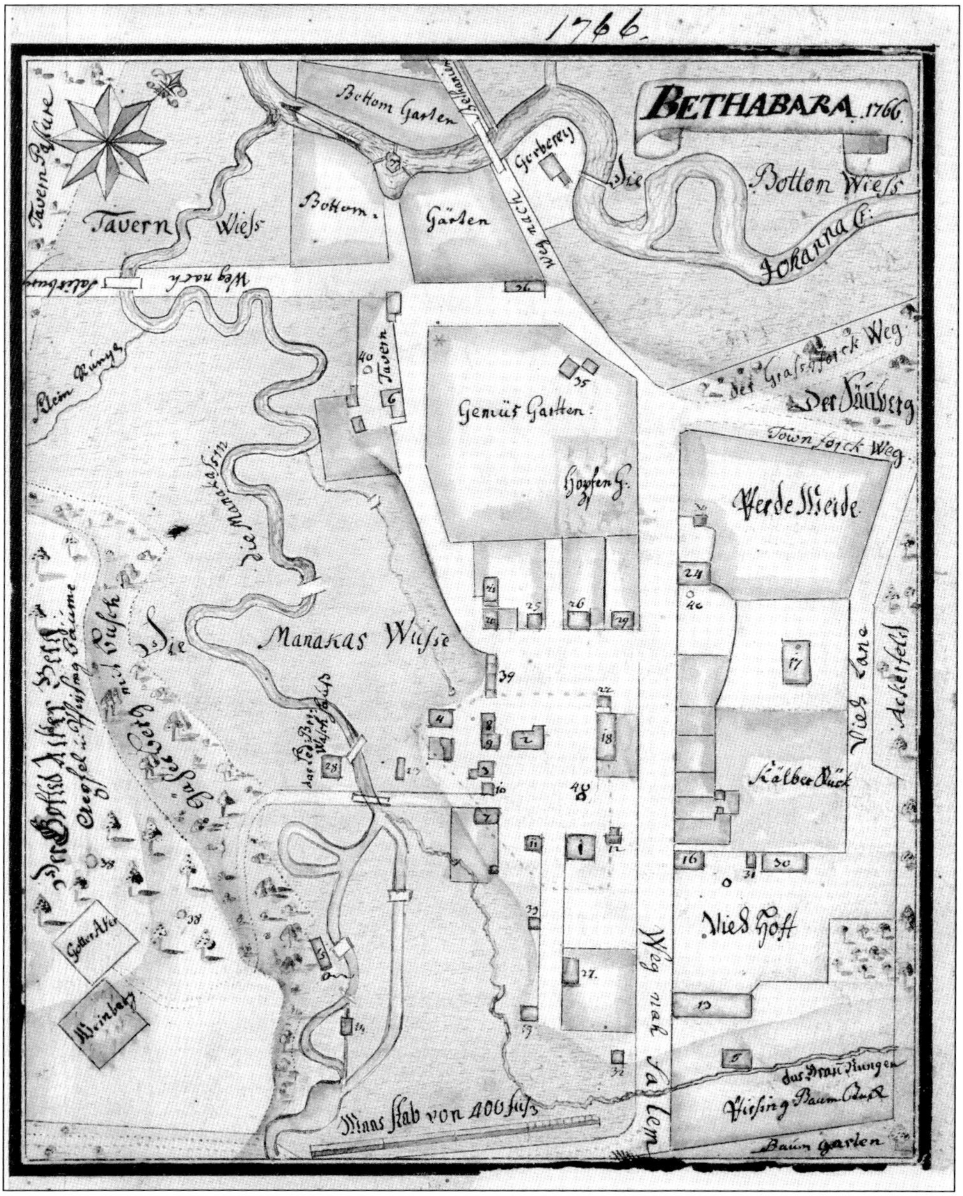

Moravian surveyor Christian Reuter made this map of Bethabara in 1766, when it was at its height as a major commercial center in the Piedmont. Thirty-nine buildings are documented here, and this is the map that archaeologist Stanley South later relied on to find the foundations of the original settlement. The palisade fort was gone by 1766, but a dotted line denoting it was added from a map of 1760. Structures that were built after 1758 and are shown on this map include a four-room family house, a store, a laboratory for the doctor, a gunsmith shop, a gun-stock maker's shop, a linen house, a horse stable, a house for the millwright (not directly by the mill anymore), an apothecary shop, a tailor's shop, a calf barn, a poultry house, a smoke house, and a cabin for the stablemen. In addition, the map shows the Gemeinhaus (church) and the Single Brothers' House inside the dotted line of the fort. There were also a brewery and distillery, a shoe shop, a pottery, and a tavern, all of which were major contributors to Bethabara's economy. (Courtesy of the Archives, Moravian Church in America, Southern Province.)

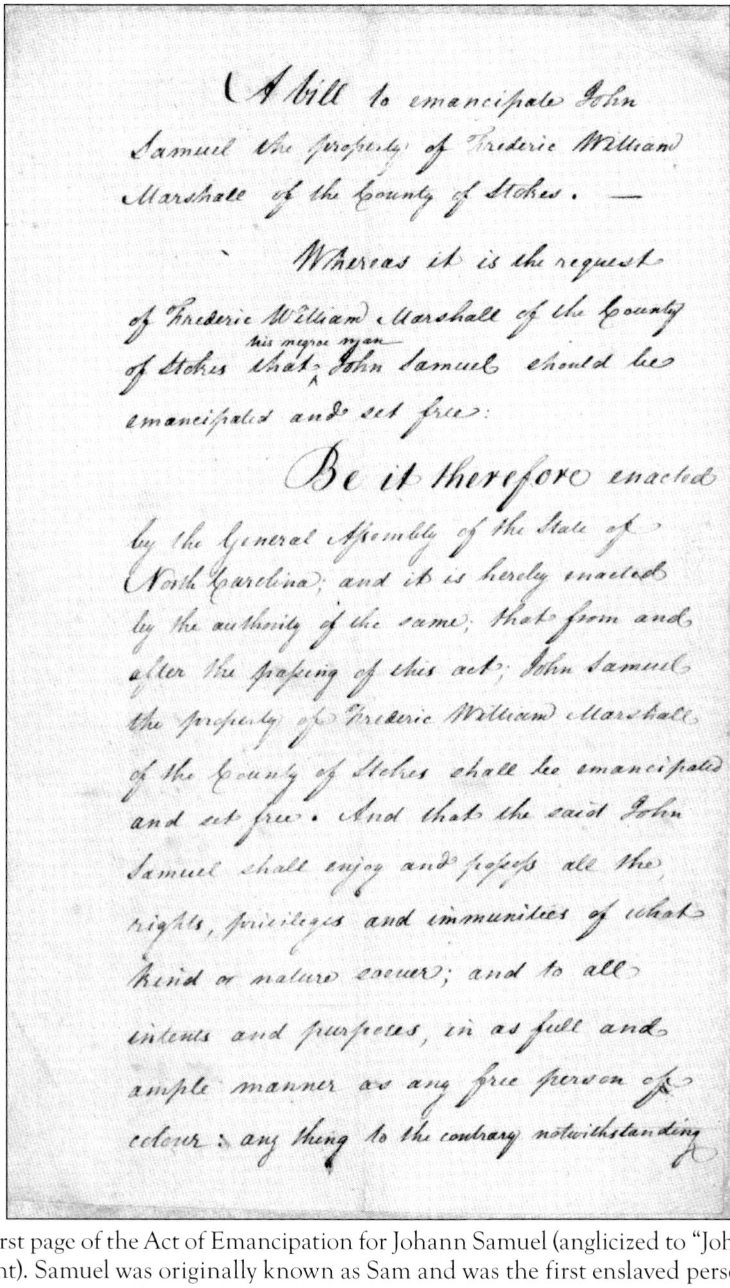

A bill to emancipate John Samuel the property of Frederic William Marshall of the County of Stokes. —

Whereas it is the request of Frederic William Marshall of the County of Stokes that his negroe man John Samuel should be emancipated and set free:

Be it therefore enacted by the General Assembly of the State of North Carolina; and it is hereby enacted by the authority of the same; that from and after the passing of this act; John Samuel the property of Frederic William Marshall of the County of Stokes shall be emancipated and set free. And that the said John Samuel shall enjoy and possess all the rights, privileges and immunities of what kind or nature soever; and to all intents and purposes, in as full and ample manner as any free person of colour: any thing to the contrary notwithstanding

This is the first page of the Act of Emancipation for Johann Samuel (anglicized to "John Samuel" in the document). Samuel was originally known as Sam and was the first enslaved person purchased by the Moravians in North Carolina. A few years later, he was baptized into their faith. Samuel worked as a teamster and farm manager. He married another enslaved Moravian named Maria and had several children. The question of Samuel's freedom first came up in 1795 in the *Records of the Moravians in North Carolina*. "We discussed the case of Johann Samuel of Bethabara. His wife will soon be free, and he would like to be free also, with his children, and make his own farm on the Bethabara plantation. The laws of the land make the situation remarkably difficult." Finally, in 1800, he received his freedom by a state senate bill. The *Records* noted, "Br. Johann Samuel, of Bethabara, has been given his freedom by the general assembly, and may now rent a farm outside the town." (Courtesy of the State Archives of North Carolina.)

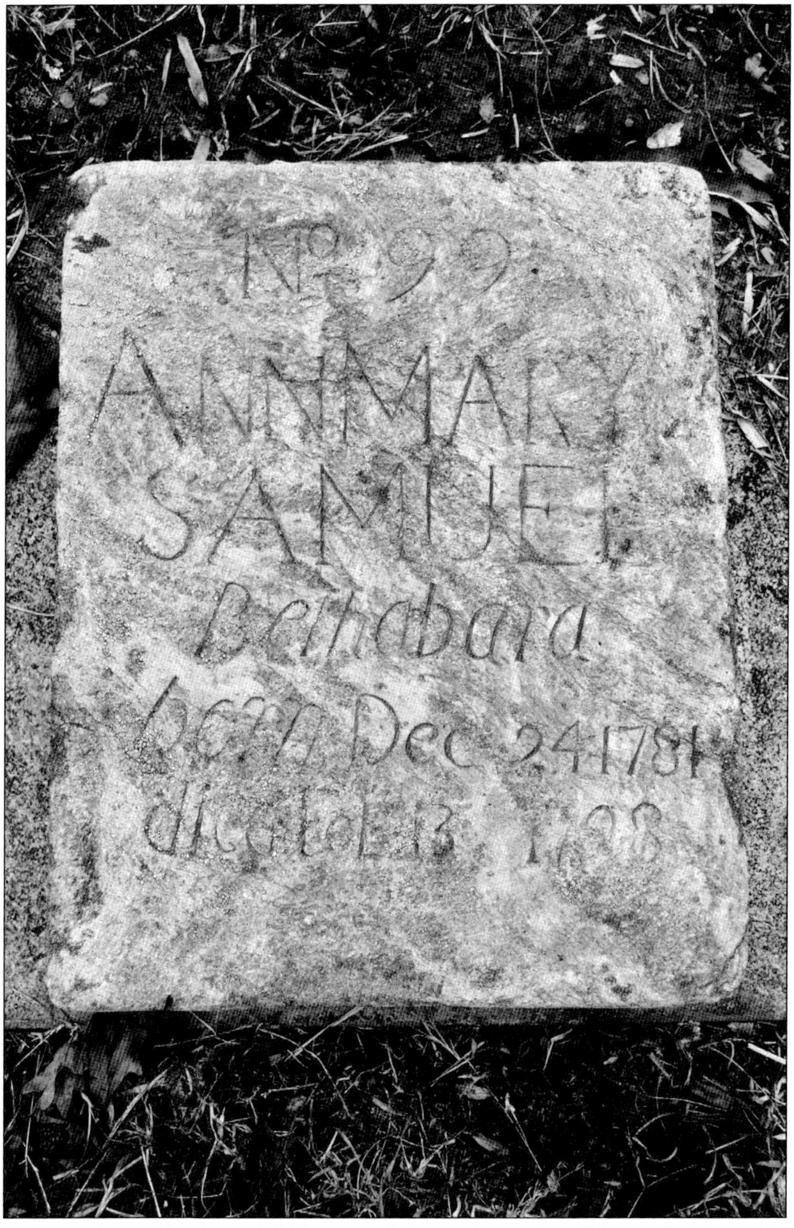

Anna Maria Samuel was the first child born to Johann Samuel and his wife, Maria. Six children would follow her, but only four of the Samuel children would live to adulthood. Anna Maria was born into the Moravian Church and attended school and church services alongside white Moravians. Her *Lebenslauf* (a spiritual memoir of a Moravian read at their funeral) stated that she had "a particular inclination for singing, and she practiced diligently to memorize the congregation verses." When she was 12, she joined the Older Girls' Choir and lived in the Single Sisters' House in Salem alongside her white peers. She would have continued to attend lessons both scholarly and spiritual, but in November 1797, she contracted consumption (tuberculosis) and was not strong enough to attend church any longer. She was cared for by her parents in Bethabara and passed away in February 1798 at the age of 17. She is buried in Bethabara's God's Acre alongside other members of her choir. (Courtesy of the Bethabara Collection.)

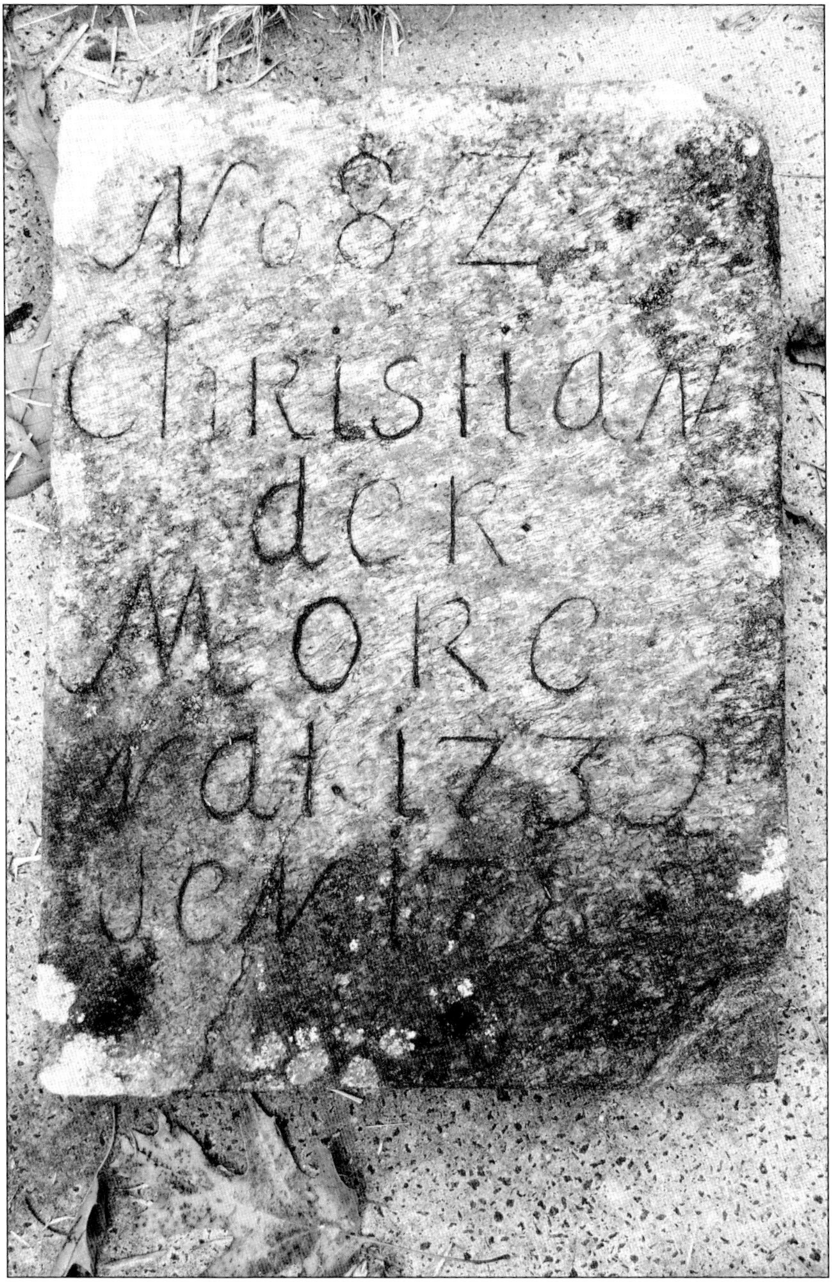

According to Christian's Lebenslauf, he was born in Guinea and as a small boy was "taken to a ship by one of his closest female friends" and sold into slavery. He arrived in South Carolina and was eventually sold to the Moravians in 1771 when he was around 20 years old. He was involved in the construction of Salem and was later baptized into the Moravian Church. In 1787, he and his wife, an African Moravian named Anna, were sent to Bethabara to work in the tavern. He passed away in 1788 after complications from a fall. Christian was given a full Moravian funeral, which included a service, followed by the reading of his Lebenslauf and a procession to God's Acre. Christian's homegoing, which was announced by trumpets on the tower of the church, was the first held in the newly built Gemeinhaus in Bethabara. (Courtesy of the Bethabara Collection.)

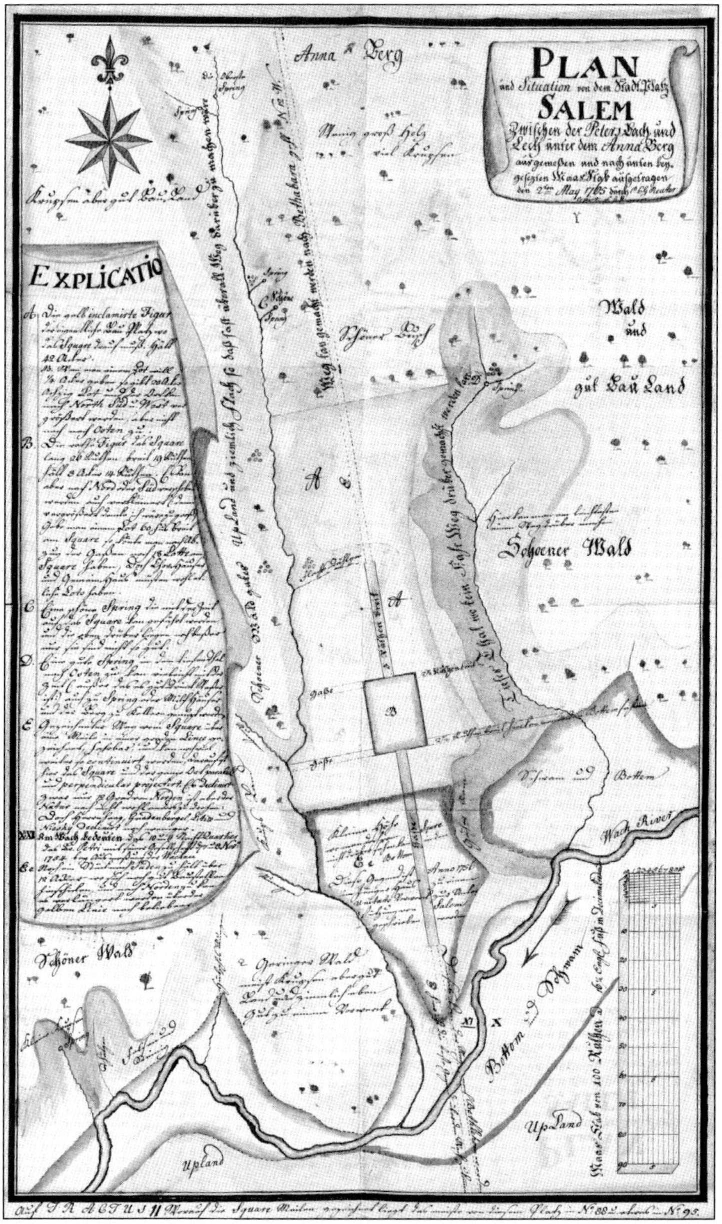

This 1765 plan of Salem was drafted by Christian Reuter and copied by Georg Wenzeslaus Golkowsky. Salem was the planned Gemein Ort, or central town, of Wachovia. The town was delayed by 13 years due to the French and Indian War and other factors. As a result, Bethabara grew much larger than originally planned. The construction of Salem began in 1766, and by 1772, most of the tradesmen in Bethabara had moved there. The *Records of the Moravians in North Carolina* chronicled this transition. "Br. Bagge, his family, and several other persons, and four wagon-loads of Store goods moved to Salem today." On February 10, "after a hearty farewell, Br. Schaaf moved to Salem. He has been in the laundry here for 12 years." This was a major adjustment for Moravians and non-Moravians alike. "People brought many deer-skins to our little Store today; they did not want to go to Salem." By mid-April 1772, the transition was complete, and Bethabara entered a new era. (Courtesy of the Moravian Archives, Bethlehem, Pennsylvania.)

Two

From Industries to Farms

19th- and 20th-Century Bethabara

In the *Records of the Moravians in North Carolina,* the Bethabara diarist recorded on April 14, 1772, "Br. Bonn and his family moved to Salem today, Br Ludwig Meinung also; all have now moved who are to go for the present, and the Congregation here is reduced to 50 members." Thus began Bethabara's transition into its second act as a farming community.

Nineteenth-century Bethabara was a far cry from what it had once been. Most residents were farmers, although a store remained with an attached post office. There were still a potter, wheelwright, and blacksmith living in the town, but these tradesmen primarily made products for the town itself.

As the century wore on, the Moravians in Wachovia increasingly adopted the customs of the strangers, or non-Moravians, around them. Church services, once integrated in Bethabara, became segregated, with a separate African American church built on the outskirts of Salem in 1823. Enslaved individuals in and around Bethabara likely would have traveled to this new church for their worship services. Services for white Moravians continued in the 1788 Gemeinhaus, although there was much concern about attendance as well as behavior among its members.

During the Civil War, Rev. Jacob F. Siewers served both Bethabara and Bethania. Church attendance was low during this period, perhaps in part due to Siewers's opposition to the conflict (by this point, many Moravians had given up their pacifist stance, and some in the Bethabara congregation were advocates of the war). Attendance improved after Siewers's departure in 1865.

By the end of the 19th century, Bethabara's congregation had grown large enough to need to expand the "audience room" (or worship space) of the Gemeinhaus. The *Wachovia Moravian*, a publication put out by the Moravian Church, noted, "It will be deeply gratifying to the readers of the *Wachovia Moravian* to learn that in our oldest congregation, so replete in historical reminiscences in connection with the founding of Wachovia, there are increasing evidences of progress."

As the 20th century arrived, Bethabara was on firmer spiritual ground. Members continued to plow the fields, unknowingly protecting the original town that would one day be unearthed.

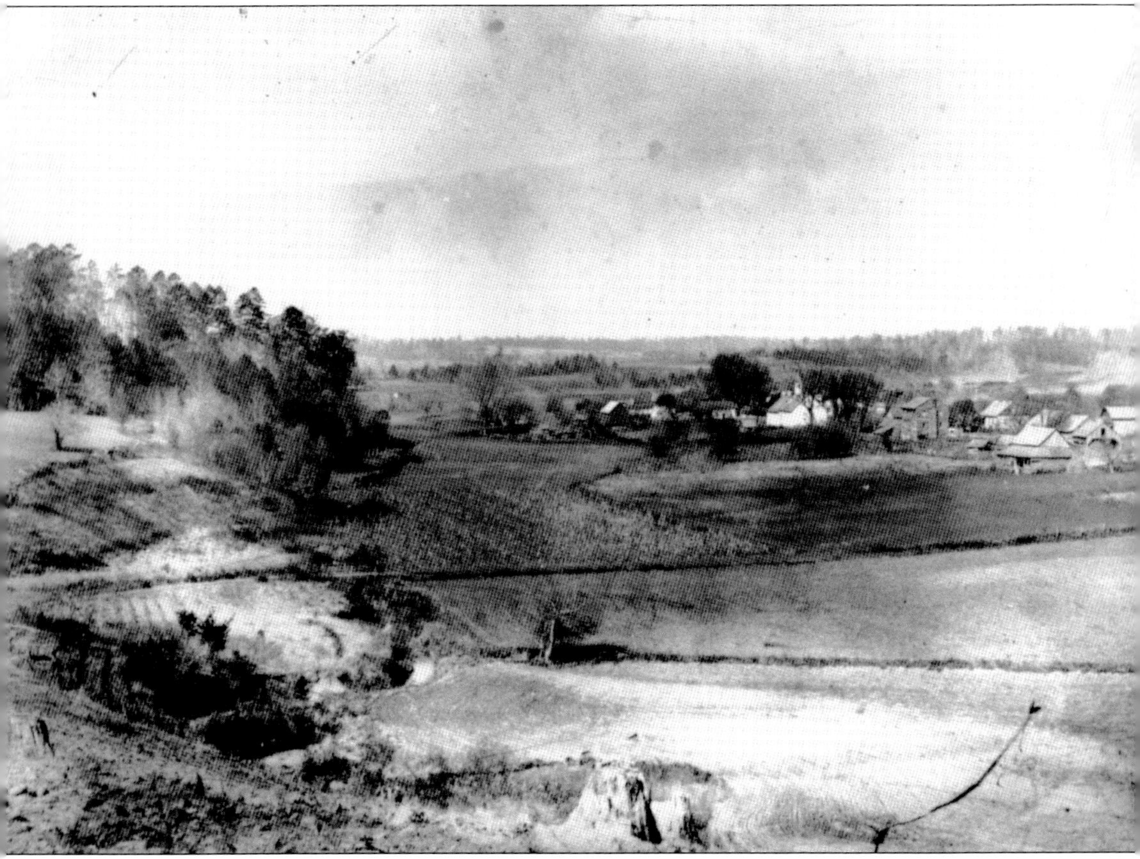

This photograph from c. 1890–1900 provides a view of Bethabara, with the Gemeinhaus and its distinctive bell tower easily seen among the other buildings. The 1803 Distiller's House can be seen toward the right in this image; it is the white house across the street from the Gemeinhaus. The 1782 Potter's House can barely be seen but is farther to the right in this image, partially hidden behind a barn. Fields of crops are found just outside the town. The hill to the left leads to God's Acre, the Moravian cemetery. In the 19th century, Bethabara and Bethania often shared a minister, who regularly commented on poor church attendance. One minister was told to not bother holding a church service at Bethabara while the competing non-Moravian Maple Springs camp meeting took place, as all the members were likely to attend it. In 1861, on at least two occasions, Reverend Siewers found himself preaching to two men and one little boy at Bethabara. (Courtesy of Old Salem Museums & Gardens.)

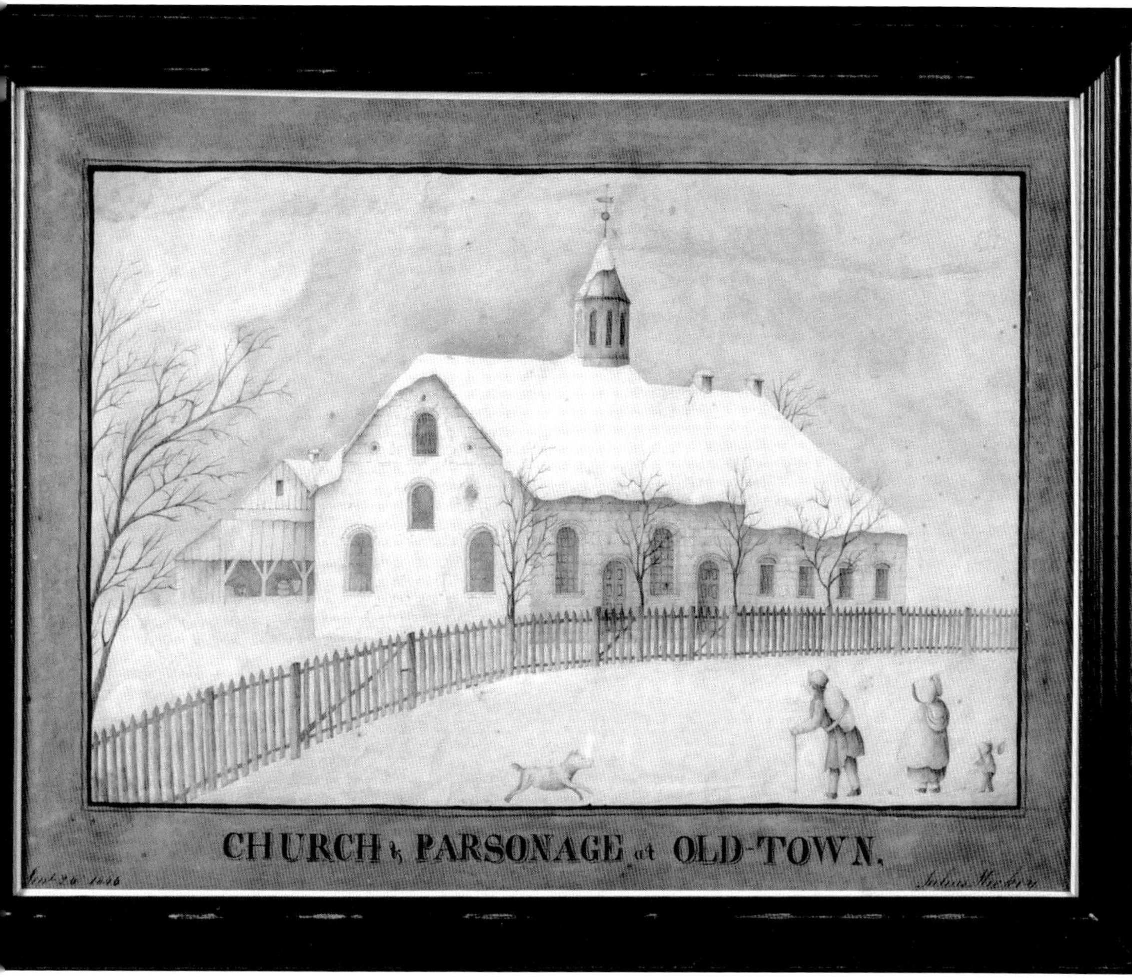

This depiction of the 1788 Gemeinhaus in the snow, entitled "Church and Parsonage at Old-Town," was drawn by Julius Mickey and dated September 26, 1846. The Gemeinhaus served as both the church and minister's living quarters (which is why Mickey labeled the Gemeinhaus as a church and parsonage). By the time of this drawing, Bethabara had become known as Old Town after the US Post Office changed its name. Julius Mickey was born in 1832 in the Distiller's House, located near the Gemeinhaus. He was 14 years old when he made this drawing. By 1858, he and his brother Samuel had moved to Salem and opened a tin shop. Their store was easily recognizable thanks to the large tin coffee pot they made and displayed outside their store. That iconic symbol of Winston-Salem now stands at Old Salem Road and South Main Street, not very far from Salem's God's Acre. (Collection of Wachovia Historical Society; photograph courtesy of Old Salem Museums & Gardens.)

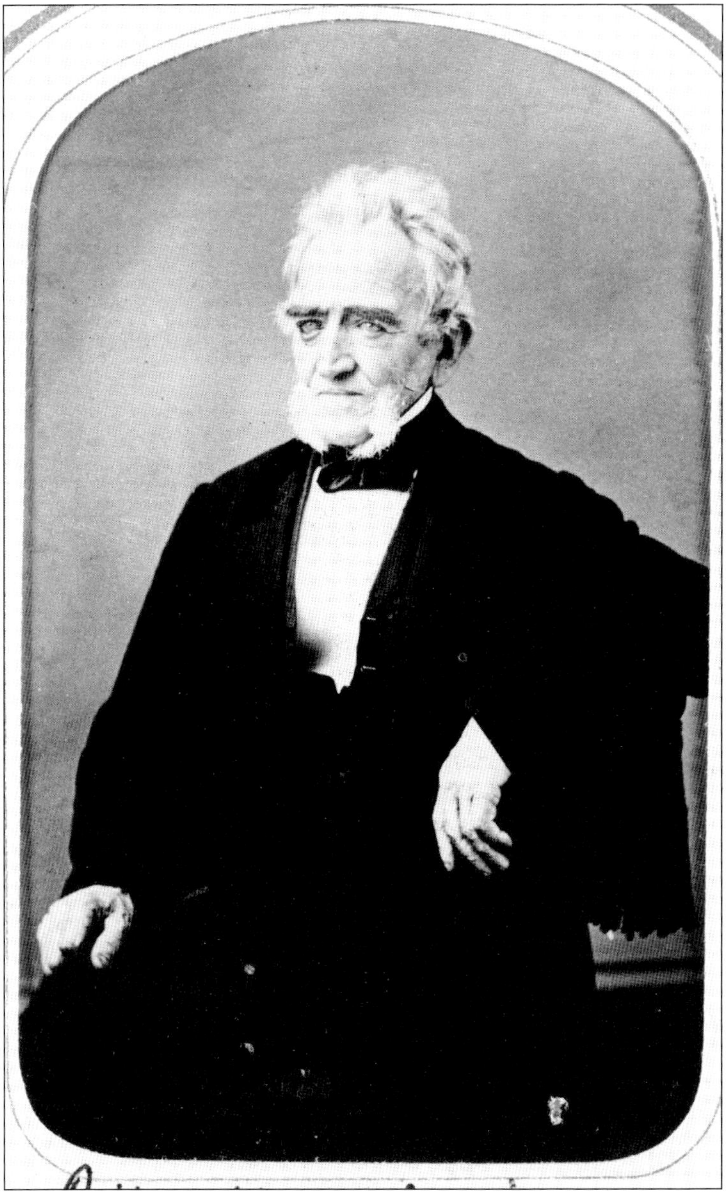

Born in Burkhall, Denmark, Bishop Johann Christian Jacobson (1795–1870) came to America in 1816 and settled first in the Moravian town of Bethlehem, Pennsylvania. He traveled to Salem, North Carolina, in 1826 and was made a deacon of the Moravian church. He and his wife settled into the parsonage at Bethania. When Br. Johann Ludwig Strohle, who had served as minister for many years at Bethabara, passed away, Jacobson began to serve both congregations. He continued to preach at both Bethania and Bethabara from 1827 until 1834, when he was replaced by Bishop George Frederic Bahnson. Jacobson became the inspector of the Girls' Boarding School and assistant pastor at Salem. He was well known for being able to preach sermons in both German and English. In 1844, Jacobson moved back to Pennsylvania to take charge of the Boys' Boarding School in Nazareth. H.P. Osborne, a photographer in Bethlehem, Pennsylvania, captured this image of Bishop Jacobson sometime between 1864 and 1866. (Courtesy of Old Salem Museum & Gardens.)

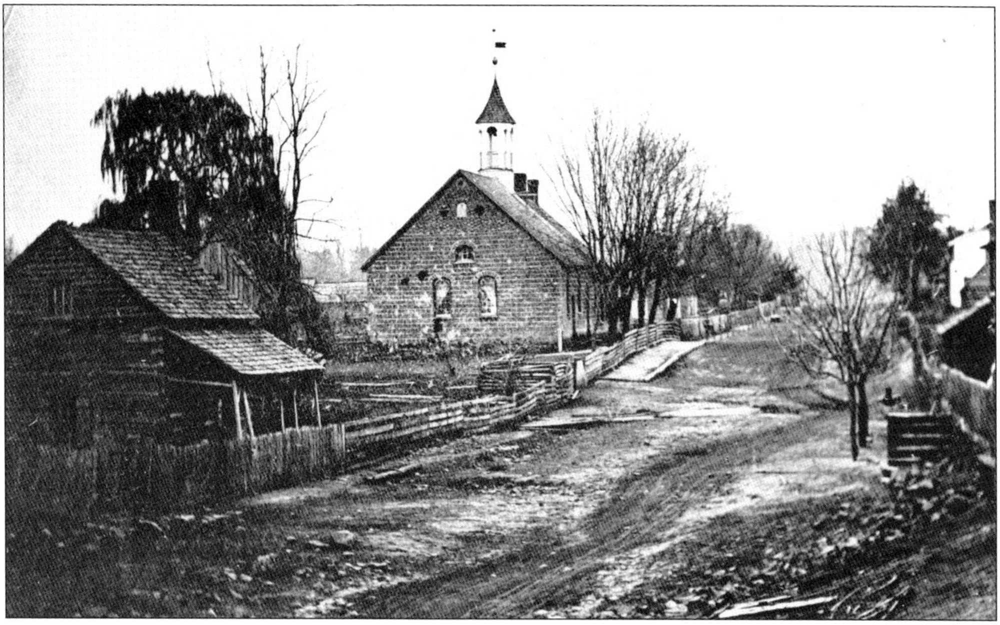

This photograph was part of a stereograph, which is a pair of images viewed through a stereoscope to create the illusion of a three-dimensional image. The viewer might have noticed the state of Bethabara's roads, which caused Rev. Eugene Grieder to remark in 1874 that Bethabara was an "ugly old town with mud up to the throat fit to kill civilization out of any man." (Courtesy of the Forsyth County Public Library Photograph Collection, Winston-Salem, North Carolina.)

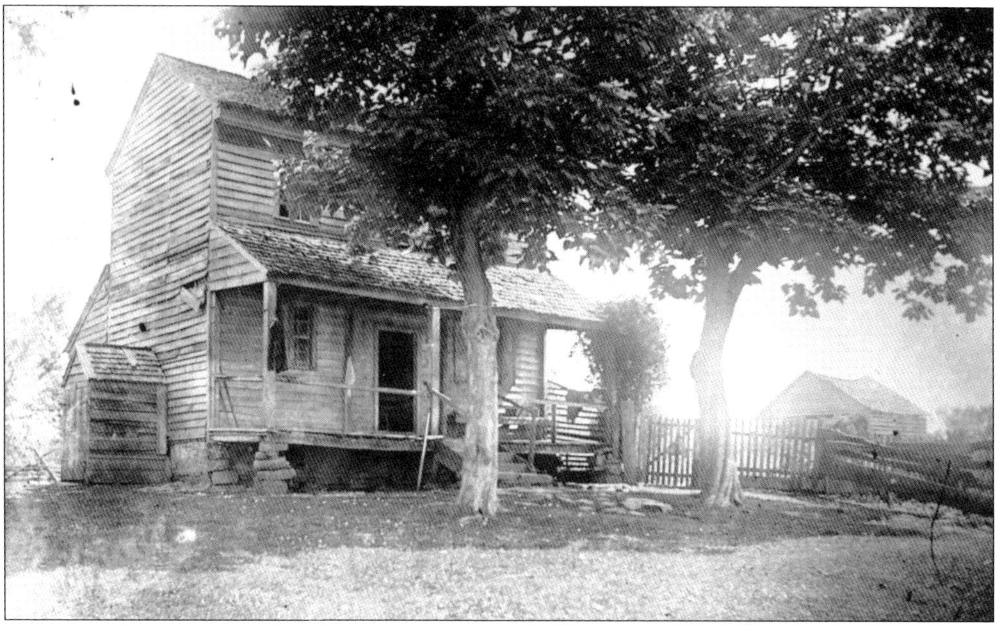

This undated photograph was labeled as "Mrs. Laura Beck's Old Home" and "Billie Beck Home" in a Peterson family scrapbook. Laura Beck (née Vogler) and other volunteer nurses from Salem went to Fauquier County, Virginia, in 1861 to nurse members of the 21st North Carolina Regiment. She married widower William Beck of Old Town in 1863. (Courtesy of the Forsyth County Public Library Photograph Collection, Winston-Salem, North Carolina.)

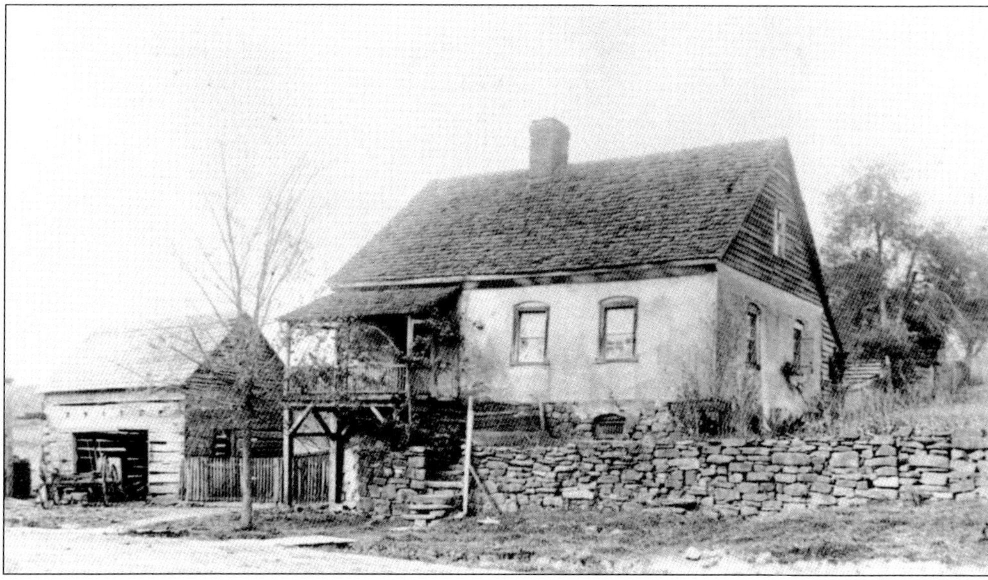

This photograph of the Distiller's House was taken around 1890. Built in 1803 to house the distiller and his family, at this point it had become a private residence and was no longer owned by the Moravian Church. A log barn and carriage can be seen next to the home. (Courtesy of Old Salem Museums & Gardens.)

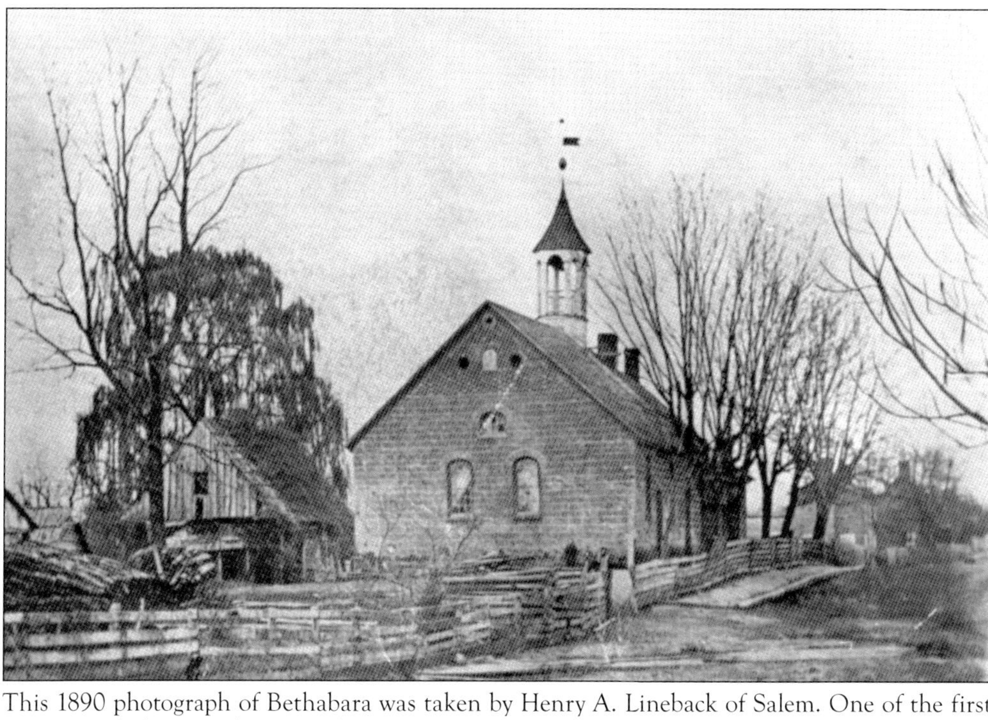

This 1890 photograph of Bethabara was taken by Henry A. Lineback of Salem. One of the first professional photographers in Salem, Lineback built a studio on the north end of his father John Henry Lineback's house. Lineback later married his assistant, Susan Elizabeth James, and had two children. He retired from the photography business in 1922. (Courtesy of Old Salem Museums & Gardens.)

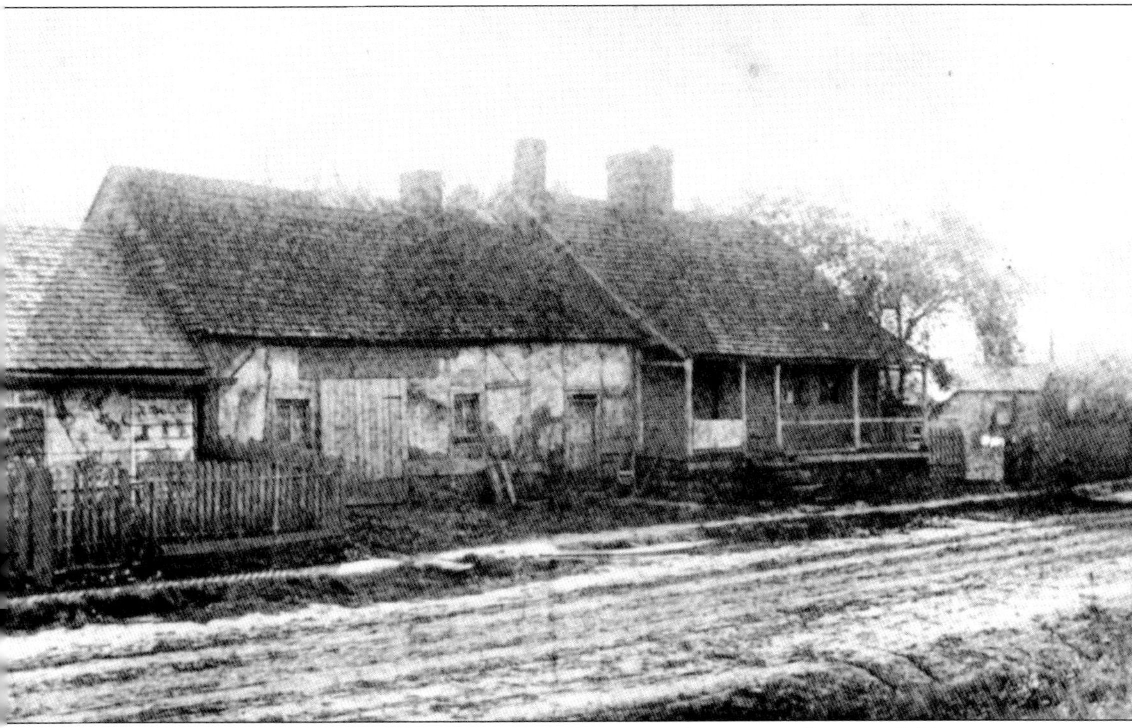

This image of the Potter's House was taken around 1890. Built in 1782, the Potter's House, as it is known today, was originally the home of Johannes Schaub Jr. Once the tavernkeeper, he later became a blue dyer and set up a shop in his new home. Schaub sold the house to Gottlob Krause, who was the first potter to live there. Krause built the half-timber addition that can be seen in the photograph. He sold his home and shop to John Butner, who moved into the house sometime after August 1802. Butner and his sons carried on the Bethabara pottery tradition well into the 19th century. The house, shop, and land remained in the Butner family until 1872, when it was sold to L.I. Hine. Ada Hine became the owner in 1924. Her estate sold the property to B. Clyde Shore in 1956, and Edwin Stockton purchased it on behalf of the Moravian Church in 1957. (Courtesy of Old Salem Museums & Gardens.)

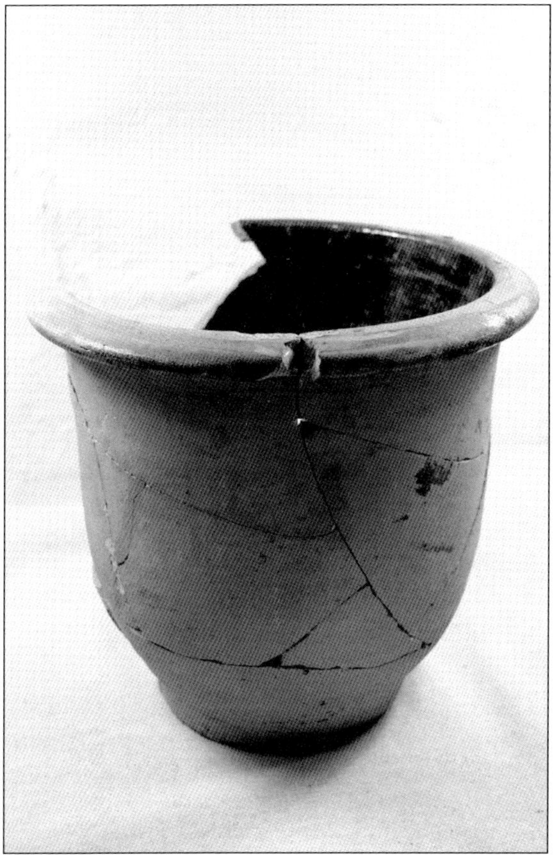

While living in the Boys' School in Salem in 1789, John Butner began his apprenticeship to master potter Rudolph Christ. His bad behavior in pottery almost got him kicked out of the congregation, but he turned things around and was allowed to stay. In 1796, he ended his apprenticeship and became a journeyman in Christ's shop. In 1802, he purchased the Potter's House and shop from Gottlob Krause and became the master potter in Bethabara. For the next 70 years, the Butners continued to make and sell pottery in Bethabara. The crock at left with lead-glazed interior is attributed to John Butner. Below is an image of a Butner pottery mark, indicating that for a time John and his son Joseph worked together as potters. (Both, courtesy of the Bethabara Collection.)

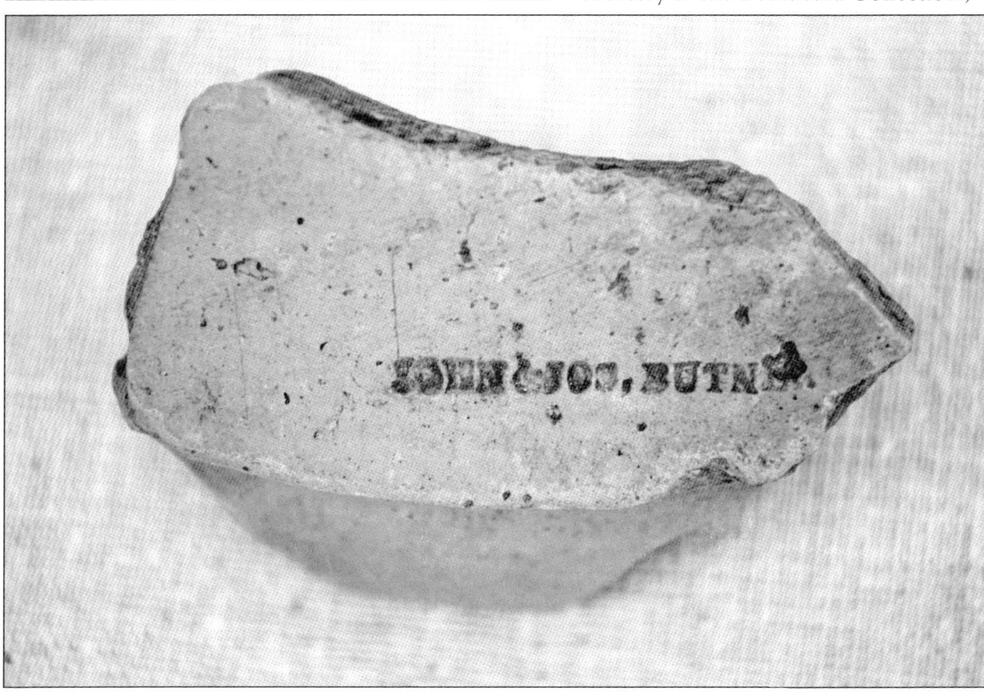

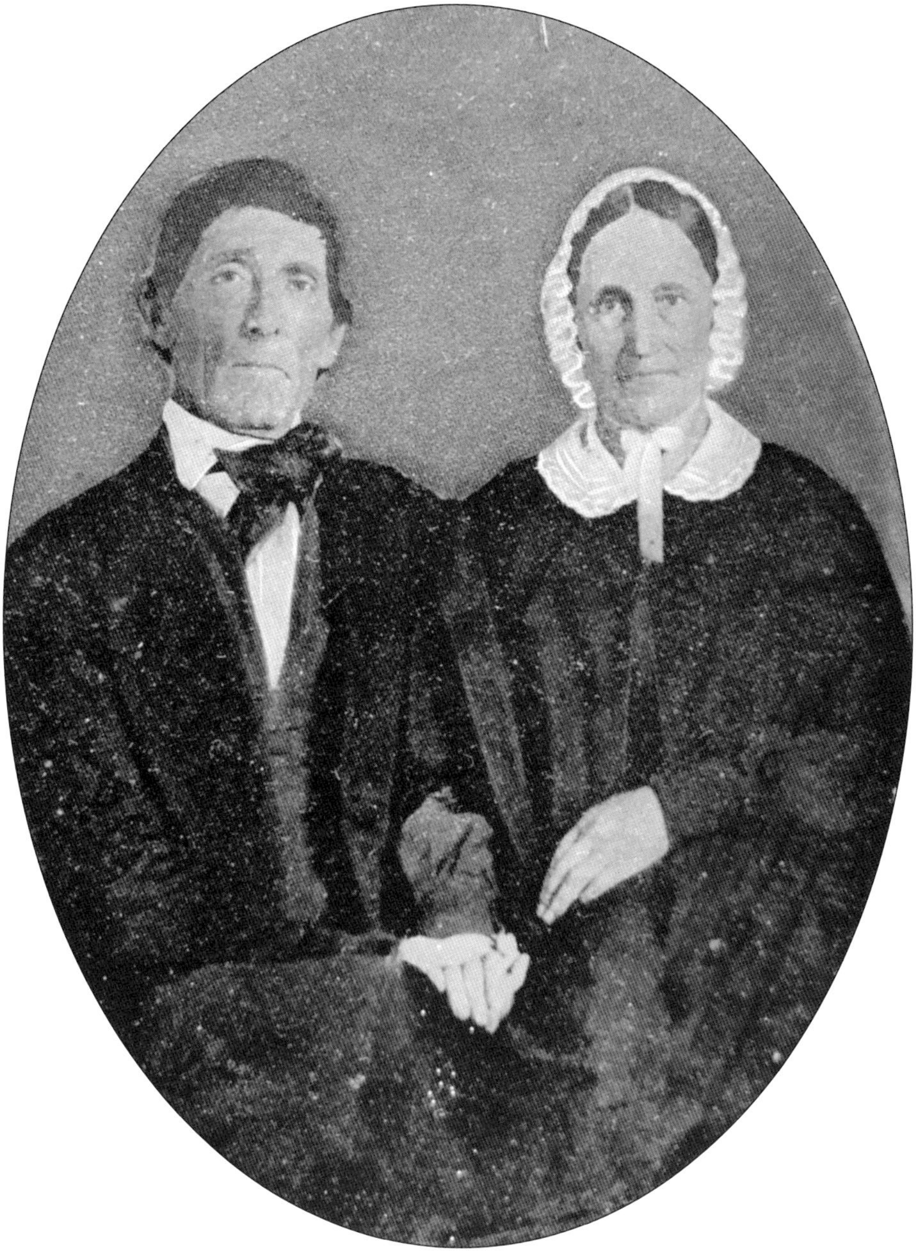

This c. 1850s tintype portrait is either of John Butner and his second wife, Elizabeth Spaugh Butner, or possibly of his son Joseph Butner and his second wife, Louise Catherine Walk Butner. John Butner was a prominent member of the town, living in the building now known as the Potter's House. He ran a pottery next to his house and a general store across the street. He was made Bethabara's first postmaster in 1832, and the post office was likely housed inside his store. On December 28, 1856, Butner suffered a stroke that left him paralyzed, and he died on January 2, 1857. In his will, Butner devised his property, which included the Potter's House, the shop, the kiln, and meadowland he used for acquiring clay, to his son Joseph. His wife, Elizabeth, moved to Salem to live in the Widows' House. Joseph Butner continued in the pottery trade until he died in 1872. (Courtesy of the Bethabara Collection.)

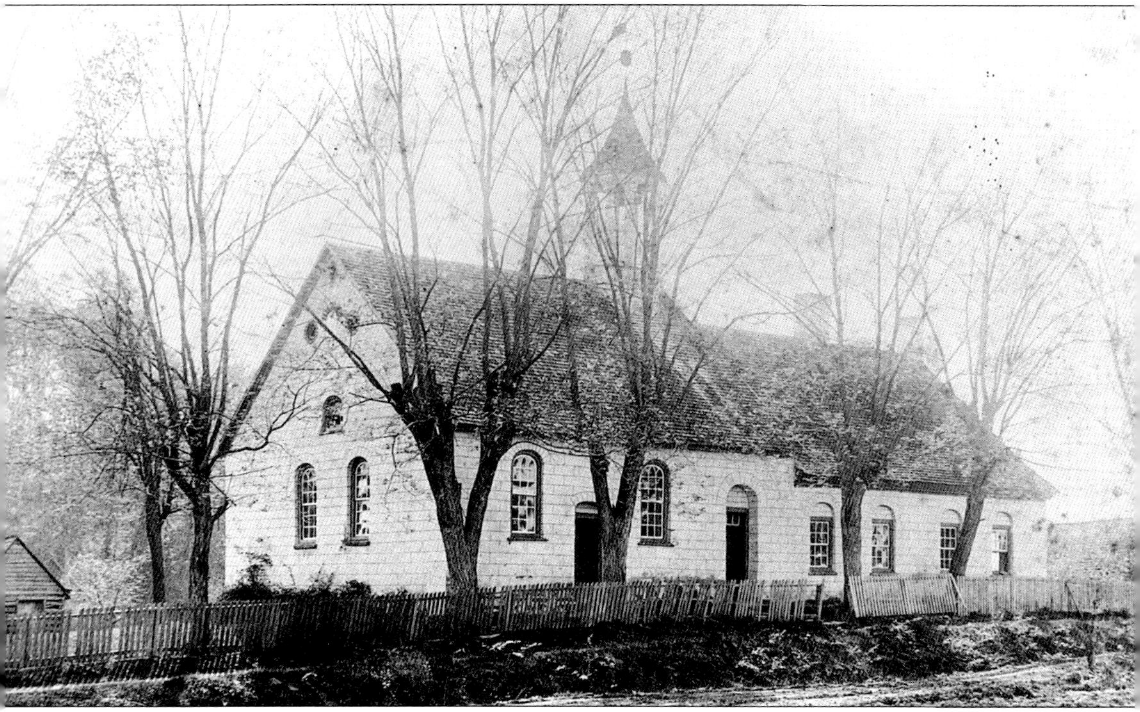

In 1847, the *Records of the Moravians in North Carolina* noted, "A meeting of the members of the congregation in Bethabara has been set to listen to the rules and regulations of the congregation which must then be signed. It is high time that those of the congregation do away with what is evil." The impact was not a long-lasting one, as two years later, John Shore was caught dancing at a corn husking event. He was spoken to about this transgression and told that he could stay in the church if he promised to improve. Attendance continued to be low, including at the November 17, 1855, celebration of Bethabara's founding. "Most of the sisters attended," the *Records* stated, but after the service, "some of the brethren slipped away." The diarist concluded that "this congregation quite definitely needs to be revived by grace." This image of the Gemeinhaus was taken in the late 1800s. (Courtesy of Old Salem Museums & Gardens.)

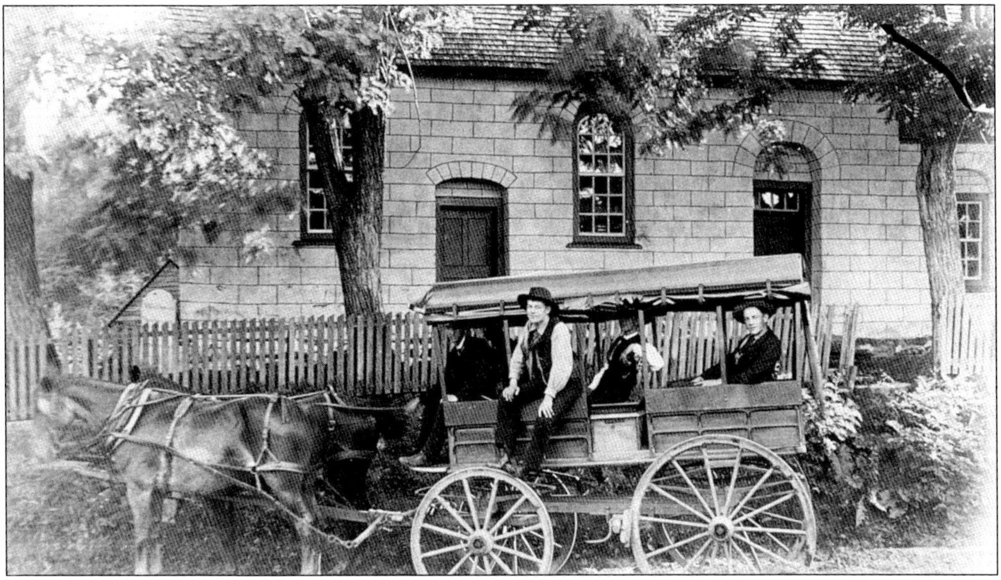

The subjects and photographers of these two images are unknown, but they were likely taken in either the late 19th or early 20th century. At this point, Bethabara's congregation had begun a major turnaround in both attendance and behavior. Much of this can be credited to Rev. John McCuiston, who became the minister of Bethabara Moravian Church in 1892. By March 1895, the *Wachovia Moravian* reported that "new life and interest is filling the congregation under Bro. McCuiston's ministrations. Extensive repairs are about to be made which will increase the size of the auditorium [worship space], and in addition to this a new floor will be laid and other changes made. The work is to commence at once." The article went on to note that "the congregational singing is improving. The nice lot of new hymn books doubtless contributed to this end." (Both, courtesy of Old Salem Museums & Gardens.)

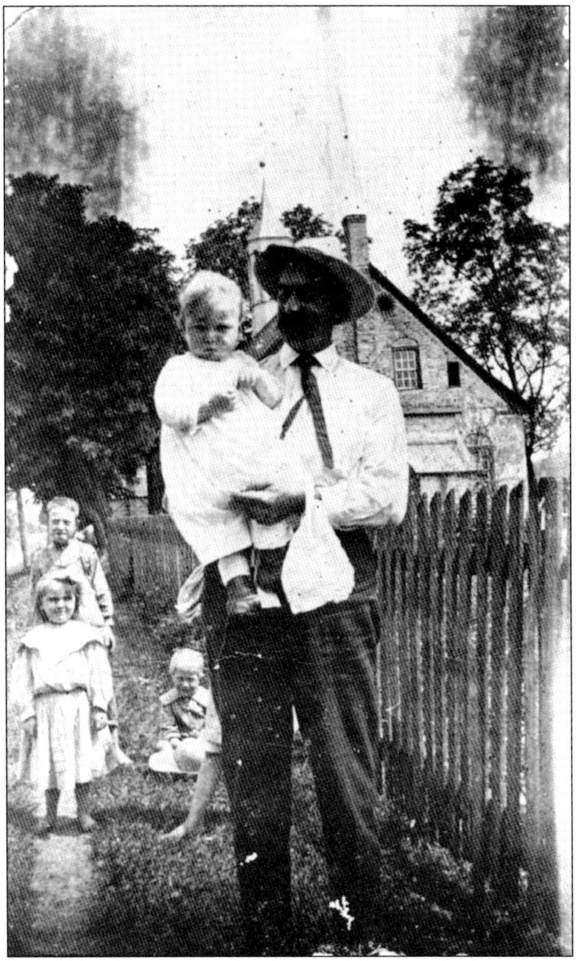

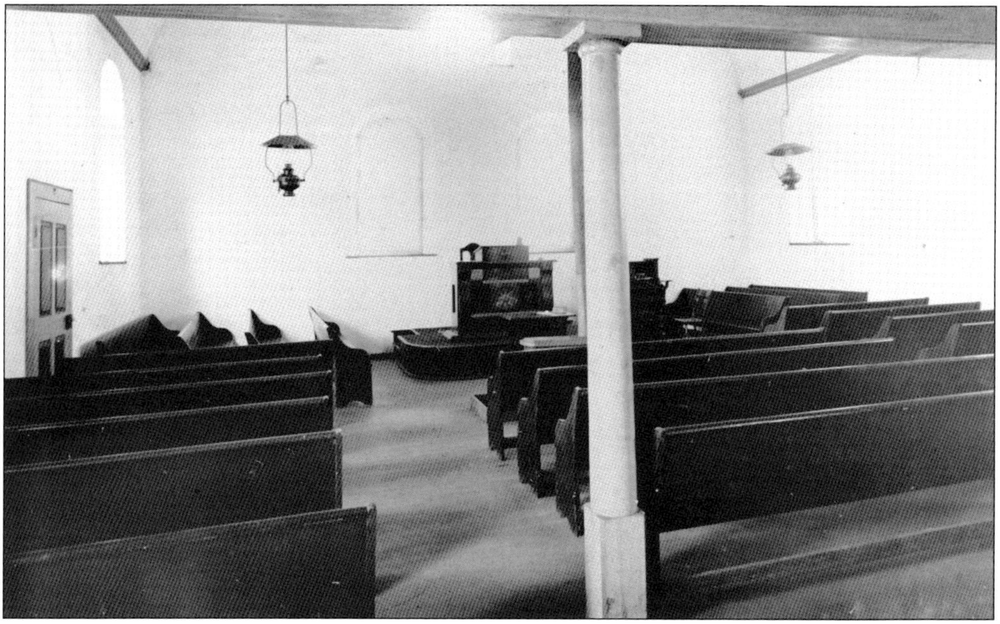

The original 1788 Gemeinhaus *Saal*, or worship room, consisted of pews that pointed toward the front of the room, where the minister's chair and table sat. The original Saal did not have a heat source or pulpit, and wall sconces provided light. By 1901, when this photograph was taken, much had changed about the Saal, including the removal of the wall for the vestibule to increase space for the growing congregation. (Collection of Wachovia Historical Society; photograph courtesy of Old Salem Museums & Gardens.)

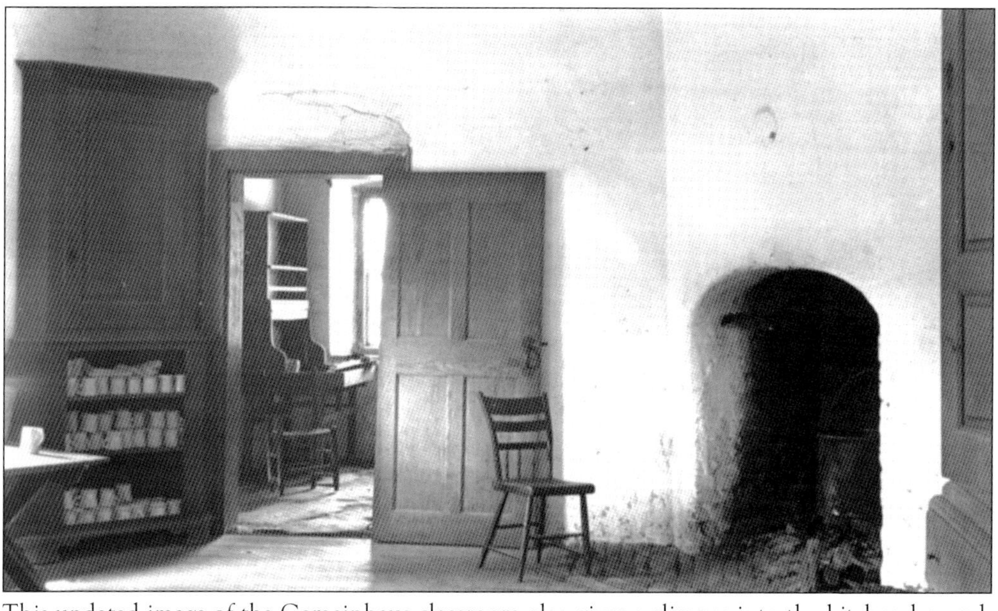

This undated image of the Gemeinhaus classroom also gives a glimpse into the kitchen beyond. The classroom served its namesake purpose in the 18th century and was also used to prepare coffee for the lovefeast, a religious singing service that is followed by a simple meal shared in fellowship. Evidence of this use can be found in the corner cabinet as well as the large kettle used for making coffee, which is thought to be original to the building. (Courtesy of Old Salem Museums & Gardens.)

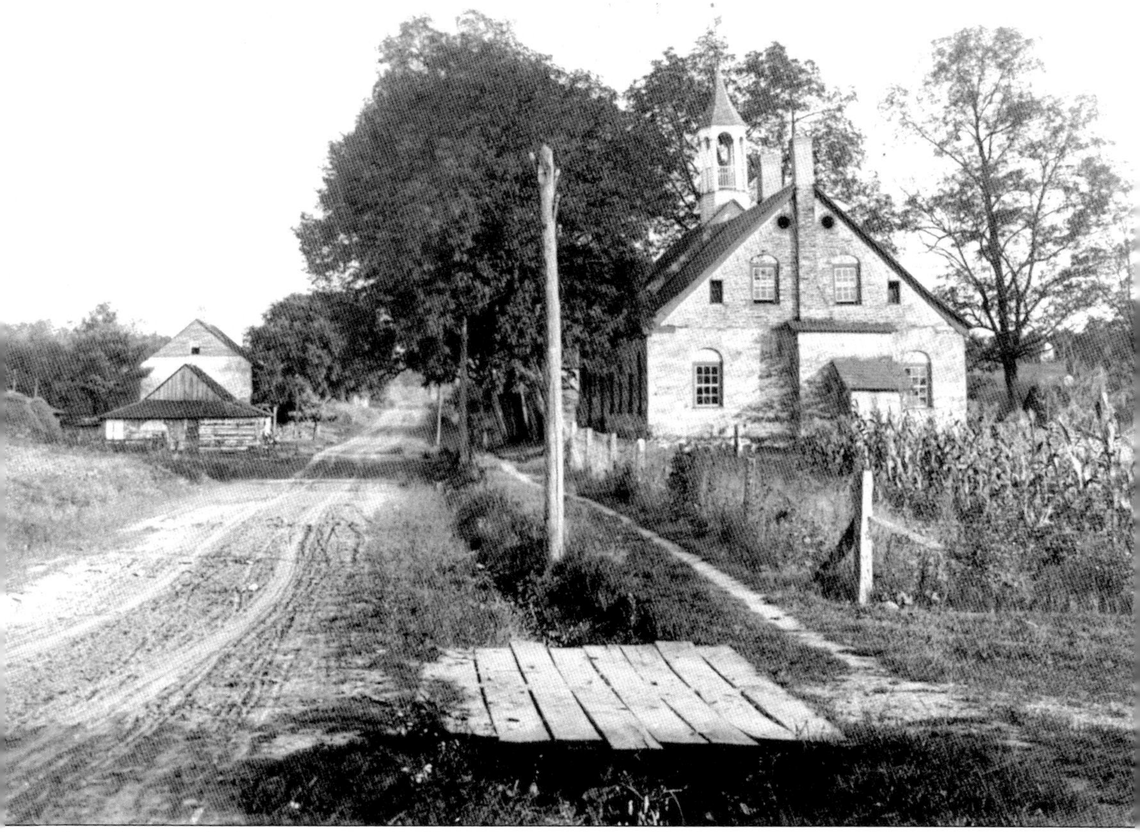

This photograph, likely from the early 1900s, shows the Gemeinhaus (right) with the Distiller's House (left) in the distance. Corn grows in front of the Gemeinhaus, and to the left of the building is a line of telegraph poles. Large haystacks stand behind the Distiller's House barn, which also has a poster for Barnum and Bailey circus displayed on its side. The circus first came to the area in October 1909. During this time, Bethabara's congregation continued to improve and expand. In that same year, the *Wachovia Moravian* noted, "Some one recently wrote to a member at Old Town, asking if the congregation was dead, that nothing had appeared in the *Wachovia Moravian* in some time. We can say that during the past year, Bethabara has been very much alive." The Young People's Christian Endeavor Society and the women's auxiliary both helped the congregation grow and become more active. (Courtesy of the Archives, Moravian Church in America, Southern Province.)

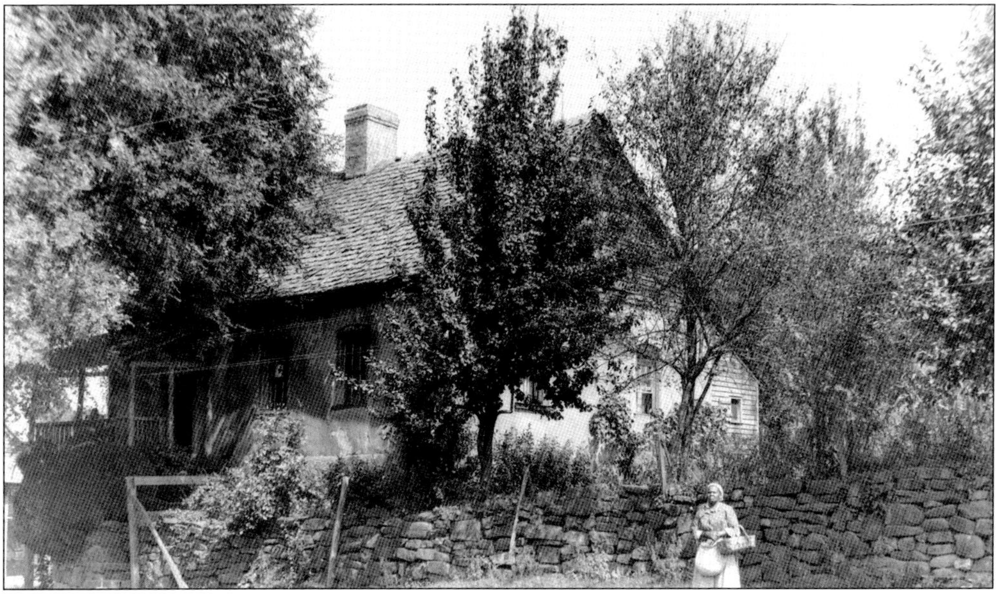

This image of the Distiller's House was taken by Irvin T. Rominger around 1918. It is believed his parents lived in the house at the time. In the front window is the symbol for the Red Cross, indicating this was likely captured during World War I. Taken from the Peterson family album, this photograph has "Aunt Kate Atkins" written on it, referring to the figure in the foreground. (Courtesy of Old Salem Museums & Gardens.)

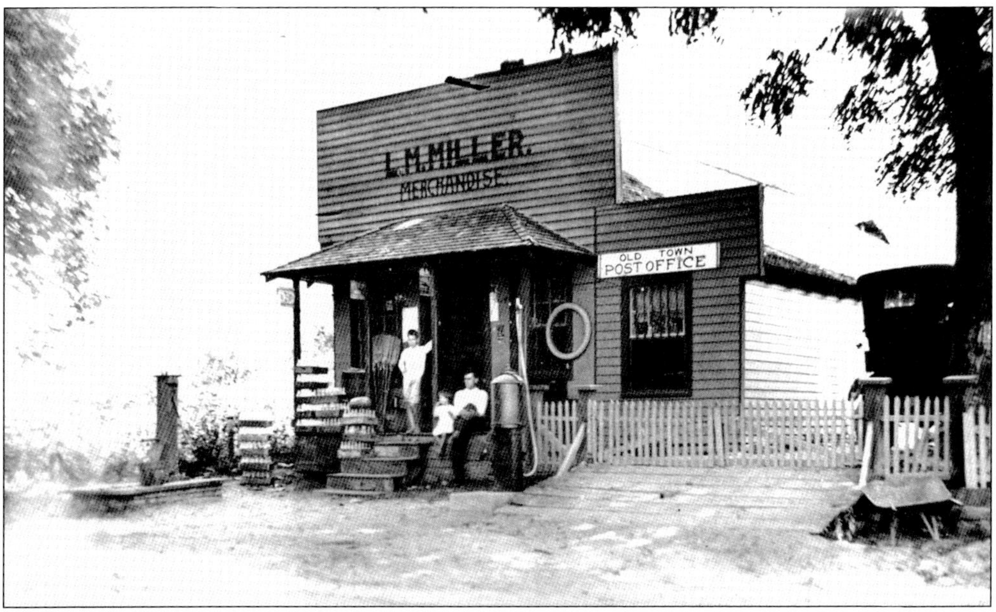

F.T. Hine sold his general store and land to Leland M. Miller in 1909. In addition to merchandise, Miller also sold produce from his store. In 1832, the US Postal Service granted Bethabara a post office, which likely operated out of John Butner's store. In 1835, the US Postal Service changed Bethabara's name to Old Town. Eventually, the post office moved into Miller's store. (Courtesy of the Archives, Moravian Church in America, Southern Province.)

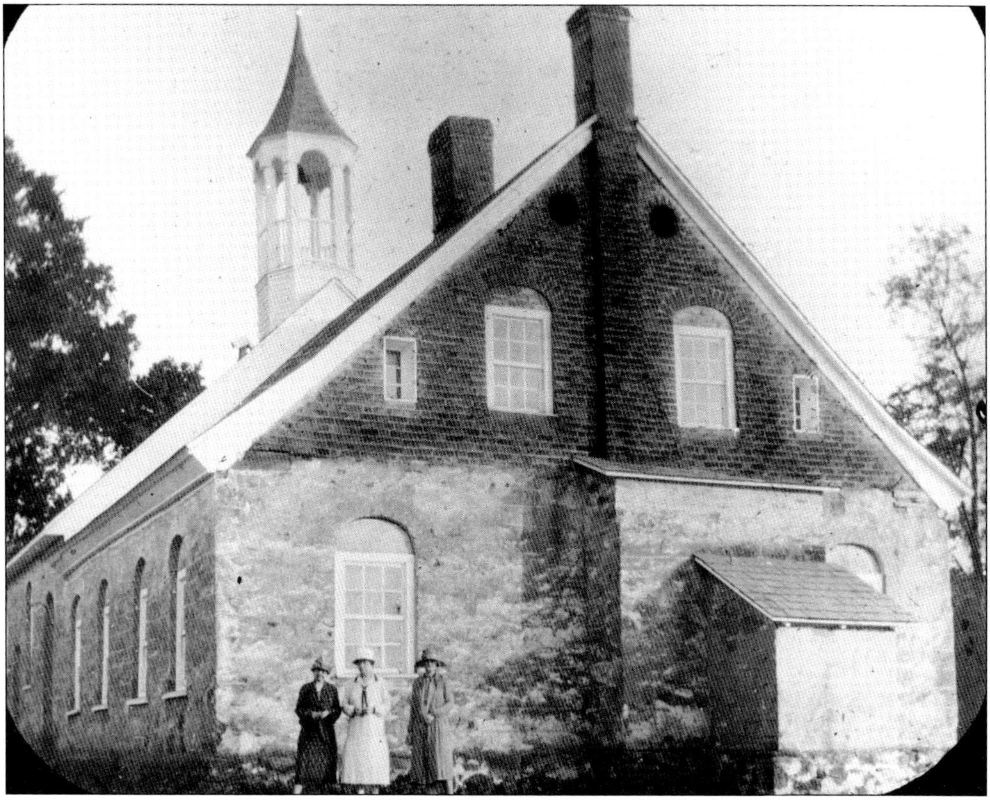

This c. 1920–1930 photograph taken by Irvin T. Rominger shows three unidentified women in front of the Gemeinhaus. The building continued to be the iconic symbol of Bethabara, and visitors often wanted to be photographed next to it. (Courtesy of Old Salem Museums & Gardens.)

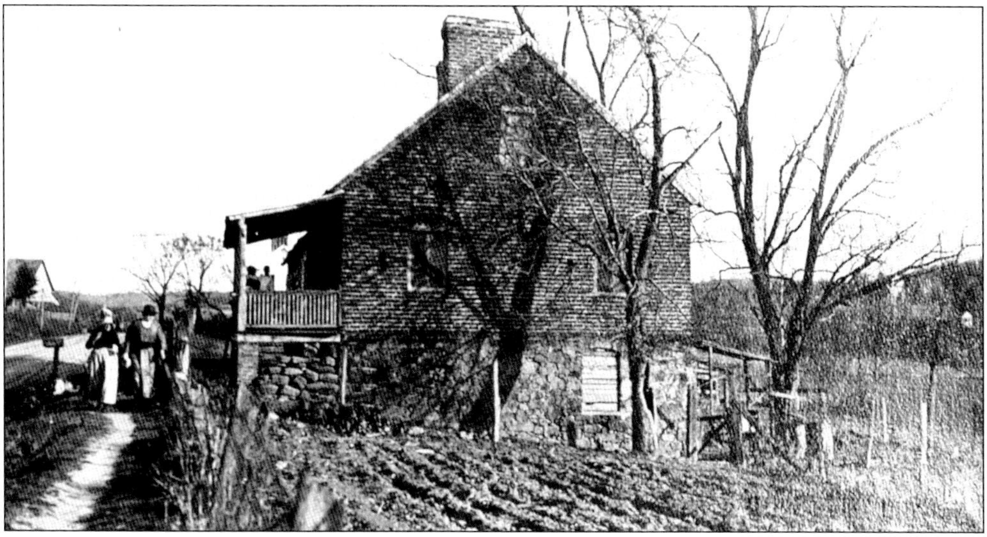

This c. 1920 photograph features the Potter's House. The photographer and individuals in the image are unidentified. The Potter's House is one of the oldest brick houses still standing in Forsyth County. In the 1920s, it was owned by the Hine family. (Courtesy of Old Salem Museums & Gardens.)

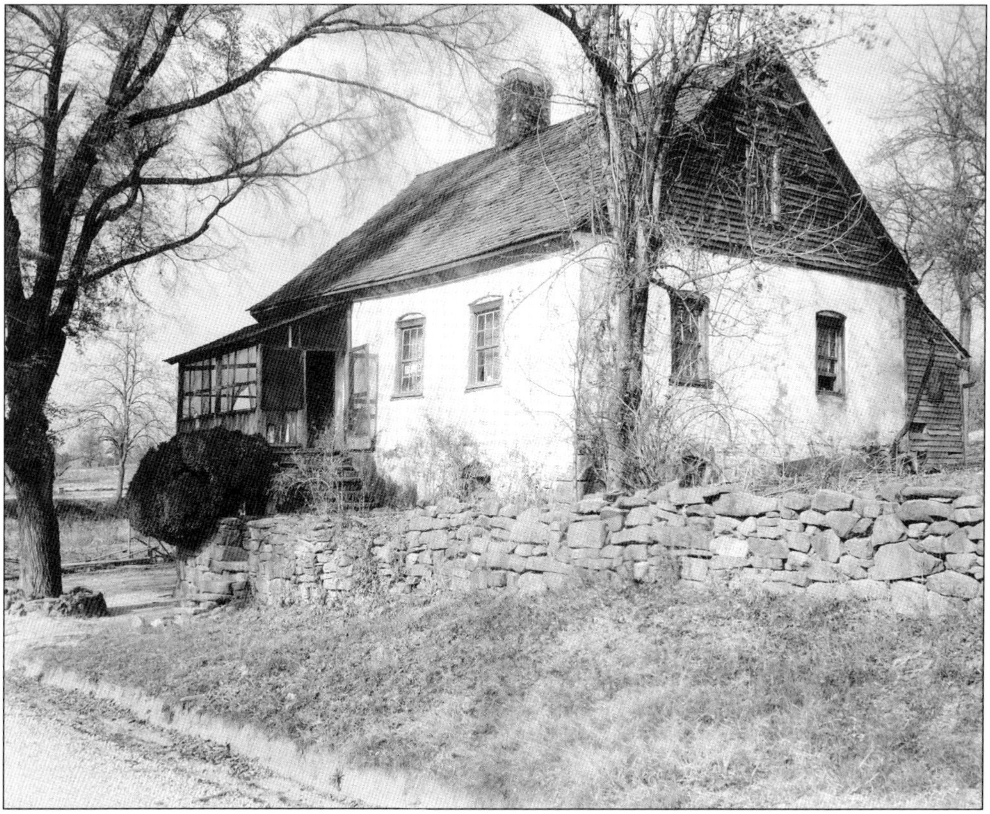

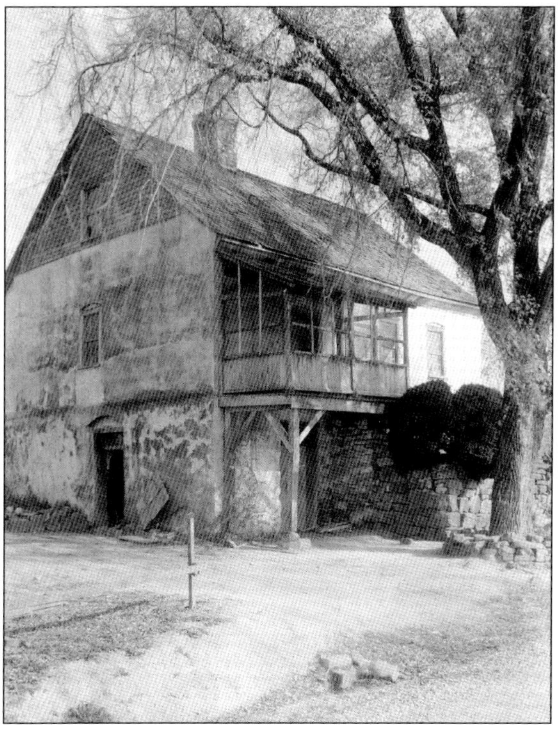

These two photographs of the Distiller's House were taken between 1935 and 1938 by the renowned photographer Frances Benjamin Johnston. Johnston began her photographic career taking portraits, including those of Susan B. Anthony, Mark Twain, and Booker T. Washington. By the 1920s, she became more interested in photographing architecture, particularly of ordinary historic buildings. She began documenting the architecture of the American South and was drawn to structures that were in states of deterioration. The state of the Distiller's House made it an attractive subject for Johnston. Fortunately, the Distiller's House was only a few years away from being renovated to serve as Bethabara's parsonage. (Both, courtesy of the Library of Congress.)

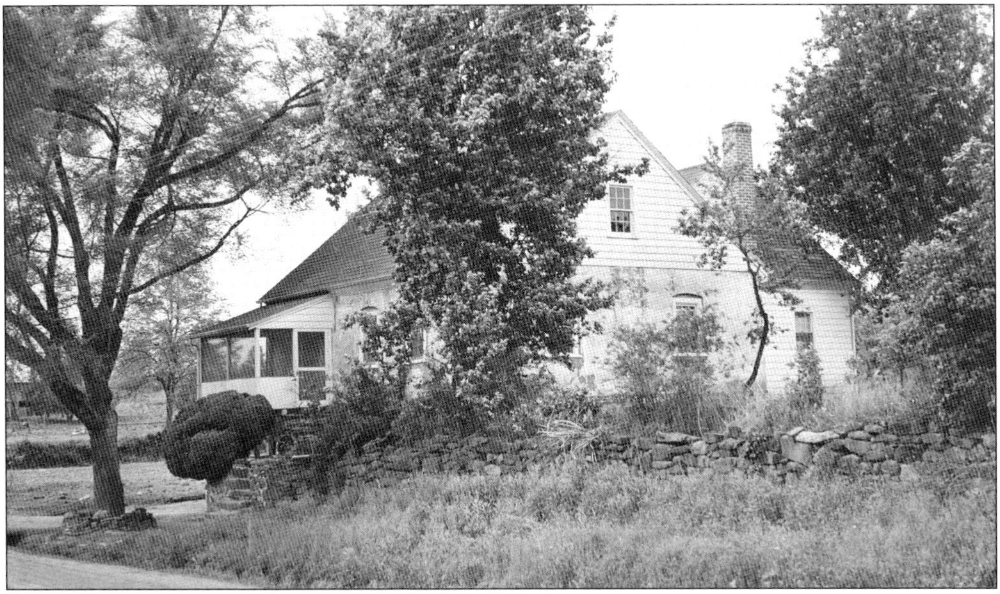

The above photograph was taken sometime after 1938, when the Distiller's House had been renovated into Bethabara's parsonage. The Gemeinhaus rooms once used as the minister's living quarters were needed for other uses as the church grew. The $3,000 Distiller's House renovations included an addition to the rear of the house, a new roof, window and door framing, indoor heating, electric wiring, plumbing, painting, and plaster and concrete work. Charles B. Adams was the minister at the time, and he and his wife were the first occupants of the parsonage. Eleanor Adams was said to have loved the large attic and hung her wash there to dry in bad weather. The photograph below was taken by Jack E. Boucher in 1962 as part of the Historic American Buildings Survey (HABS) project. (Above, courtesy of the Forsyth County Public Library Photograph Collection, Winston-Salem, North Carolina; below, courtesy of the Library of Congress.)

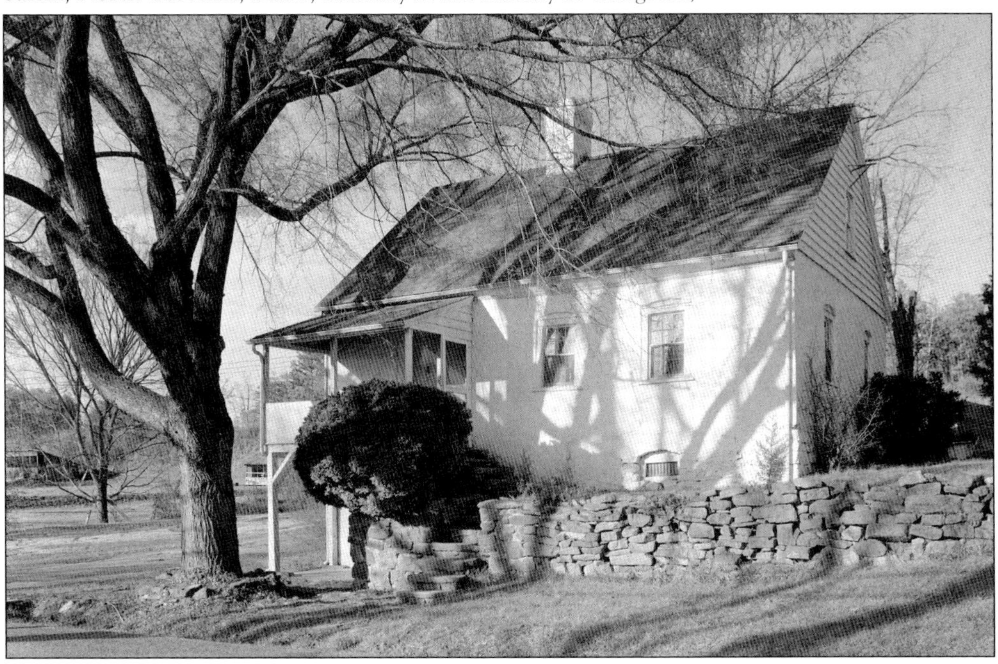

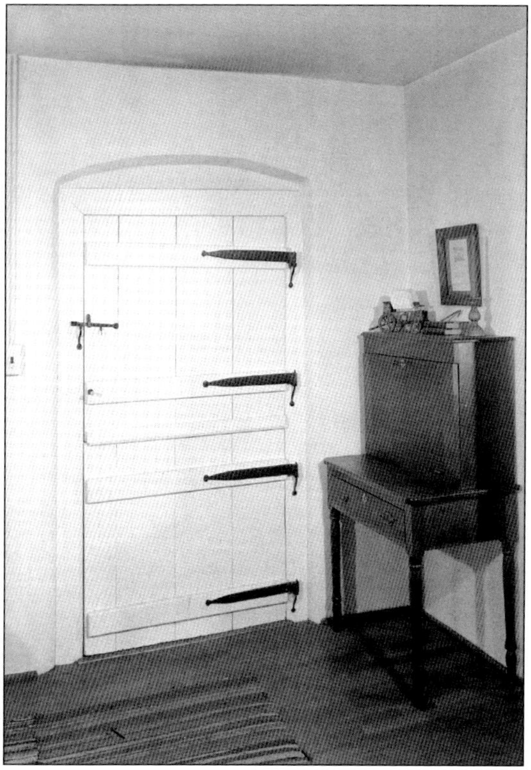

These two 1962 photographs of the interior of the Distiller's House were taken by the HABS project. The image at left is of the interior double door of the main floor. The image below is of the fireplace in the main room. In addition to photographs of the building, HABS also created architectural drawings as part of its study. HABS began its efforts to document achievements in architecture, engineering, and landscape design in 1933 as part of the National Park Service. The Distiller's House is one of 43,000 structures HABS has documented. (Both, courtesy of the Library of Congress.)

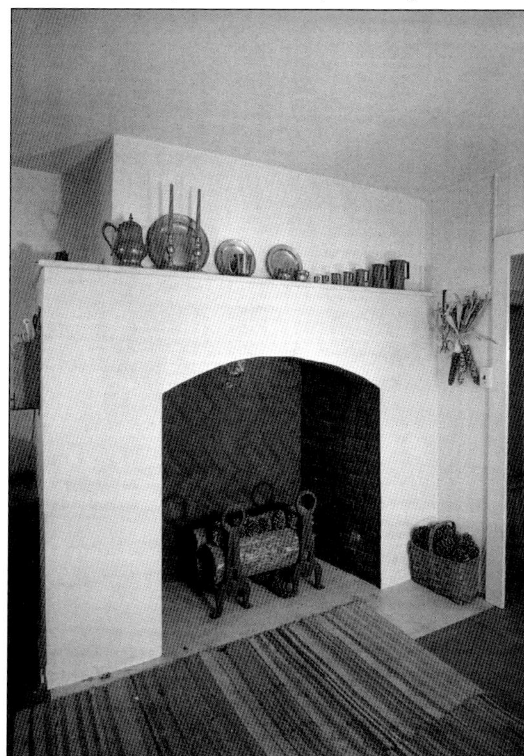

These two photographs of the interior of the Saal, or worship space, of the Gemeinhaus were taken by Frances Benjamin Johnston in 1936. The photograph at right shows the pulpit, which was likely given as a gift in the early 1890s by Br. Augustus Fogle of Salem. The photograph below clearly illustrates how the vestibule was incorporated into the worship space by removing a wall. Pillars were put in its place, and a small entryway room was added to enclose the front door. A "Register of Attendance and Offering" can be found on the back wall, noting that in 1936 Bethabara's congregation numbered 75, and the offering collected the previous Sunday came to a total of $3. The cord for the bell can be seen dangling from the upper floor. (Both, courtesy of the Library of Congress.)

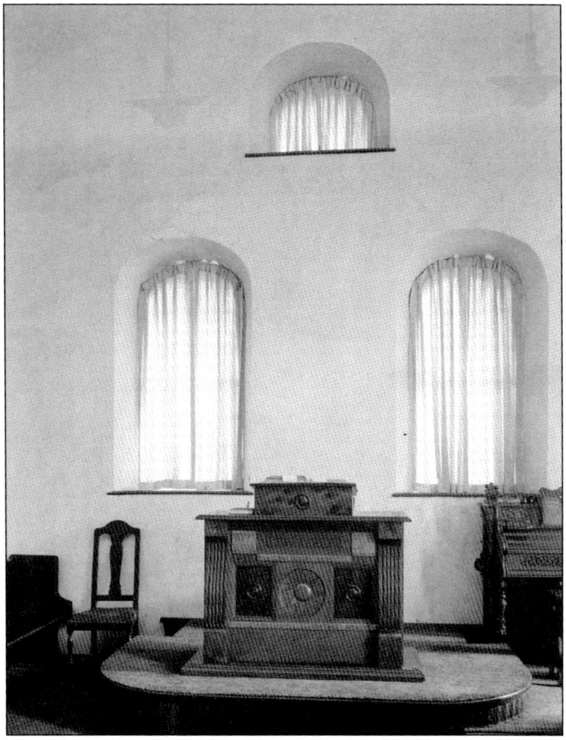

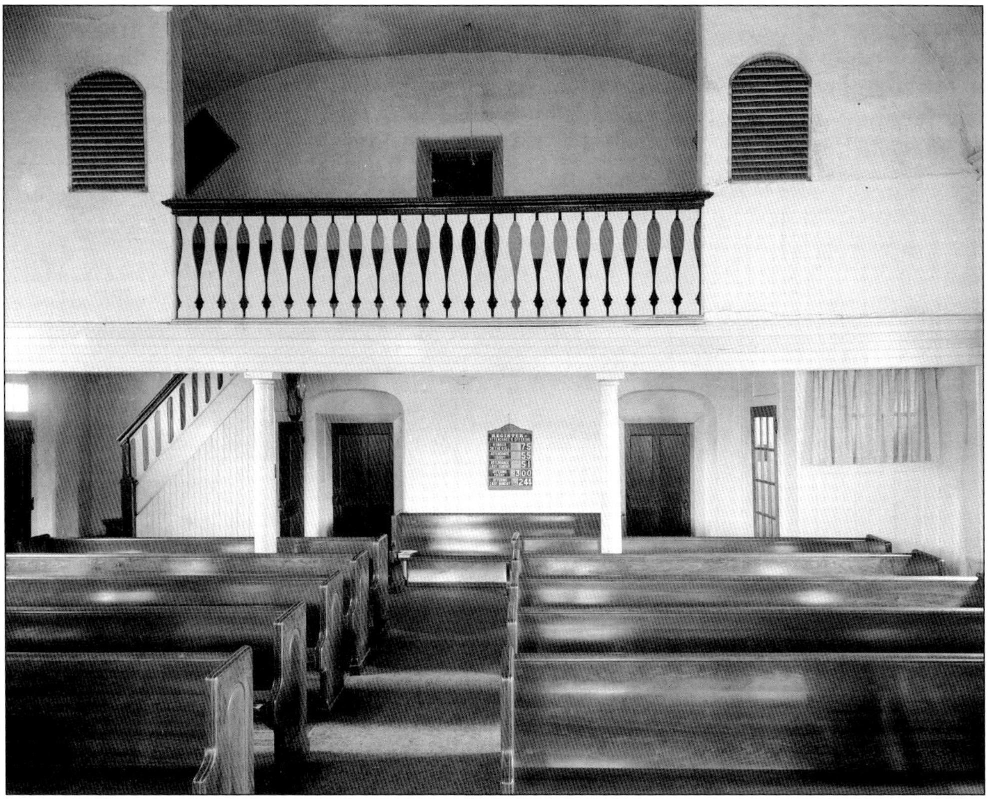

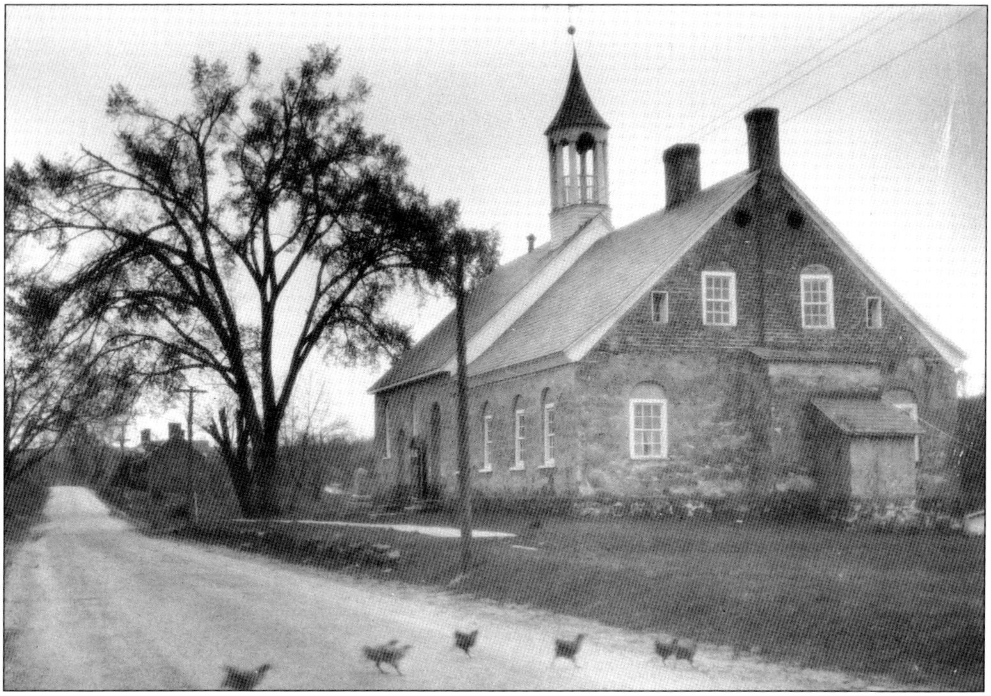

These two photographs capture the rural setting of the 1788 Gemeinhaus. The photograph above was taken in the 1930s, while the photograph below was taken in the 1950s, prior to the building's restoration. By this time, Bethabara's congregation had grown so large that the old church could no longer accommodate them. They wanted more space for worship and more rooms for their active Sunday school classes. The congregation thought about expanding the church by building a new addition to it but ultimately decided to construct an entirely new church just up the street. (Both, courtesy of the Forsyth County Public Library Photograph Collection, Winston-Salem, North Carolina.)

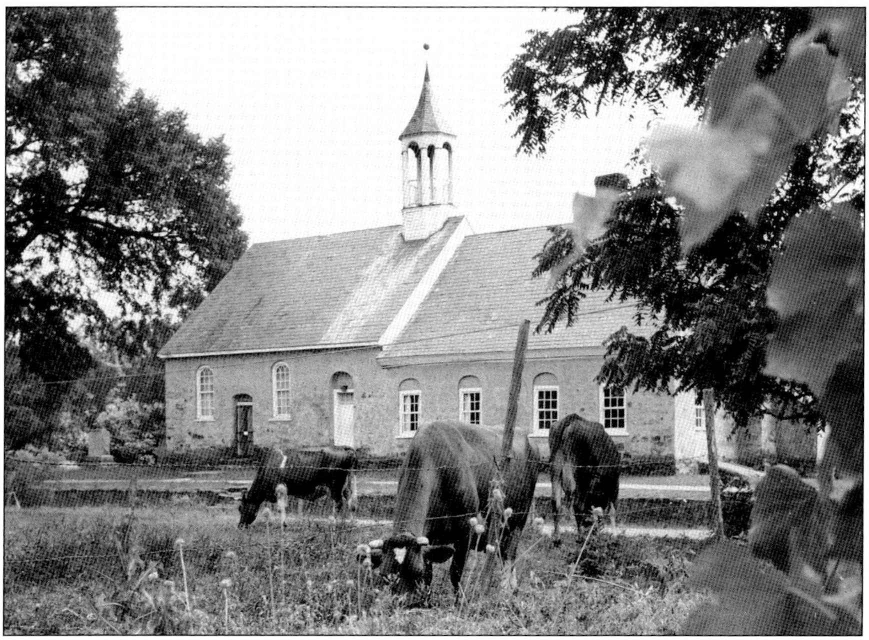

Three

Remembrances and Celebrations
20th-Century Bethabara

The year 1903 marked the 150th anniversary of the founding of Bethabara. To commemorate this occasion, preparations were made and committees were formed, including the Bethabara Memorials and Celebration Committee and the Memorials and Locations Committee. In September 1903, the *Western Sentinel* noted that the Memorials and Locations Committee met in Bethabara, where it located the palisade fort site along with the sites of the original mill and the Hans Wagner cabin, all of which were on land owned by Calvin Hauser. It was decided that the Sunday school classes of the Moravian churches in the South would raise money to help mark the location of the palisade fort, while the men's Bible class of Home Moravian Church would raise money for a new marker for the Hans Wagner cabin location.

"Bethabara Day," as the sesquicentennial event was called, took place on Friday, November 13, 1903. The morning exercise included hymns and an address from Bishop Edward Rondthaler. The first of three monuments was unveiled by Theodore Hine and Calvin Hauser, both long-standing members of Bethabara Moravian Church. After lunch, two more memorials were unveiled at the site of the Hans Wagner cabin and the palisade fort. The bands from Salem and Bethania provided music throughout the event and led the group up to God's Acre, where the final exercise of the day was held. On the actual anniversary of the founding on November 17, ministers from all of the Wachovia Moravian churches were encouraged to hold services of prayer and praise at 3:00 p.m.

Bethabara was also celebrated in quieter ways in the 20th century. Students from Salem Academy and College went there to escape the city and enjoy a country picnic. In 1938, a special Easter service was recorded by the Winston-Salem *Journal and Sentinel*, noting the significance of the site as the birthplace of Wachovia. In a little over two decades, that significance would be recognized through a substantial archaeological dig and the creation of a historic site.

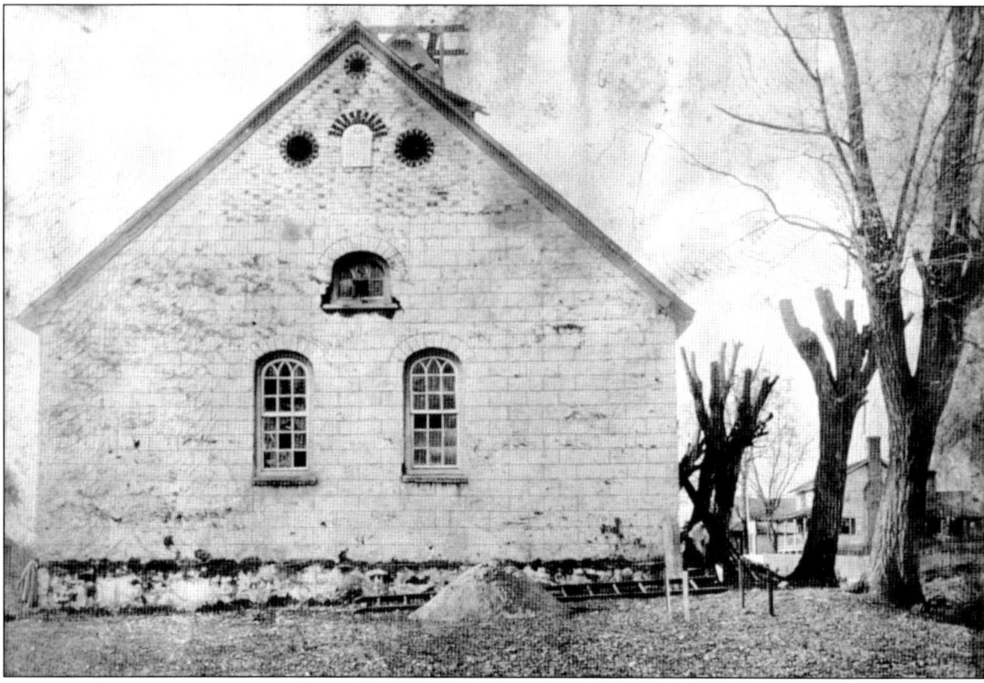

These two images of Bethabara were taken prior to the sesquicentennial. In the above photograph, work appears to be underway to get the Gemeinhaus ready for the big day. It was decided the building should have a new slate roof. Other improvements included a new fence around God's Acre cemetery. A large pile of sand sits where one of the monuments would be laid and was likely used to level it. In the background is L.M. Miller's general store as well as the Pou House (later restored and known as the Log House). In the photograph below, the various outbuildings around the Gemeinhaus can be seen, along with fields that have been freshly plowed. (Above, courtesy of Old Salem Museums & Gardens; below, courtesy of the Moravian Archives, Bethlehem, Pennsylvania.)

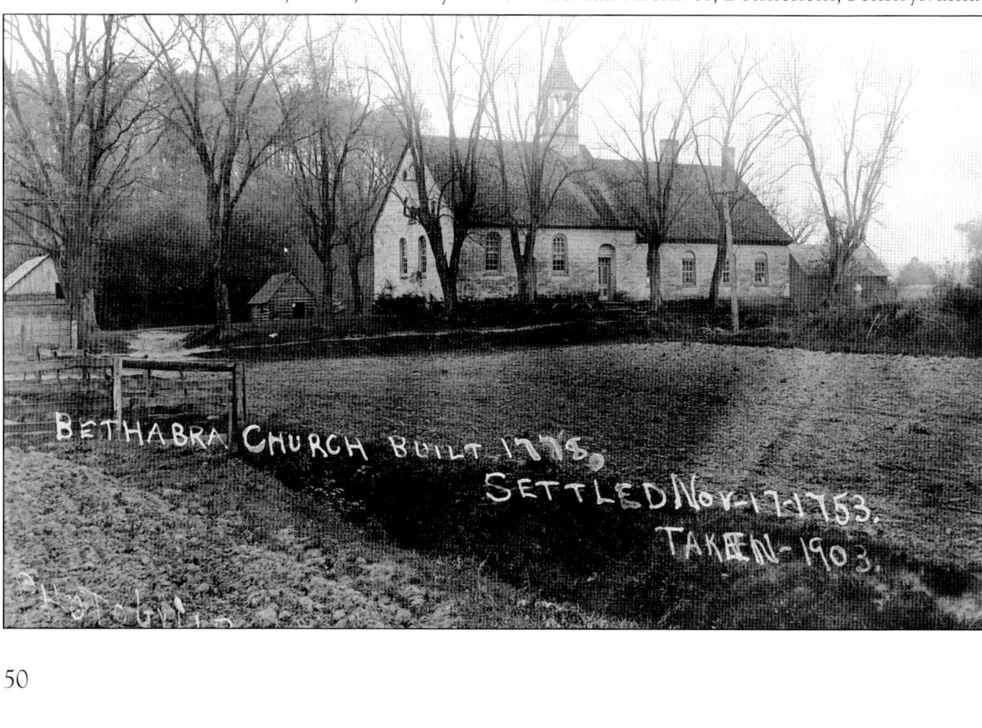

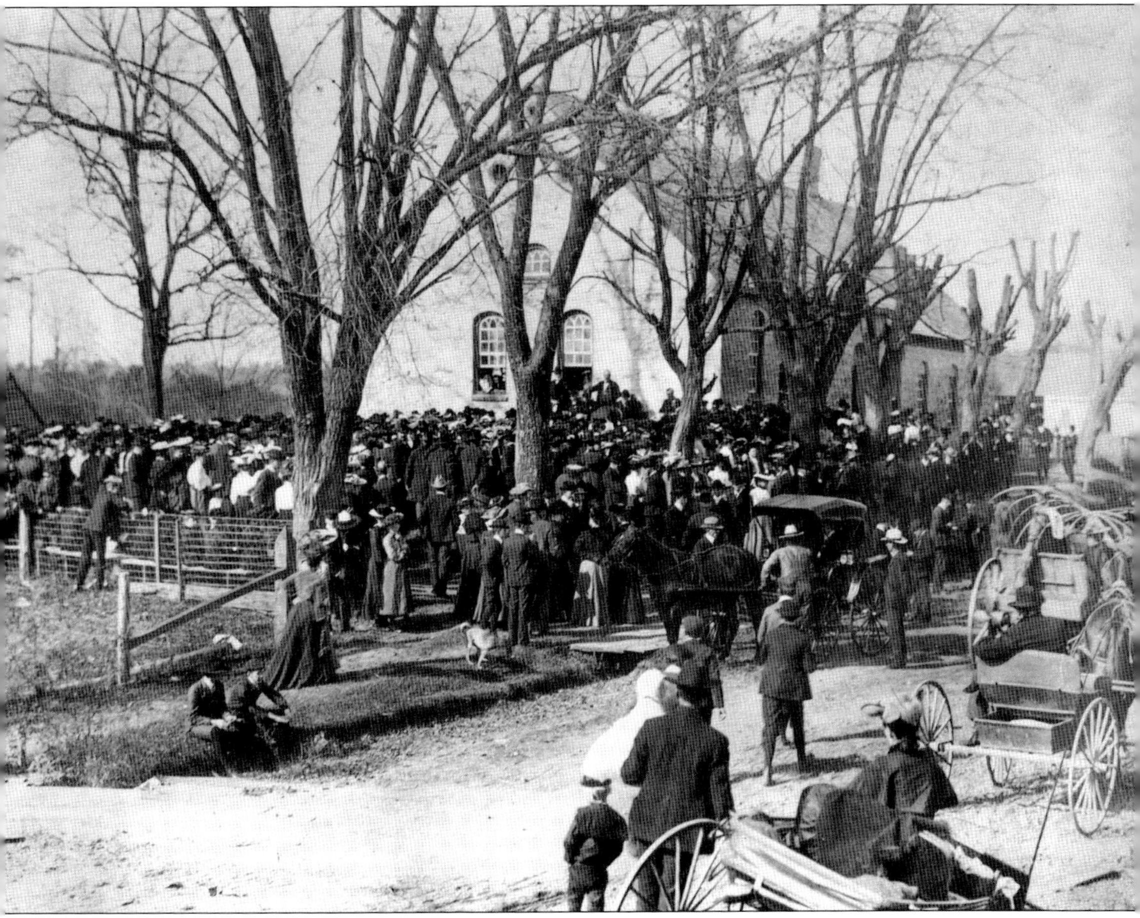

On November 13, 1903, a special train of 10 coaches brought the Salem delegation, including pupils of Salem Academy and College and Salem Boys' School, to Bethabara. The *Wachovia Moravian* newspaper estimated over 3,000 in attendance, while the *Union Republican* gave a more conservative number of 2,000. Opening exercises began at 10:30 a.m., which included the unveiling of a large memorial commemorating the first settlers who came to Bethabara on one side and the surveying party led by Bishop Spangenberg on the other. The monument was located just south of the Gemeinhaus, where a large crowd is gathered in this photograph. Brethren Theodore Hine and Calvin Hauser unveiled the monument, which contained a copper box that held a Moravian hymn book, Moravian periodicals, and a sesquicentennial medal. Bishop Rondthaler presided over the ceremony, while Reverends Hall, Clewell, Crosland, Spaugh, and de Schweinitz and the Honorable C.B. Watson occupied the platform. The monument stood next to the Gemeinhaus for many years but was eventually lost. (Courtesy of the Forsyth County Public Library Photograph Collection, Winston-Salem, North Carolina.)

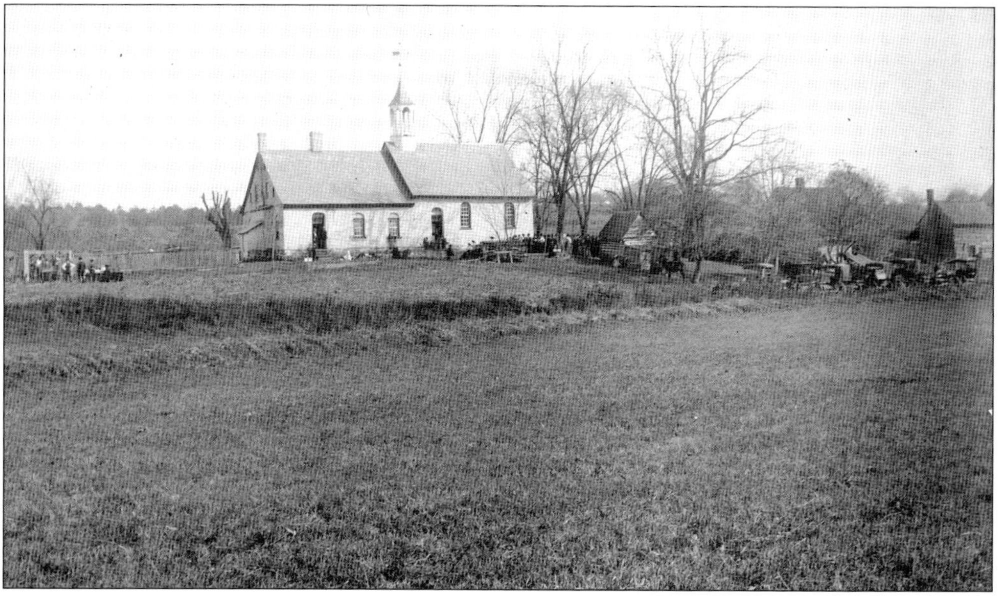

The above photograph, attributed to Ada H. Allen, shows the Gemeinhaus from the back. Many are gathered next to the south side of the building, where the morning address and monument unveiling took place. To the north, a group of men and women stands around a large steaming pot, which can be seen better in the photograph below. Water was heated over an open fire and coffee was made for the crowd gathered to celebrate the sesquicentennial. The Pou House can be seen at left in this photograph. (Both, courtesy of Old Salem Museums & Gardens.)

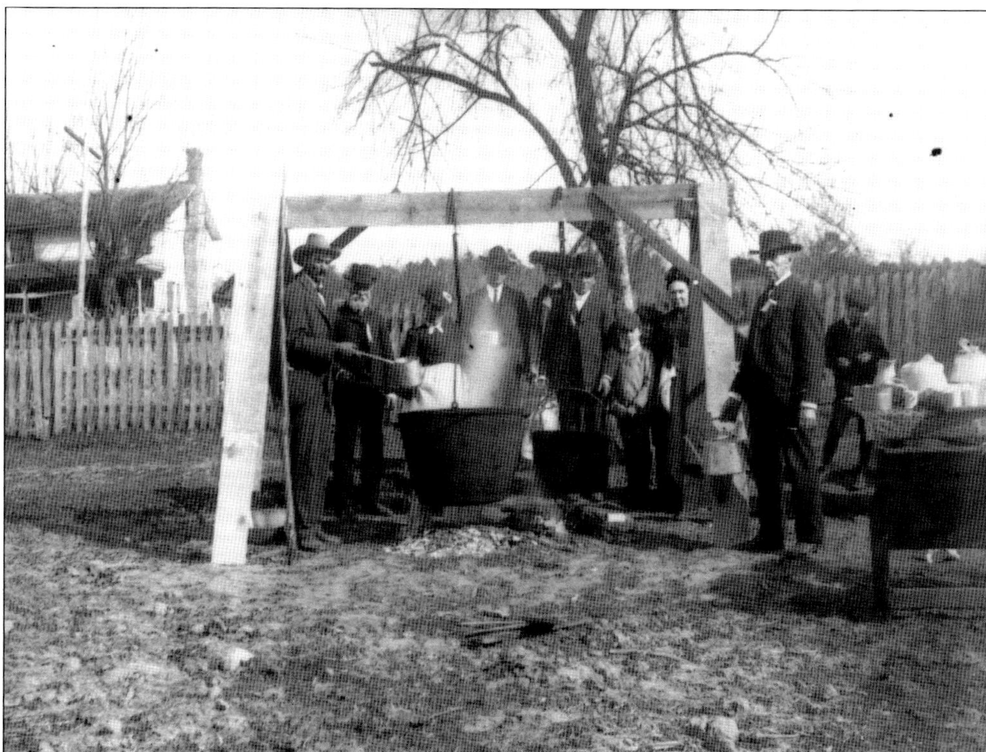

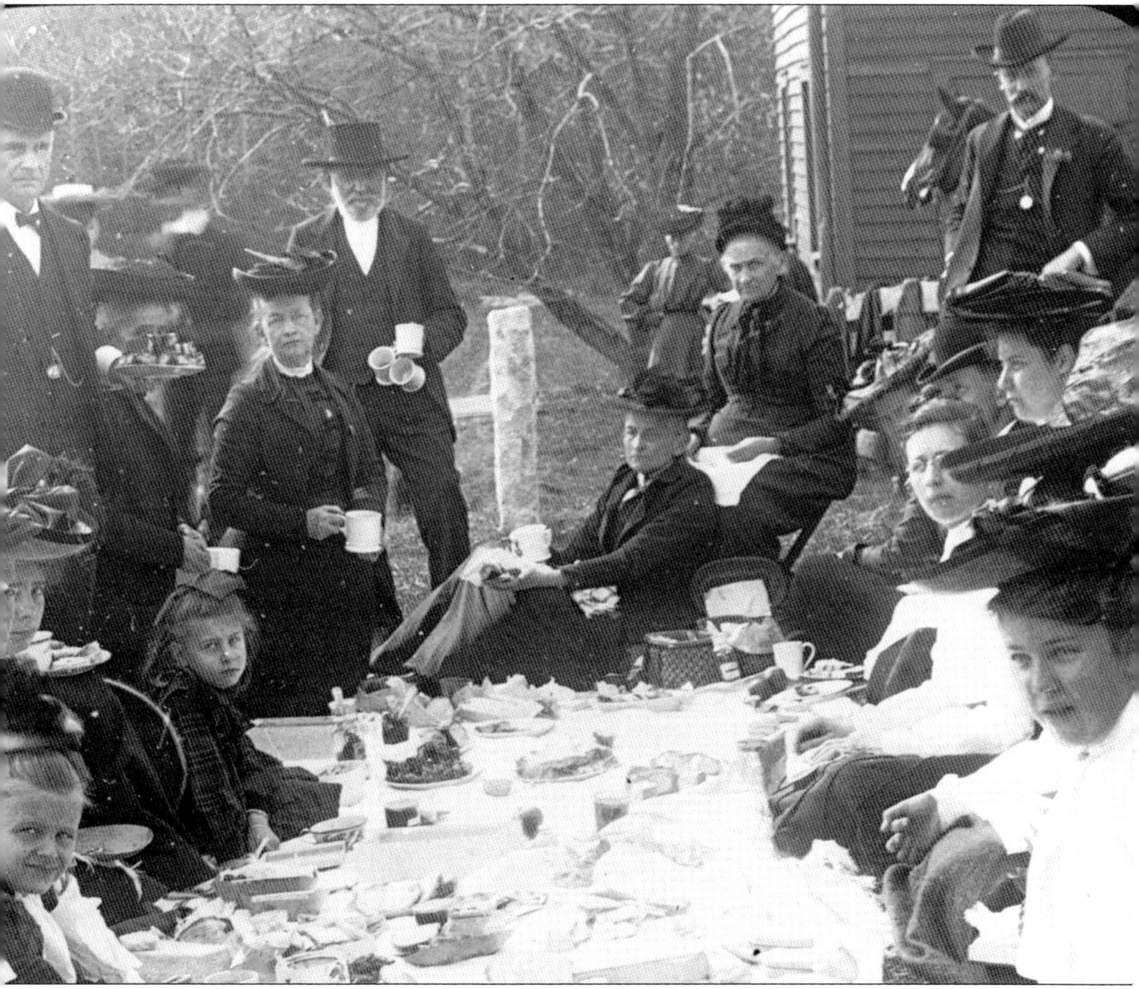

After the morning speeches and monument unveiling were complete, the crowd took a break for lunch. The group here paused for a photograph. Several are holding the white coffee cups that were housed in the old classroom inside the Gemeinhaus. They were likely brought out and used to serve the large quantity of coffee being made outside next to the north end of the Gemeinhaus. The little girl at the front left of the photograph is Gertrude Vogler, and the woman directly to the right of her is Amanda W. Spach. William T. Vogler stands to the back left. The woman with glasses to the right of him is Mary Horton, with Maria Vogler seated to the right of her. Martha Peterson is seated directly behind her. (Courtesy of Old Salem Museums & Gardens.)

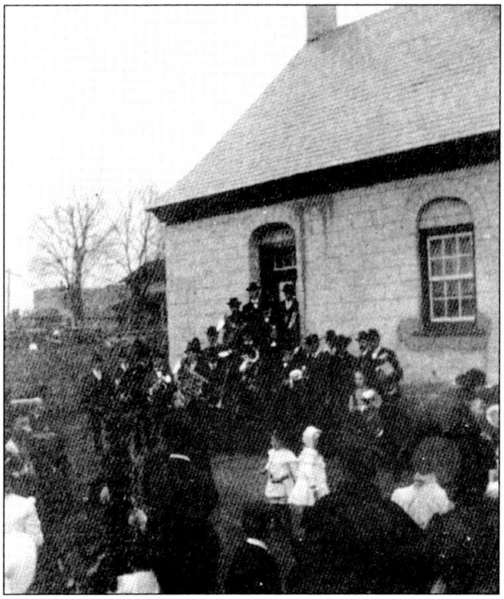

The Salem Home Church Band and the Bethania Church Band provided the music for the sesquicentennial's festivities. At left, band members are gathered on the steps leading out of the kitchen of the Gemeinhaus. Below, the bands lead a processional, likely to God's Acre, the Moravian cemetery. The graves of the first settlers were marked with a cross and crown of evergreens. A speech was read by Rev. E.S. Crosland. The bands also played as the crowd gathered at the site of the Hans Wagner cabin, which was the first dwelling the Moravians stayed in when they arrived in 1753. A second monument was unveiled, and the audience listened to a speech by C.D. Crouch, who stated, "Where with interest and pleasure you gaze upon boulder and tablet, they gazed upon the Hans Wagner hunter hut." (Both, courtesy of Old Salem Museums & Gardens.)

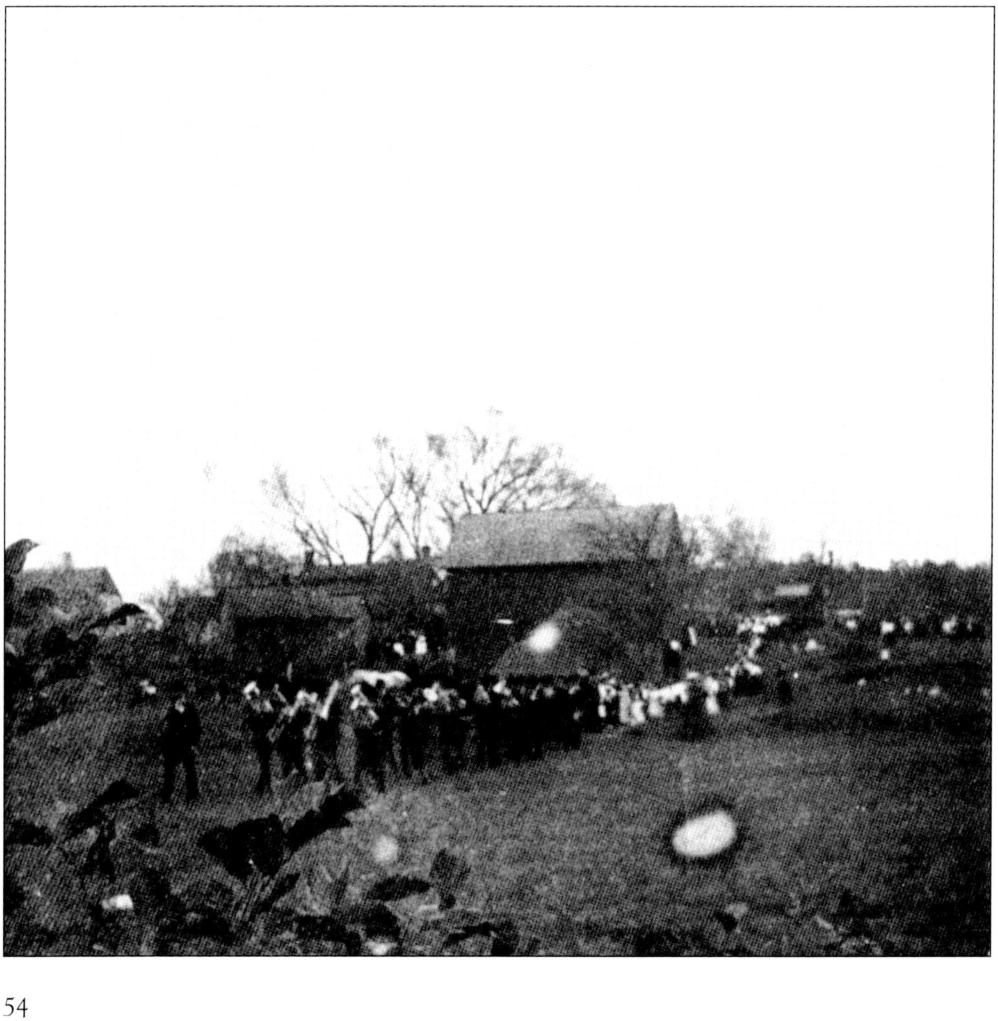

After the unveiling of the monument where the Hans Wagner cabin stood, the celebration continued at the site of the original palisade fort. Two months prior to the sesquicentennial, a group of Moravian men from Salem, including B.J. Pfohl, J.T. Lineback, and J.A. Lineback, went to Bethabara to meet with Calvin and Albert Hauser. They located the original fort on Calvin Hauser's land and marked the outline of it with stone pillars. In the southeast corner, they placed a plaque attached to one of the original millstones that described the fort. B.J. Pfohl read an account of the fort and mill to the crowd. The photograph at right is likely from one of the speeches given during the sesquicentennial, and the photograph below shows the fort plaque. (Both, courtesy of Old Salem Museums & Gardens.)

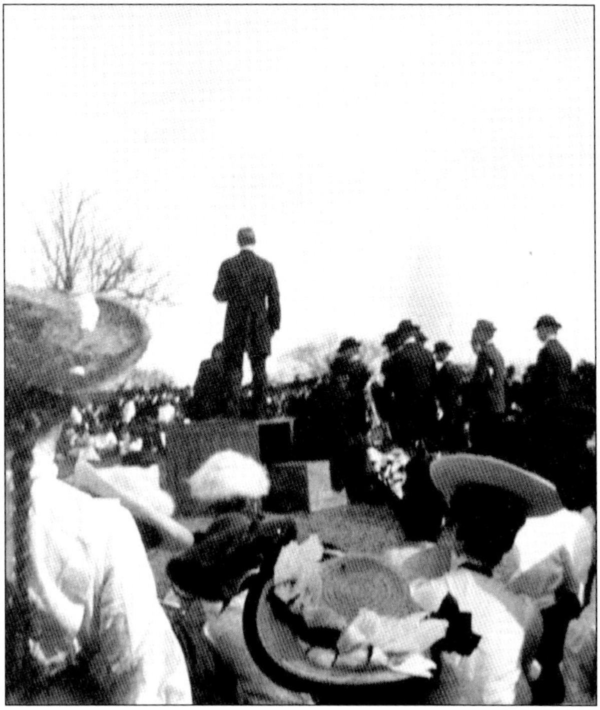

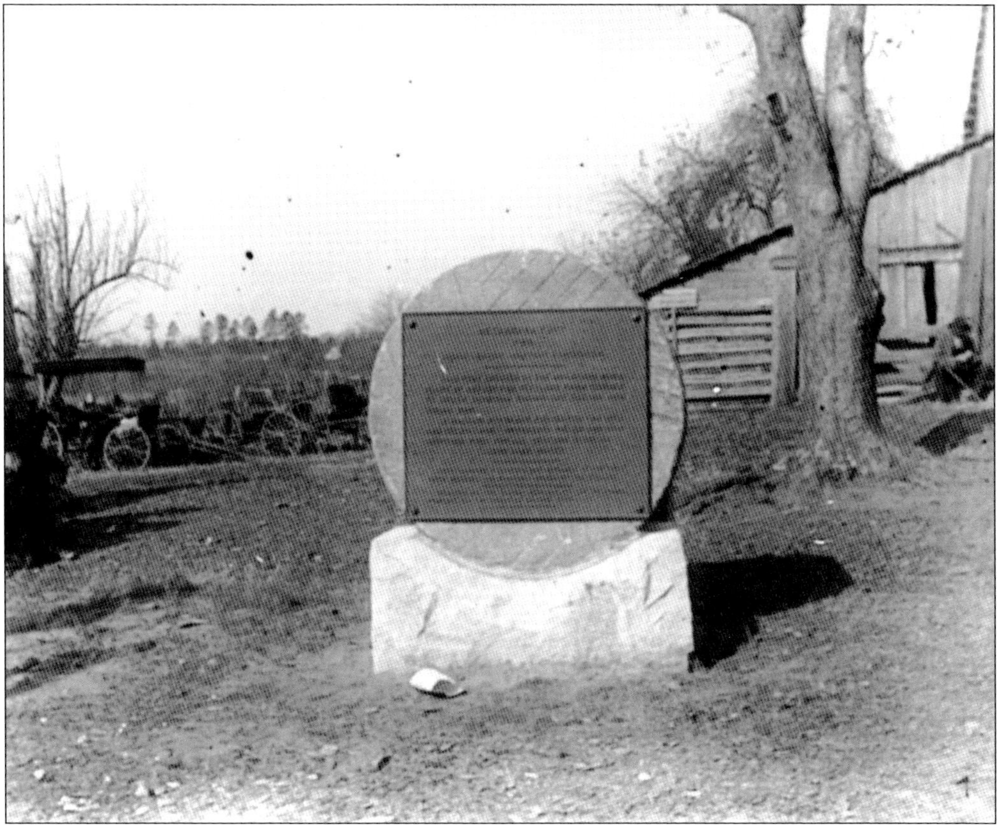

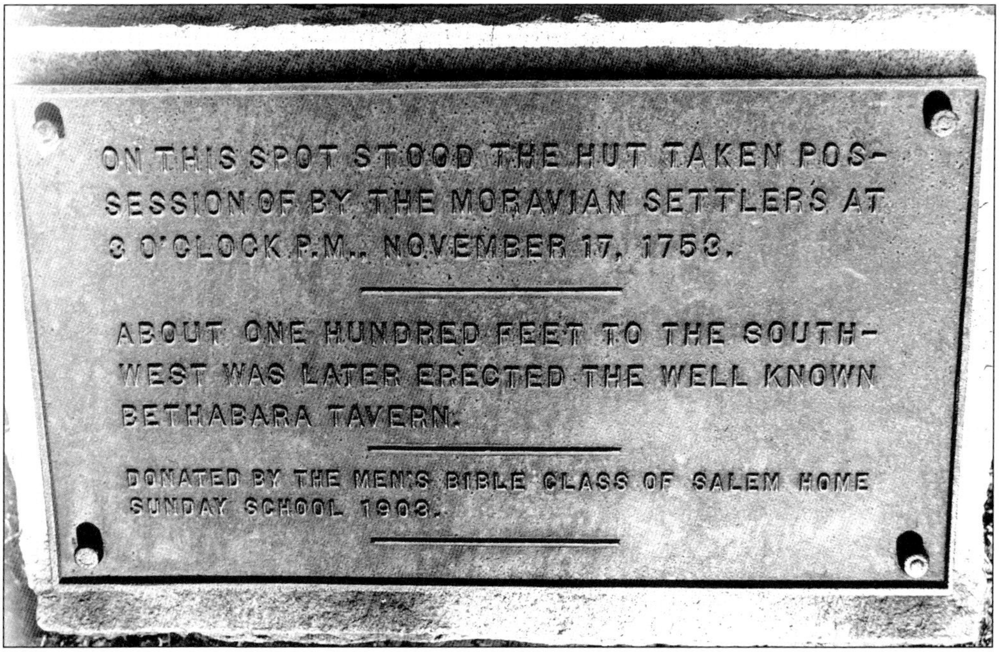

This plaque marked the location of the Hans Wagner cabin. The inscription reads, "On this spot stood the hut taken possession by the Moravian settlers at 3 o'clock p.m., November 17, 1753. About one hundred feet to the southwest was later erected the well-known Bethabara tavern. Donated by the men's Bible class of Salem Home Sunday School 1903." Today, this plaque is located by Bethabara's visitor center. (Courtesy of Old Salem Museums & Gardens.)

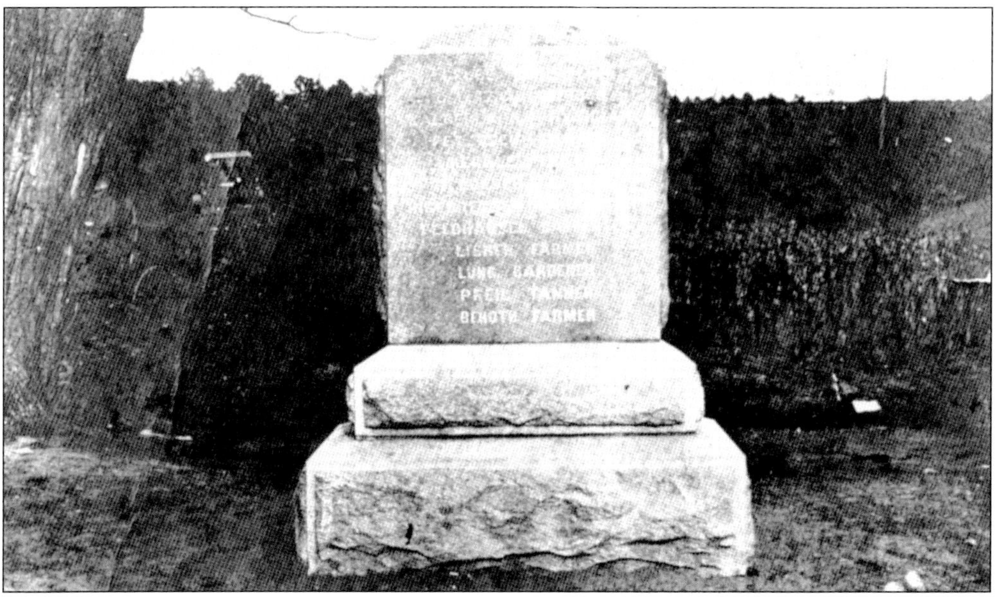

This is the plaque placed next to the Gemeinhaus, which was dedicated to the first Moravian men who lived in Bethabara and the surveying party who chose its location. It cost $142 and was given by the Wachovia Historical Society. When the Bethabara site was cleared for archaeological excavation in 1963–1964, the monument was moved but was never put back. Its whereabouts today are unknown. (Courtesy of Old Salem Museums & Gardens.)

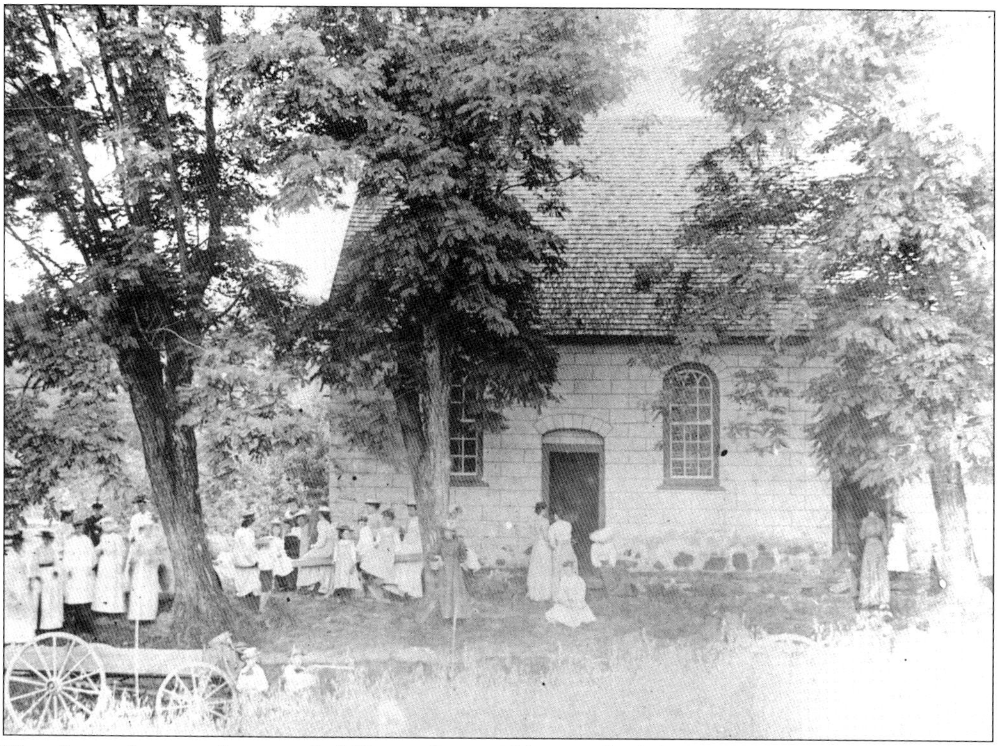

The above photograph is entitled "Picnic Party Old Town," while the photograph below features unidentified Salem College students posing by the Gemeinhaus sometime between 1900 and 1920. Students from Salem College often visited Bethabara for a special day out in the countryside. One such trip was documented by O. Farrow for the *Charlotte Observer* in 1903. Eleven students and one teacher traveled by wagon from Salem to Bethabara. It was a rainy morning, and they worried their picnic would be spoiled. When they arrived in Bethabara, they were welcomed into the Gemeinhaus, where they ate in the dining room (now the kitchen) and were charmed by the "old-fashioned fireplace" where a fire smoldered. (Both, courtesy of Old Salem Museums & Gardens.)

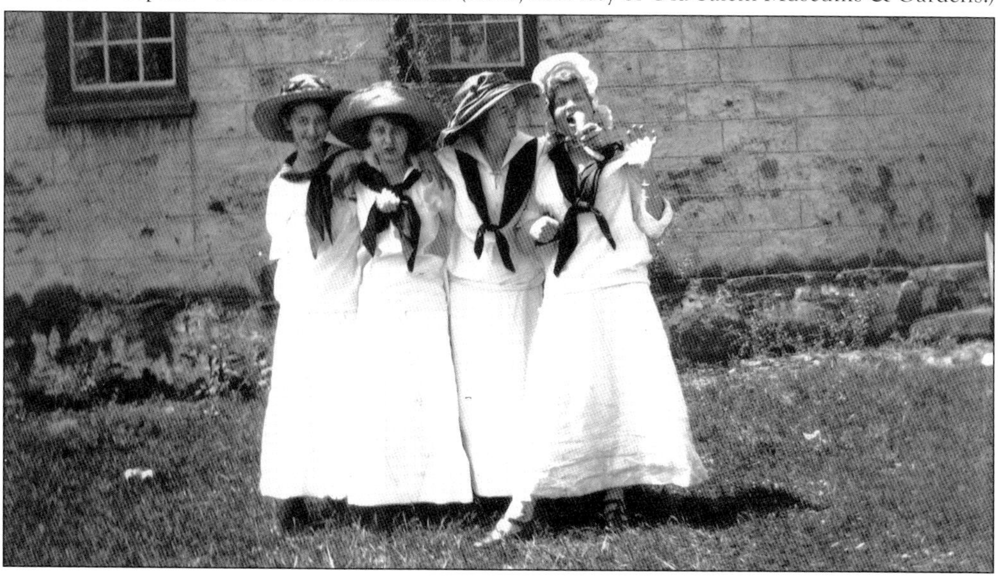

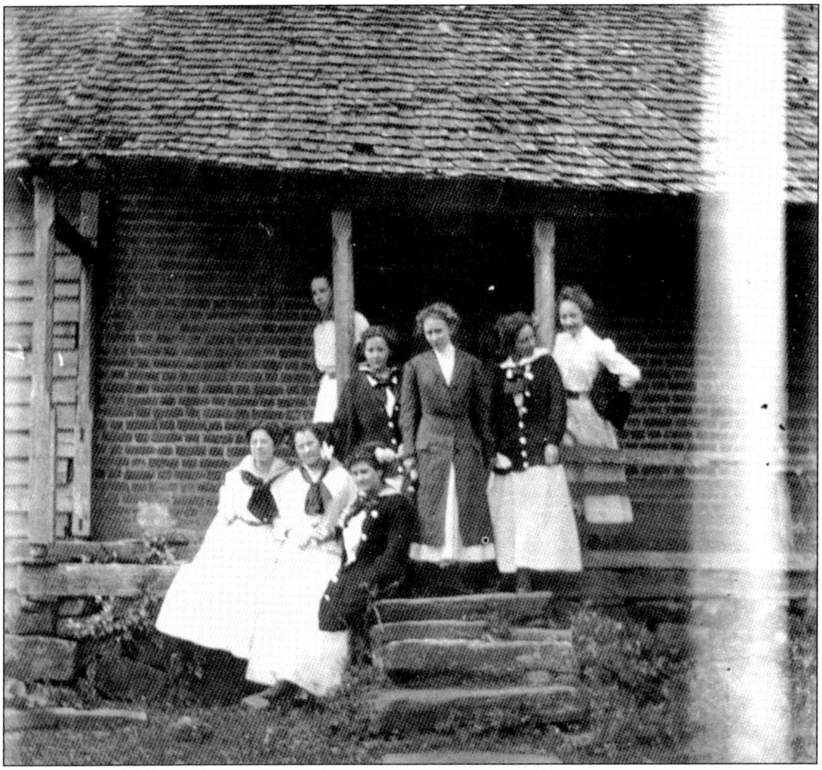

Above, Salem College students pose on the Potter's House porch at an unknown date. The two students at right are also unidentified. Most Salem College students knew about the history of Bethabara from reading Dr. John Henry Clewell's *History of Wachovia*. They were aware of the palisade fort and the Hans Wagner cabin, and they often ventured up to God's Acre. Along the way, they would find flowers like anemone and Jack-in-the-pulpit. The picnickers from the 1903 *Charlotte Observer* article used flowering dogwood branches to decorate their wagon for the trip back to Salem. (Both, courtesy of Old Salem Museums & Gardens.)

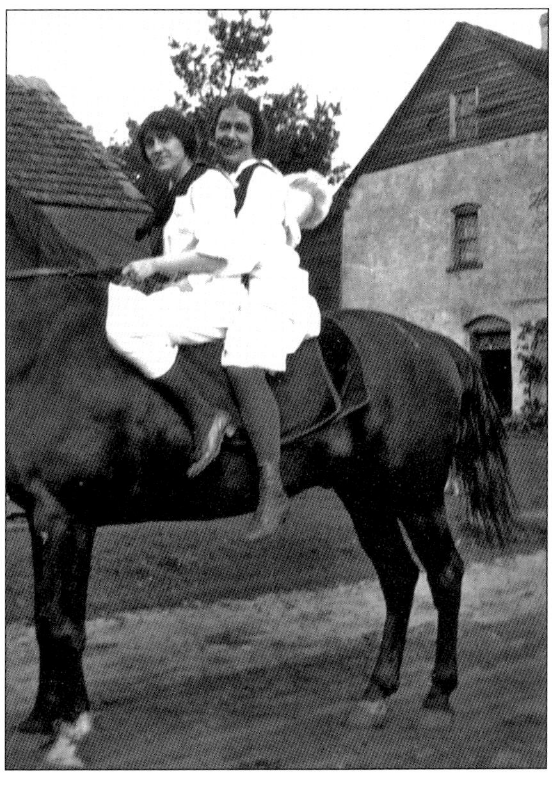

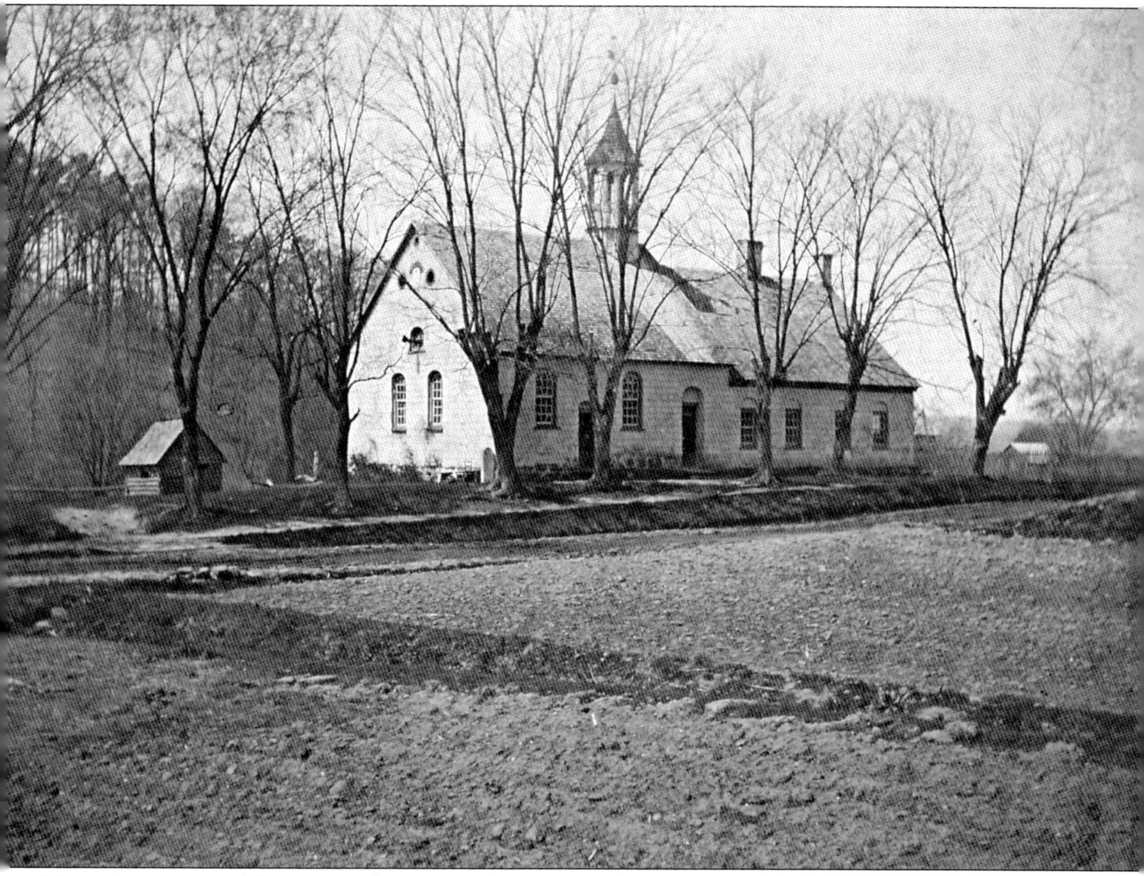

This photograph of the Gemeinhaus was taken in 1903 by Dr. Anna M. Gove. Gove was born in Whitefield, New Hampshire, in 1867. Her father was a physician, and she wanted to become one herself. Her father ensured she had the best education possible, and she took premedical courses at the Massachusetts Institute of Technology before graduating in 1892 from the Woman's College of the New York Infirmary. The following year, she moved to Greensboro, where she became the resident physician for the State Normal and Industrial School (later renamed the University of North Carolina Greensboro). She was the third woman in the state to receive her medical license. Under her guidance, an infirmary was built and a study department of health was formed. She taught physiology and physical culture as well as physiology and hygiene. She was a pioneer in her field and helped pave the way for more women to follow. This photograph from her visit to Bethabara was donated to Salem College in 1948. (Courtesy of the Salem Academy and College Archives.)

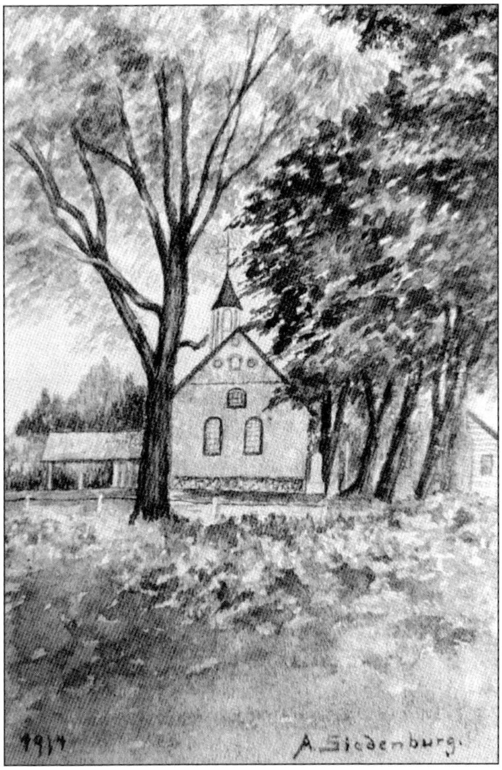

This illustration of the Gemeinhaus was made in 1914 by Anna Magdelene Siedenburg, who is seated on the right in the photograph below with Pauline Bahnson next to her. Born in Bremen, Germany, in 1854, Siedenburg moved to the United States in the 1890s, living in Cincinnati, Chicago, and New York while drawing for the *Art Amateur* publication. She also published her own illustrative work, called *Fairy Tales and Fancies*. In the early 1900s, she taught drawing and painting at Elizabeth College and Salem Academy and College, along with French and German. The illustration, made while she was teaching at Salem Academy and College, was given to Pauline Uzzell Green, who later donated it to Historic Bethabara Park. (Left, courtesy of the Bethabara Collection; below, courtesy of the Salem Academy and College Archives.)

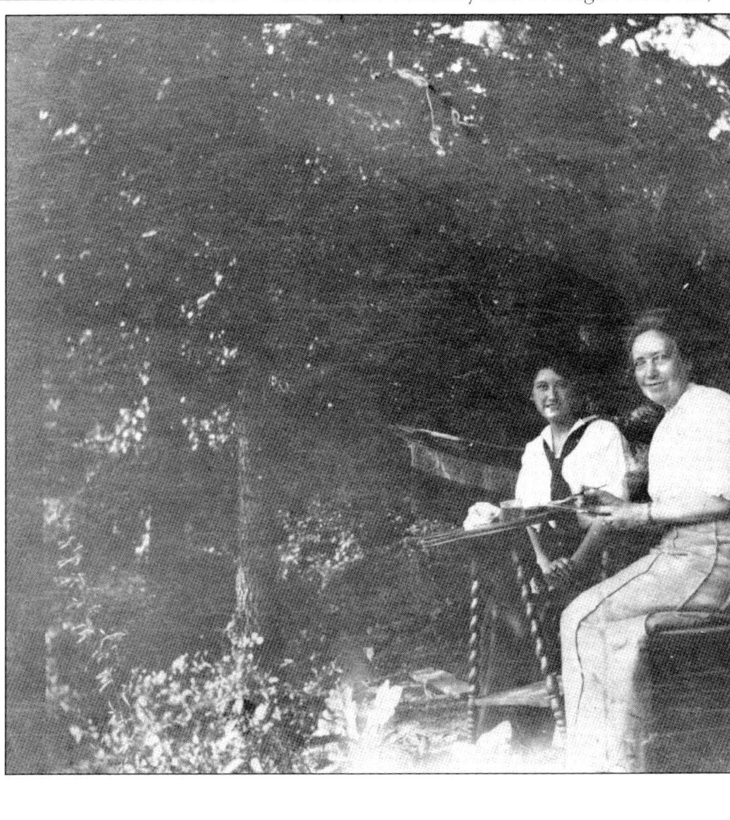

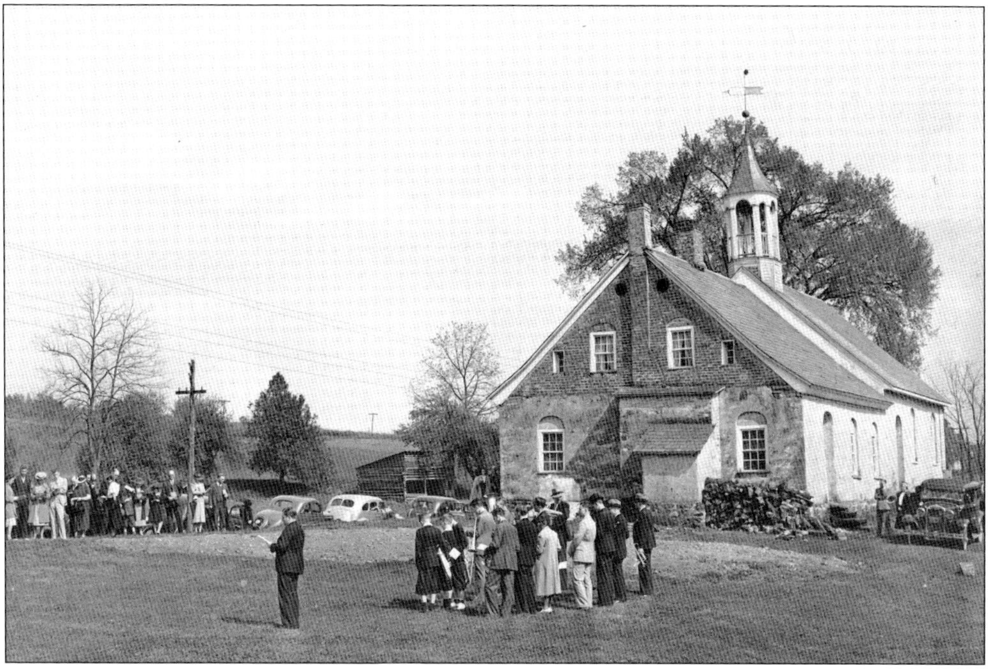

Both of these photographs were taken by Frank Jones in April 1938. They were for the *Journal and Sentinel*, which ran a front-page story about Moravian Easter celebrations. Bethabara was included in one of the articles, which read, "The Moravian Easter Litany will be prayed at 3 o'clock this afternoon on the oldest Moravian graveyard in the South, when a large congregation will gather at Bethabara Church, out of Old Town. This service will be a replica, in miniature, of the more widely known services held at dawn at the Home Church and on the Salem Graveyard." The Calvary Moravian brass band provided music for the day and can be seen in the above photograph next to the minister. In the photograph below, the processional makes its way toward God's Acre. (Both, courtesy of the Forsyth County Public Library Photograph Collection, Winston-Salem, North Carolina.)

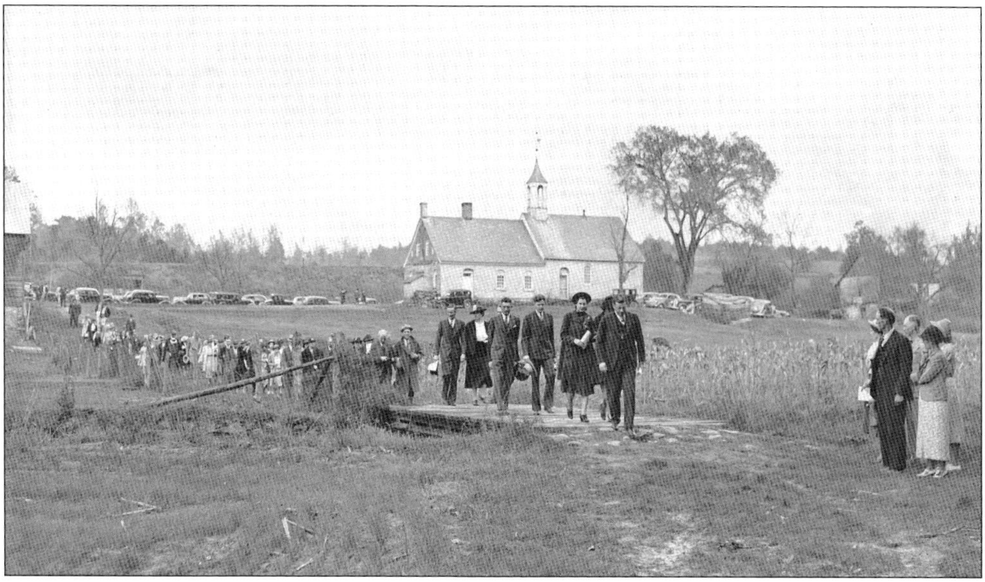

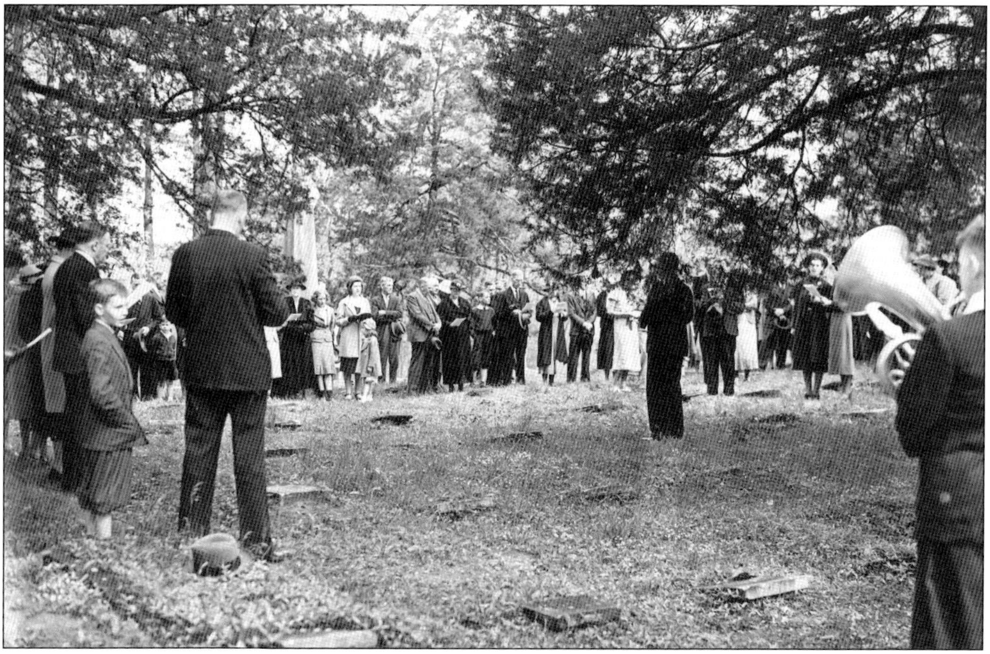

Once they arrived at God's Acre, the Calvary Moravian brass band accompanied hymns sung by the participants. Both of these photographs were taken by Frank Jones for the *Journal and Sentinel* in April 1938. Below, Ben Cahill (far right) leans against the fence. The newspaper article pointed out that this was the 181st Easter service since the first grave appeared in God's Acre, that of Anna Maria Opiz, who was buried there in 1757. After the Easter service concluded, the 1788 Gemeinhaus was opened to visitors. (Both, courtesy of the Forsyth County Public Library Photograph Collection, Winston-Salem, North Carolina.)

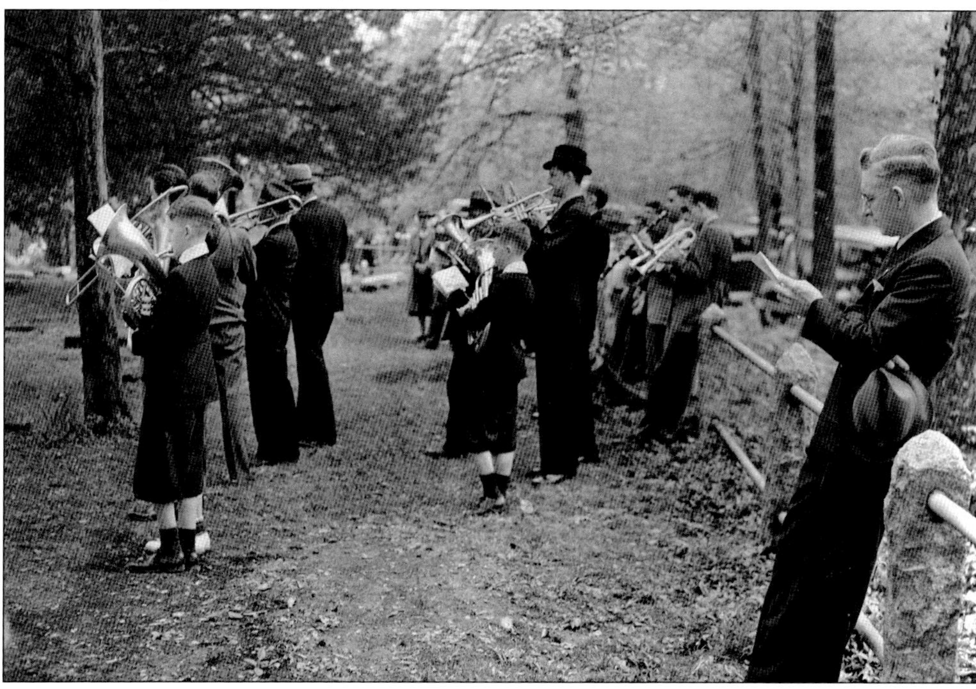

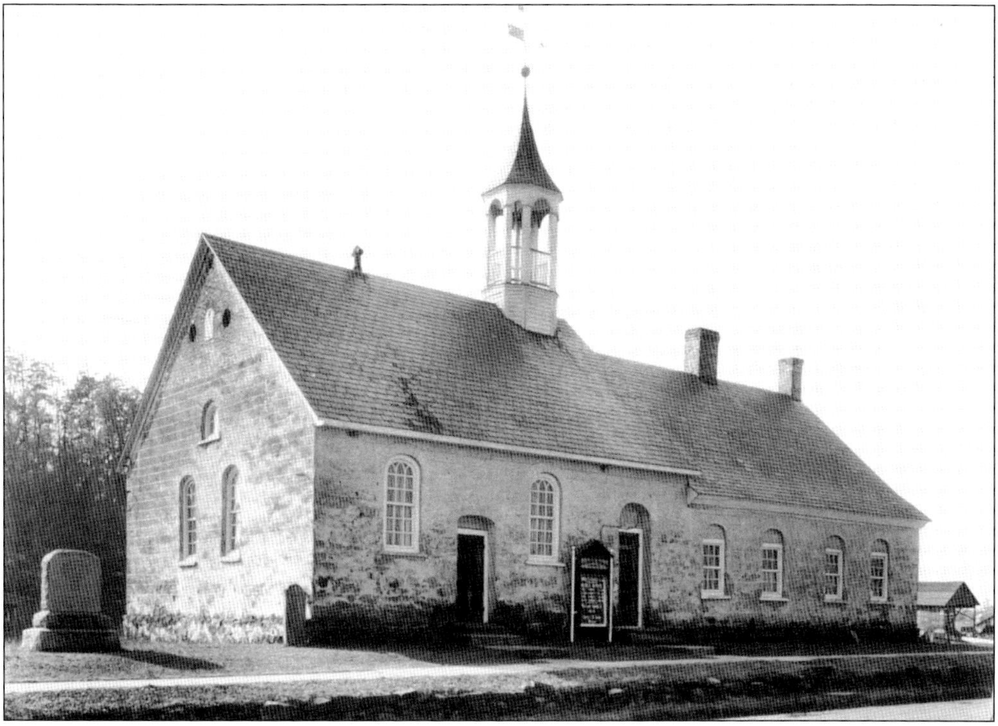

The above photograph of the Gemeinhaus was taken by Frances Benjamin Johnston in 1936, two years before Frank Jones documented the Easter service at Bethabara. The larger stone to the left of the Gemeinhaus is the 1903 monument dedicated to the original Moravians who arrived in 1753. To the right of the Gemeinhaus, just before the first outbuilding, is the monument for the fort, still attached to a millstone. The image below was taken by Frank Jones and captures an open house held in the Gemeinhaus in April 1949. The woman serving Moravian sugar cake is Mrs. E.F. Barton. On the right are R.O. Howard and Mrs. M.A. Stewart. They are sitting in the old schoolroom of the Gemeinhaus, where coffee was prepared for Moravian lovefeasts. (Above, courtesy of the Library of Congress; below, courtesy of the Forsyth County Public Library Photograph Collection, Winston-Salem, North Carolina.)

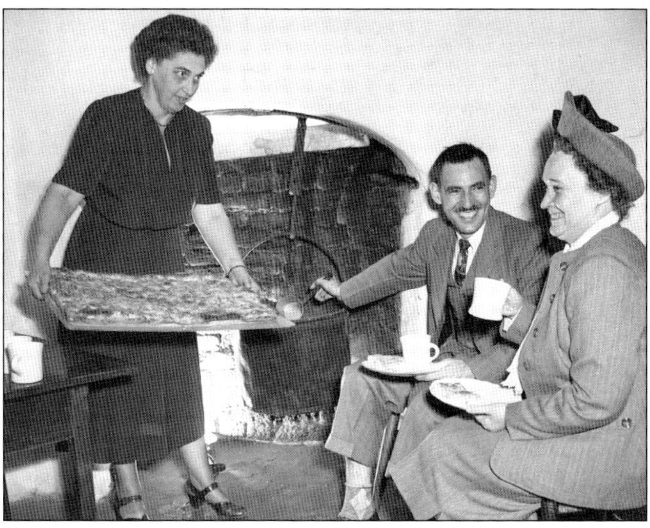

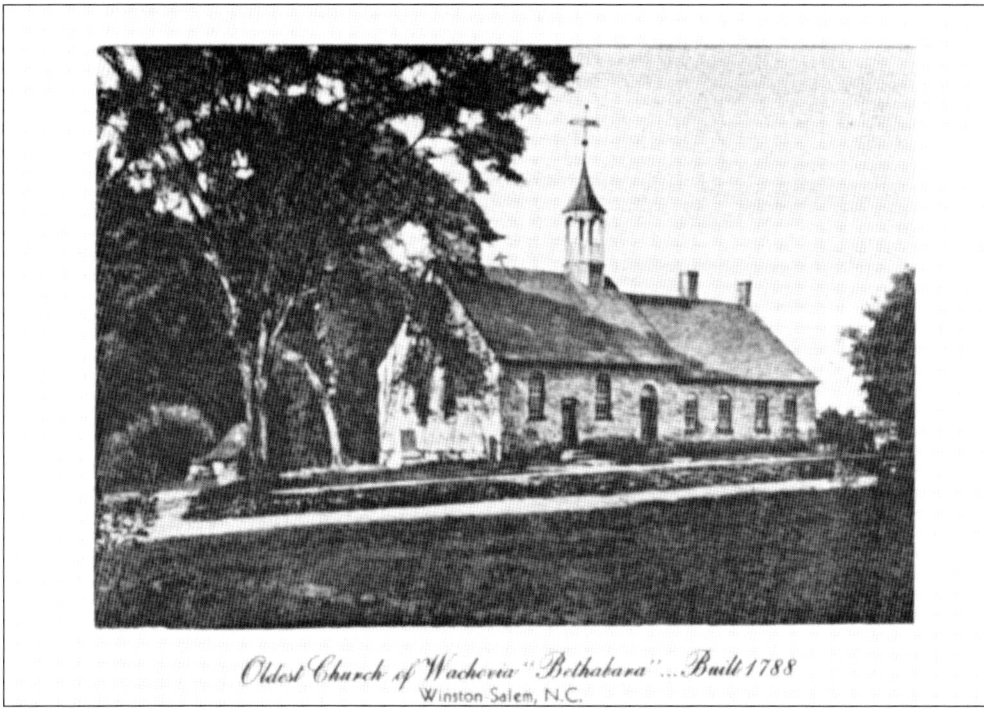

This postcard of the 1788 Gemeinhaus was sent on November 3, 1957. The sender thanked Mrs. Luckenbach for a birthday present she sent. Even before Bethabara became a historic site, it was already seen as significant enough to be placed on a postcard. By the 1950s, there were plans for the Gemeinhaus to be fully restored, and the Bethabara congregation prepared to build a new worship space just up the street. Bethabara's importance grew in the public mind through the celebrations of the 20th century, setting the stage for the creation of Historic Bethabara Park. (Both, courtesy of the Moravian Archives, Bethlehem, Pennsylvania.)

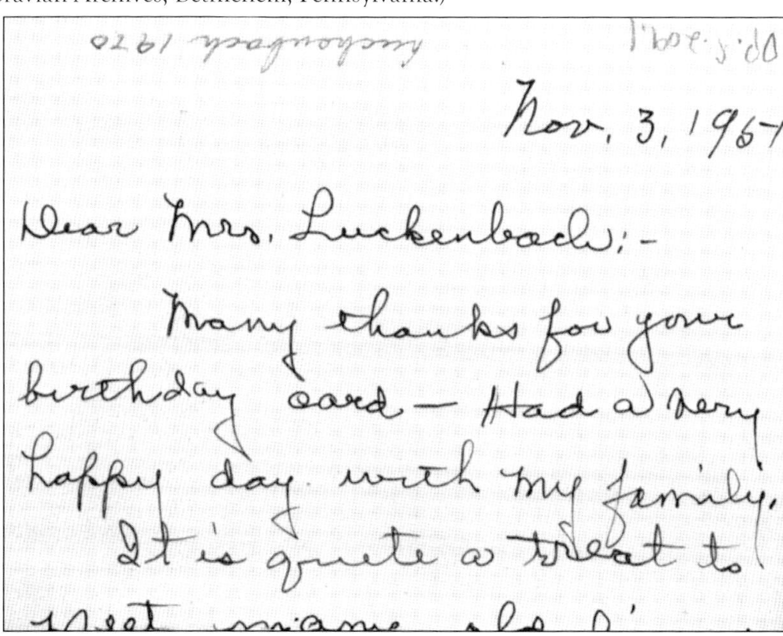

Nov. 3, 1967

Dear Mrs. Luckenbach:-
Many thanks for your birthday card — Had a very happy day with my family.
It is quite a treat to

Four

Unearthing Bethabara
20th-Century Archaeology

In late 1963, archaeologist Stanley South; his wife, Jewell; and Dr. Frank Albright and Frank Horton of Old Salem stood at the site of the Hans Wagner cabin. South pulled at the briars that had overgrown the 1903 monument marking the location of the beginning of Wachovia. He had been tasked with unearthing a 210-year-old town preserved under cornfields.

In 1951, Edwin L. Stockton, treasurer of the Southern Province of the Moravian Church, became interested in preserving the land of the former settlement, hoping to purchase plots so they could not be developed. He found financial backing in philanthropist Charles H. Babcock, and they slowly began buying the farms and fields that made up the original townsite. The ultimate goal was to create a historic site, but first they had to uncover the town's history. They contacted the Historic Sites Division of the State Department of Archives and History, which worked with various sites that needed archaeological assistance. This is how Stanley South became involved.

Studying two maps of Bethabara created by surveyor Christian Reuter in the 1760s, South was able to use Bethabara Road and the contours of the land noted on the maps as reference points to locate the shops, religious buildings, and homes that had been covered over. Exploratory trenches were cut, during which the floor of Gottfried Aust's pottery was located as well as a waster dump where unusable pottery was thrown out. These early findings proved to South that an archaeological dig would be a worthwhile endeavor. From 1963 to 1966, South and his team uncovered 27 features related to the first three decades of Bethabara, including the major buildings of the original town.

Other archaeological digs would follow. Jacqueline Fehon and John Clauser Jr. excavated around the 1782 Potter's House. Alan N. Snavely directed a dig of the mill site and stranger's cemetery in 1985. John Clauser Jr. returned in 1985 and 1988 to uncover the location of the community garden. These archaeological investigations helped uncover the history of early Bethabara, which would be of great value as the former town was turned into a historic site.

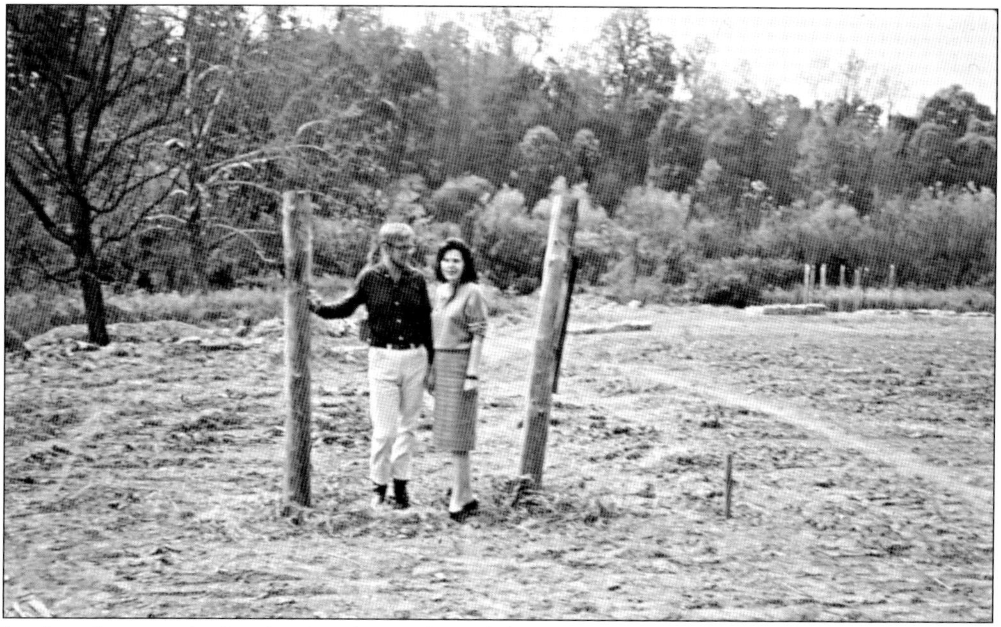

In this photograph, Stanley South stands with his wife, Jewell South, at the very start of the archaeological project, likely in 1963. Jewell South worked as the laboratory supervisor during the excavation and helped catalog and restore hundreds of pottery pieces that were found. She also occasionally helped her husband with the excavation. (Courtesy of the Bethabara Collection.)

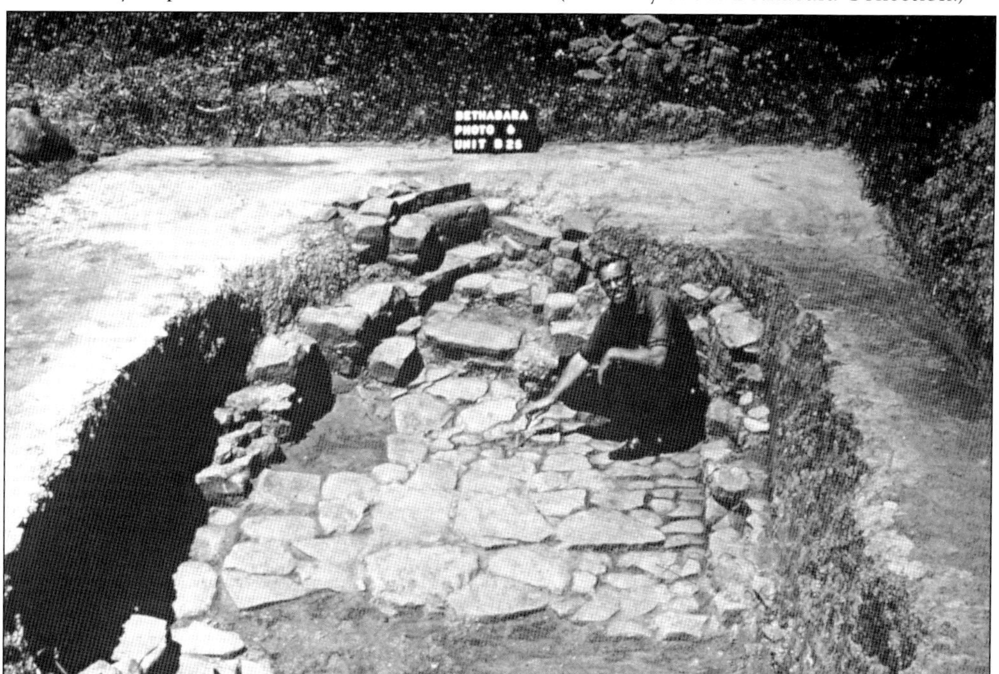

Stanley South is seen here in the excavated cellar of the smith's house. Before any excavation work could begin, a grid system had to be created around a permanent object. South chose the 1903 monument dedicated to the Bethabara palisade fort. This image was taken in 1964. (Courtesy of the Bethabara Collection.)

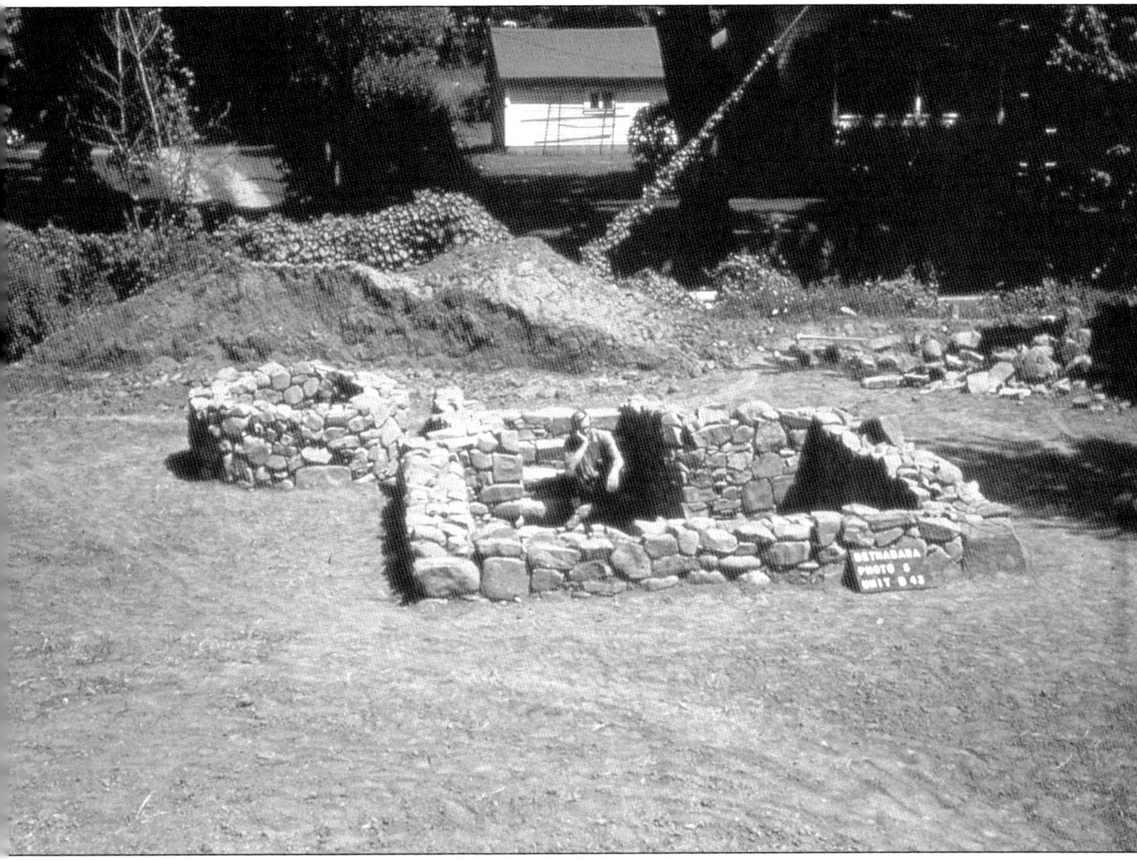

In this 1964 photograph, Stanley South sits on the stairs leading down to the cellar of the tailor's shop. A native of Boone, North Carolina, South would become the state's archaeologist and a major proponent for processual archaeology, an archaeological theory that states that the goals of archaeology are to answer questions about humans and human culture. This philosophy can easily be seen in South's work, not just in the Bethabara dig but throughout the Southeast. When interviewed by the *Journal and Sentinel* in 1963, South stated, "What we do today and the care with which we accomplish our goals will determine how future generations view us as well as the story we are trying to reveal through the ruins of Bethabara." When excavating the tailor's shop cellars, South and his crew found straight pins and thimbles, clues to the shop's original use. (Courtesy of the Bethabara Collection.)

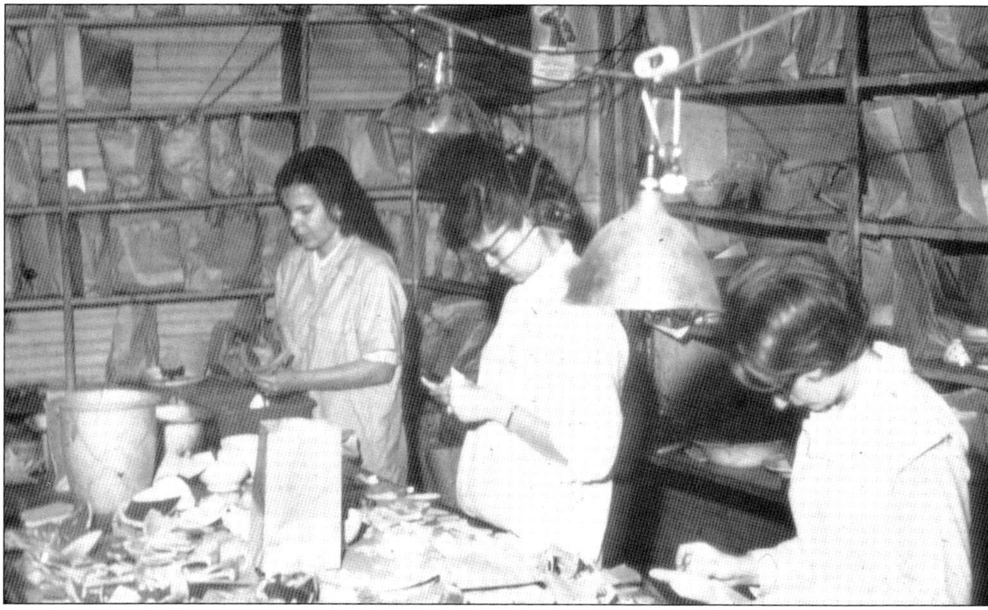

In addition to Jewell South (left), Mrs. William M. Drummond (center) and Patricia Grace (right) helped with the cleaning and restoring of pottery pieces. The laboratory was in one of the old stores along Bethabara Road that was later torn down to create the historic site. (Courtesy of the Bethabara Collection.)

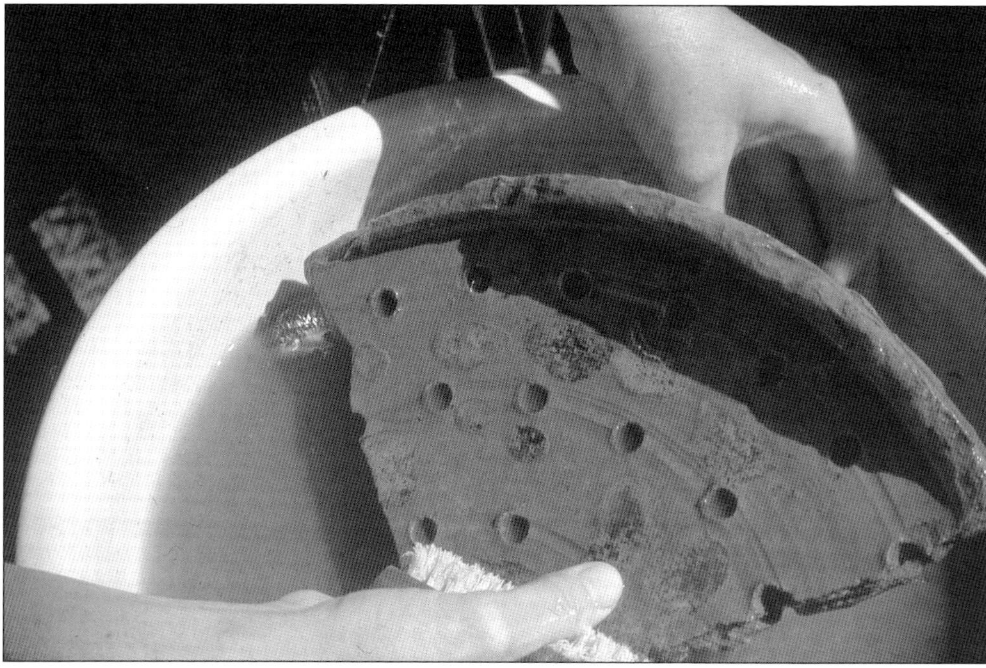

A sagger like this one was used for holding pottery pieces inside a kiln. Excavated artifacts were cleaned and cataloged, and many objects were then pieced together like a puzzle to create a whole (or close to whole) item. Objects were then measured, drawn, and photographed, which provided data for the archaeologists to use for things like figuring out the relationship between the wares created by different potters in Bethabara. (Courtesy of the Bethabara Collection.)

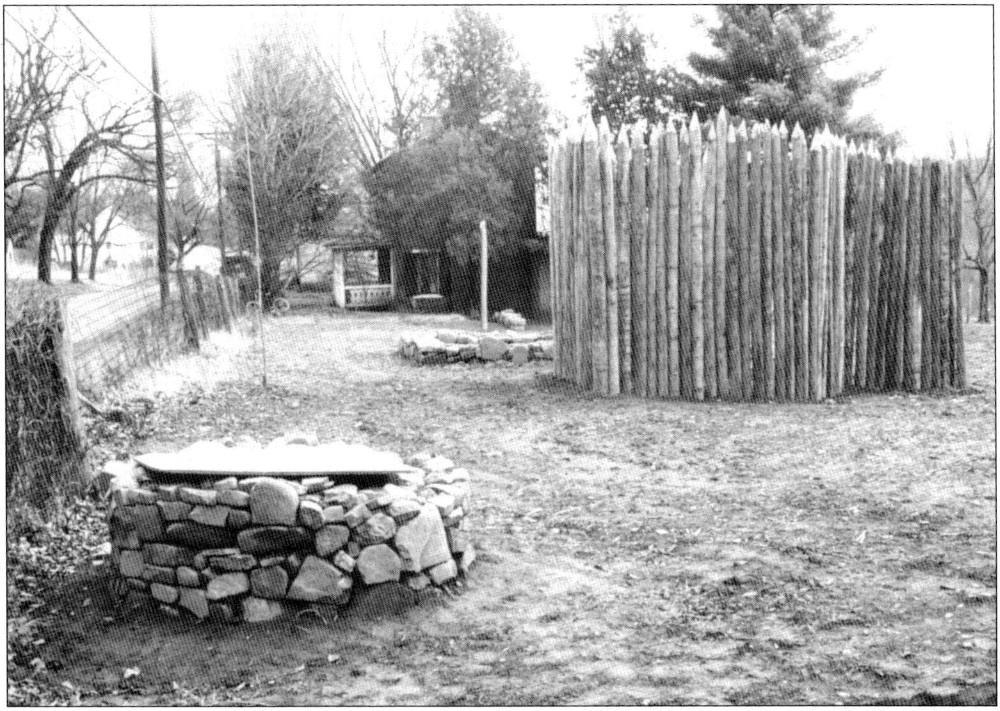

During the dig at Bethabara, Stanley South found the original postholes for the palisade fort. He recommended that the fort be rebuilt in the exact same location, which would create a dramatic backdrop for the stabilized cellar ruins. Treated wooden poles were purchased and sharpened at one end before being placed where the original postholes were. South hoped that visitors would see the relationship between the buildings and the palisade fort that provided protection during the French and Indian War. The palisade fort South envisioned began taking shape in late 1964, and while the posts had to be replaced in 1990 and again in 2013, a reconstructed palisade fort still stands in Historic Bethabara Park today. Frank Jones took these images of the first fort reconstruction in December 1964. (Both, courtesy of the Forsyth County Public Library Photograph Collection, Winston-Salem, North Carolina.)

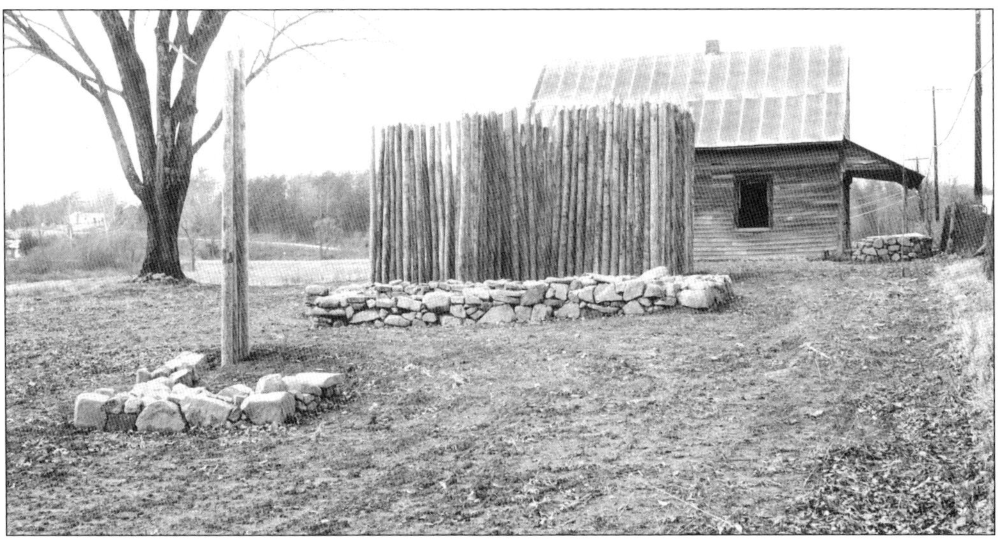

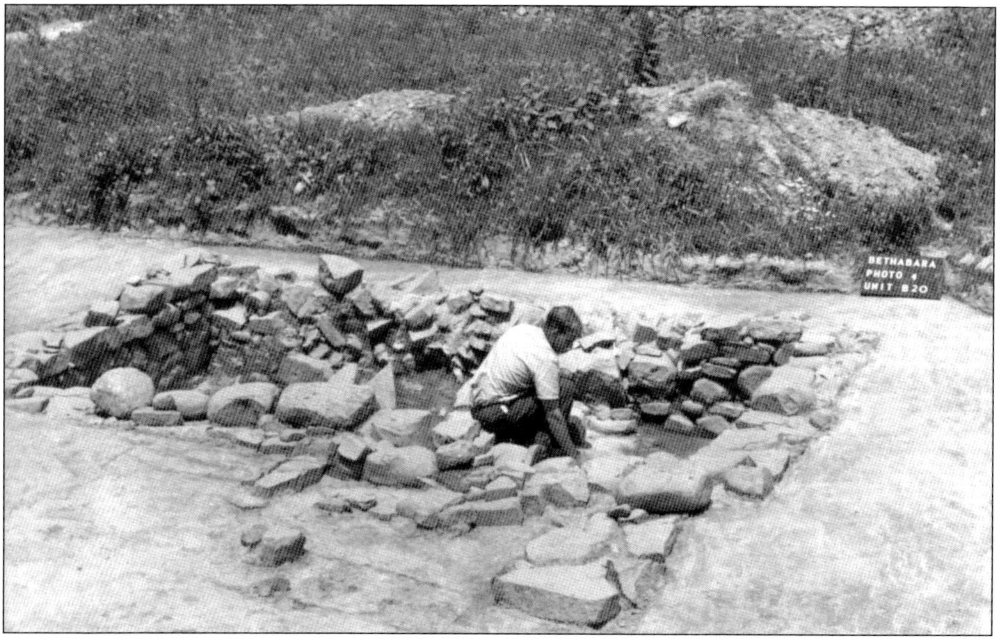

In this photograph, assistant archaeologist Brad Rauschenberg removes soil from the cellar of the gunsmith shop. Rauschenberg supervised the Bethabara dig crew when Stanley South had to be off-site for other projects. South noted in his book *Historical Archaeology in Wachovia* that Rauschenberg "worked with a love of a project that is most gratifying." Rauschenberg also supervised the stabilization of the cellar ruins. (Courtesy of the Bethabara Collection.)

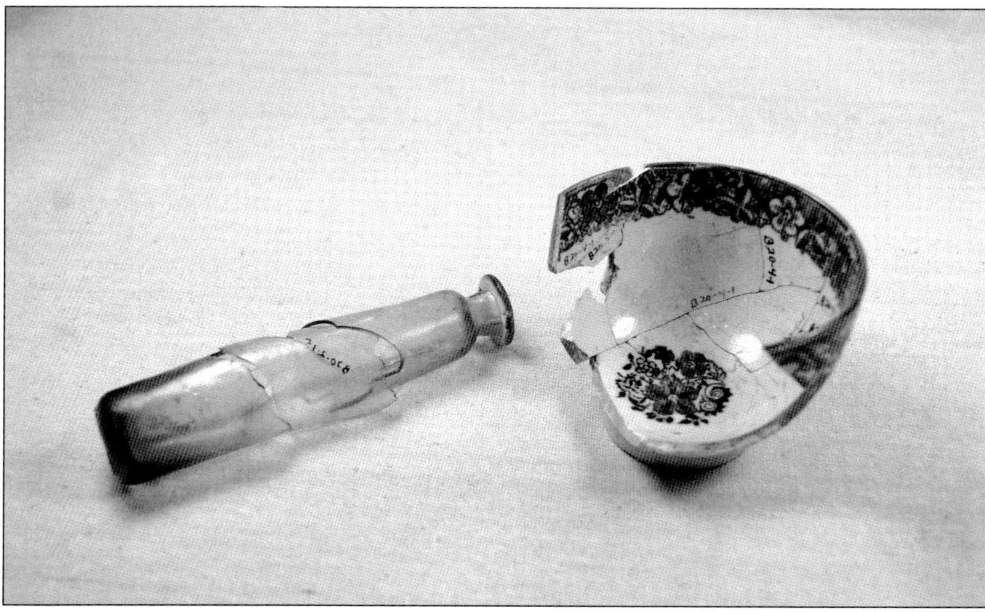

These fragments of an apothecary bottle and 19th-century teacup were found in the cellar of the gunsmith shop. When the structure was no longer needed and removed, the remaining cellar was used as a dump in the early 19th century. Besides the objects photographed here, pottery fragments, bones, glass tumblers, and creamware ceramics were found during the excavation of this cellar. (Courtesy of the Bethabara Collection.)

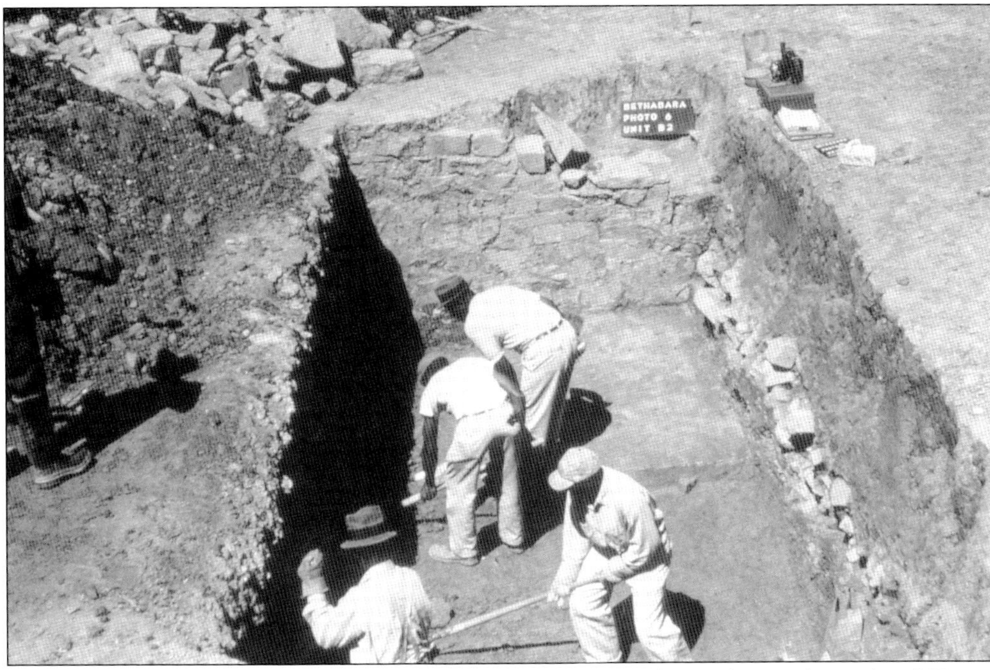

This 1964 image shows members of the crew excavating the cellar of the Single Brothers' House. The crew discovered the cellars by removing the plowed soil and looking for a dark outline of fill dirt that contrasted with the undisturbed red subsoil. The Single Brothers' House cellar was the largest excavated during the dig, measuring slightly larger than 16 by 18 feet. (Courtesy of the Bethabara Collection.)

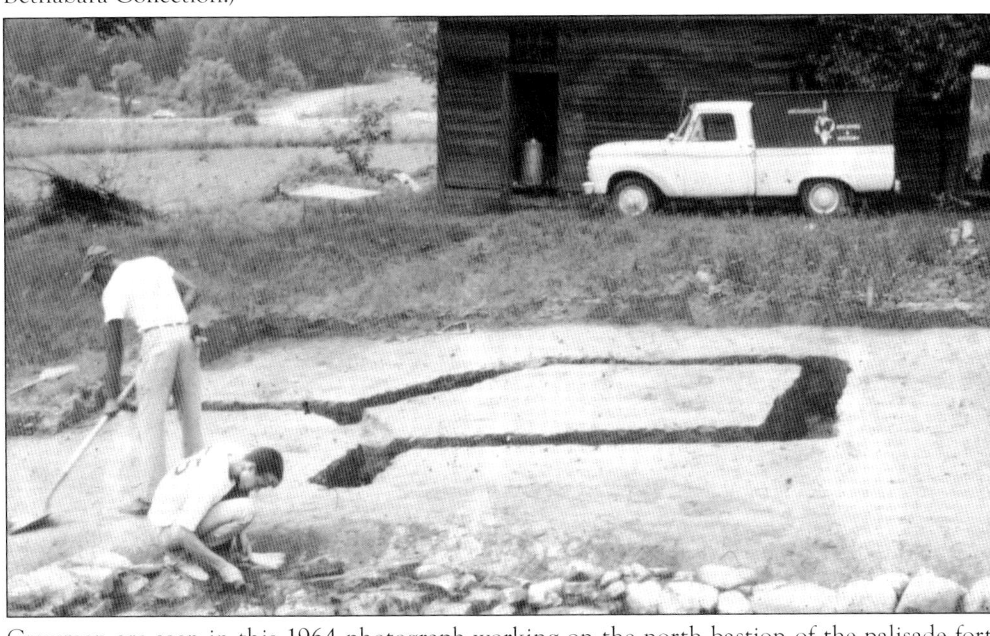

Crewmen are seen in this 1964 photograph working on the north bastion of the palisade fort. Many of the crewmen were hired locally to work on the project. In the background, a truck is parked with a logo on the side that reads, "Archaeology, Archives & History." (Courtesy of the Bethabara Collection.)

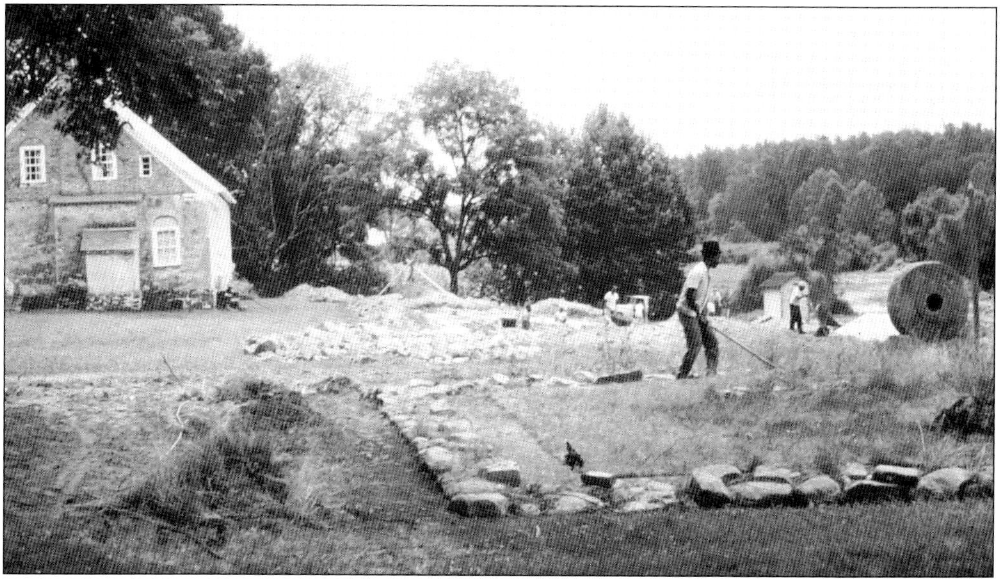

These images show the ruins of the 1756 Gemeinhaus, not too far away from the current Gemeinhaus, built in 1788. The Bethabara fort millstone monument from 1903 can be seen to the right in both photographs. The walls of the foundation of the first Gemeinhaus had been discovered during the first trench dig of the site. The partition wall foundation featured arms for the hearths in two of the rooms, which indicated a central chimney. In the photograph below, the old store can be seen that was used as the archaeological laboratory during the dig. (Above, courtesy of the Bethabara Collection; below, courtesy of the Forsyth County Public Library Photograph Collection, Winston-Salem, North Carolina.)

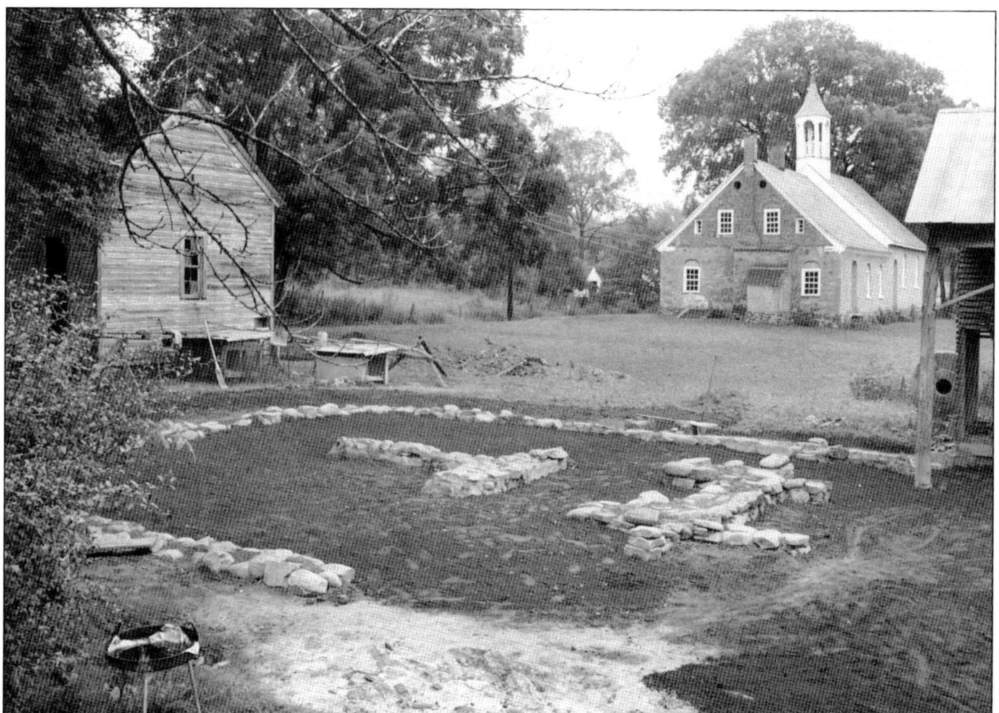

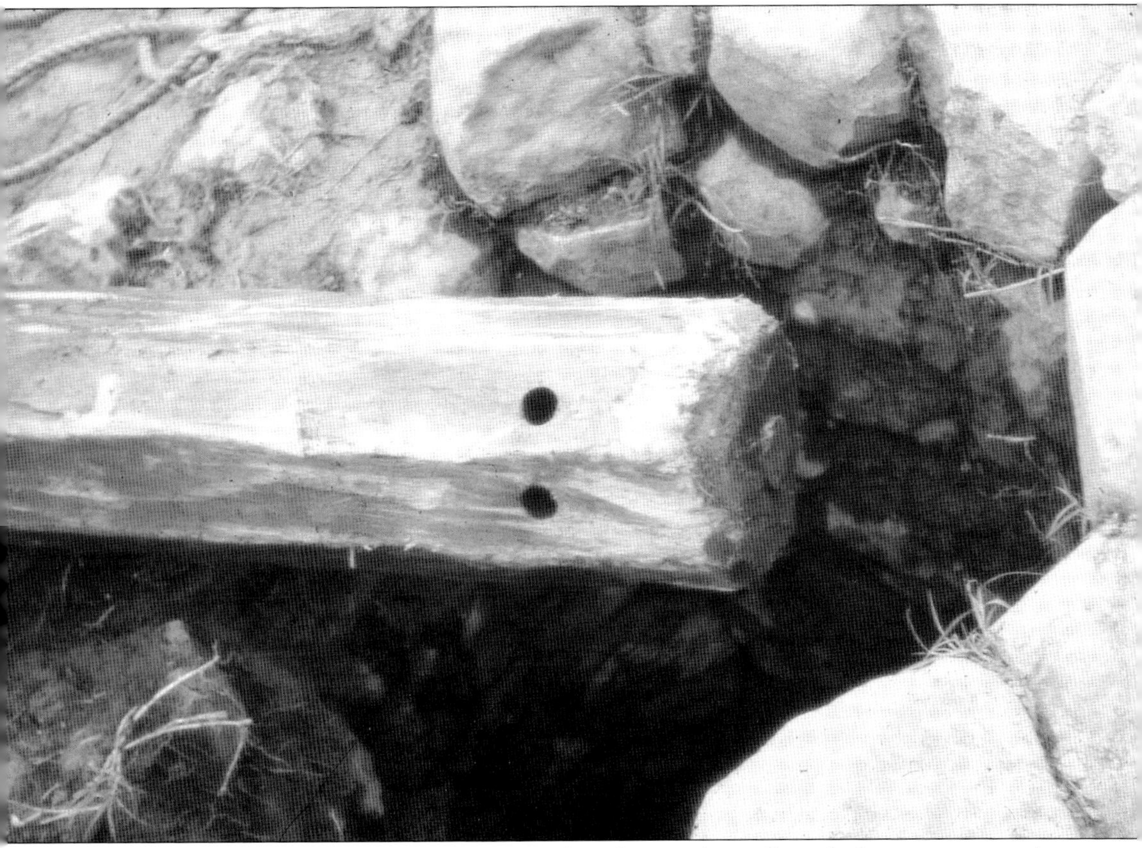

This July 1965 photograph shows the bottom end of the wooden well stock that was recovered from the excavated well of the 1788 Gemeinhaus. Water would enter at the intake holes seen on the side of the well stock. These logs were hollow so that water could enter and travel upwards with the aid of a piston that was controlled by a handle above the ground. In 1754, the Moravians in Bethlehem, Pennsylvania, built the first pressurized waterworks in North America. The Moravians who traveled to Bethabara were therefore already familiar with this system. A total of six wells were located during the Stanley South dig, two of which had pieces of wooden well stocks inside. The wells were disappointing to the archaeologists, as they had hoped to find artifacts that might have been thrown in once the well no longer produced good water. The Bethabara wells were in use so long that by the time they were replaced, the items thrown in were too modern to be of interest. (Courtesy of the Bethabara Collection.)

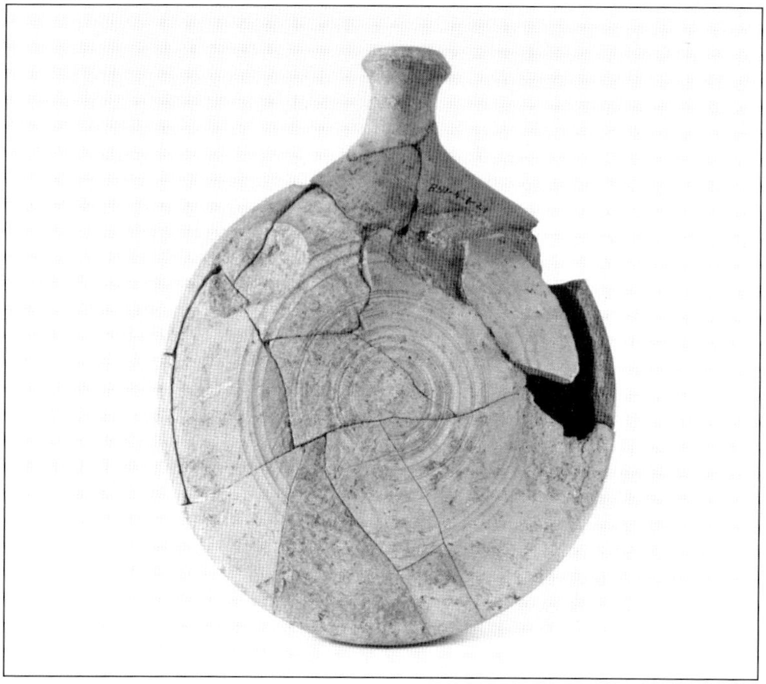

This bottle was recovered from the Aust pottery site during Stanley South's dig and was pieced back together. Bottles came in many forms, this one being a plain flask type that was likely the most common in Wachovia. Gottfried Aust was the first potter in Bethabara, and his wares helped make the town a successful trades center. (Courtesy of Old Salem Museums & Gardens.)

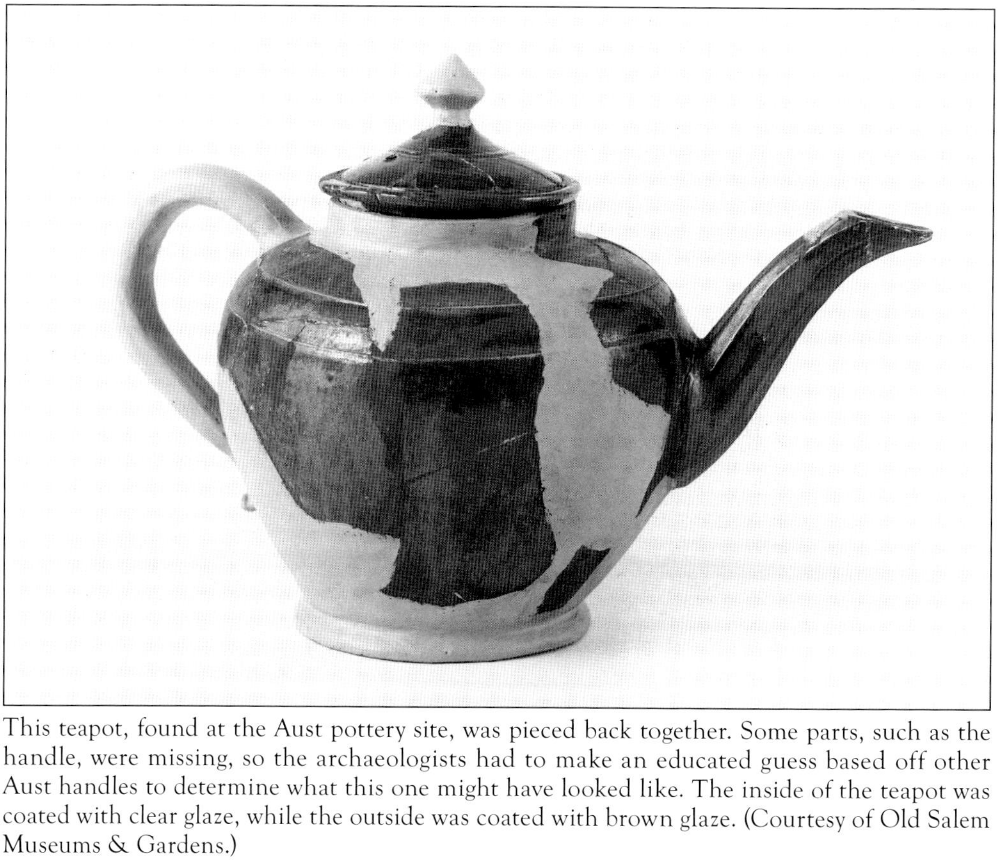

This teapot, found at the Aust pottery site, was pieced back together. Some parts, such as the handle, were missing, so the archaeologists had to make an educated guess based off other Aust handles to determine what this one might have looked like. The inside of the teapot was coated with clear glaze, while the outside was coated with brown glaze. (Courtesy of Old Salem Museums & Gardens.)

Recovered from the Aust pottery site, this brazier was a complex piece for potters to make. Braziers were filled with hot coals from the fire to keep vessels of food warm. No American form of brazier looks like the one found at Aust's site, so he likely learned how to make this type while still in Germany. (Courtesy of Old Salem Museums & Gardens.)

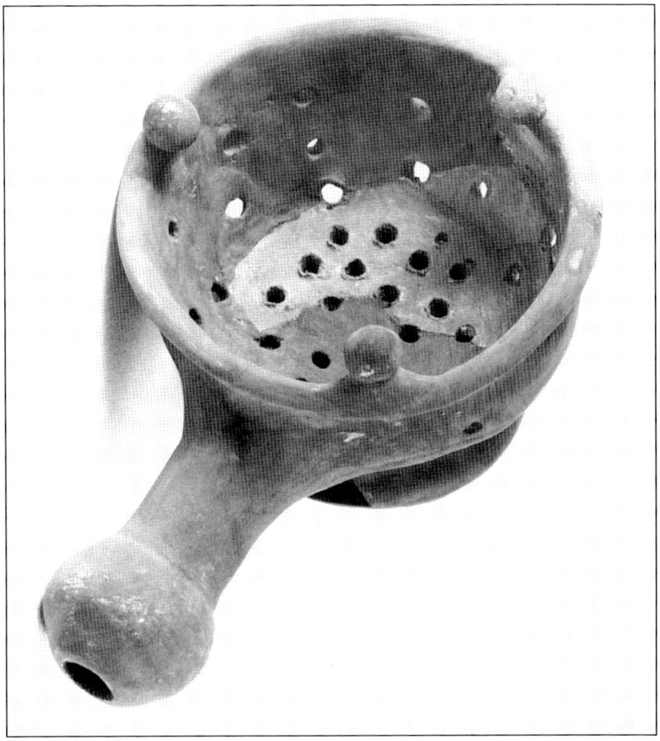

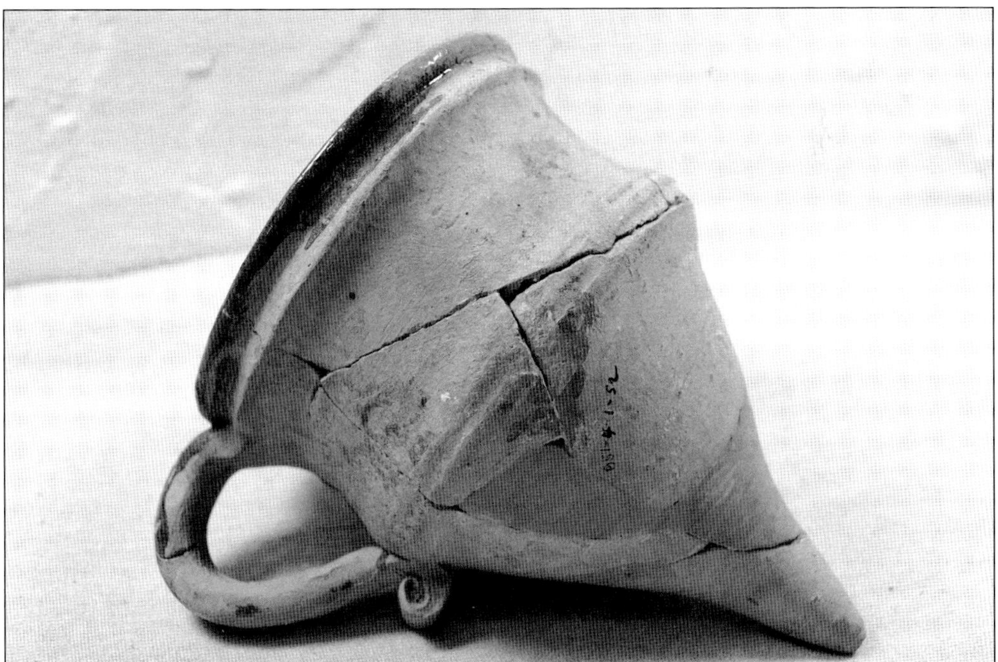

This funnel was made by Gottfried Aust and was recovered from the kiln waster dump. This dump was an unfinished basement Stanley South found that was filled partly with kiln furniture and pieces that cracked during firing and partly with other items from the nearby kitchen, including animal bones. (Courtesy of the Bethabara Collection.)

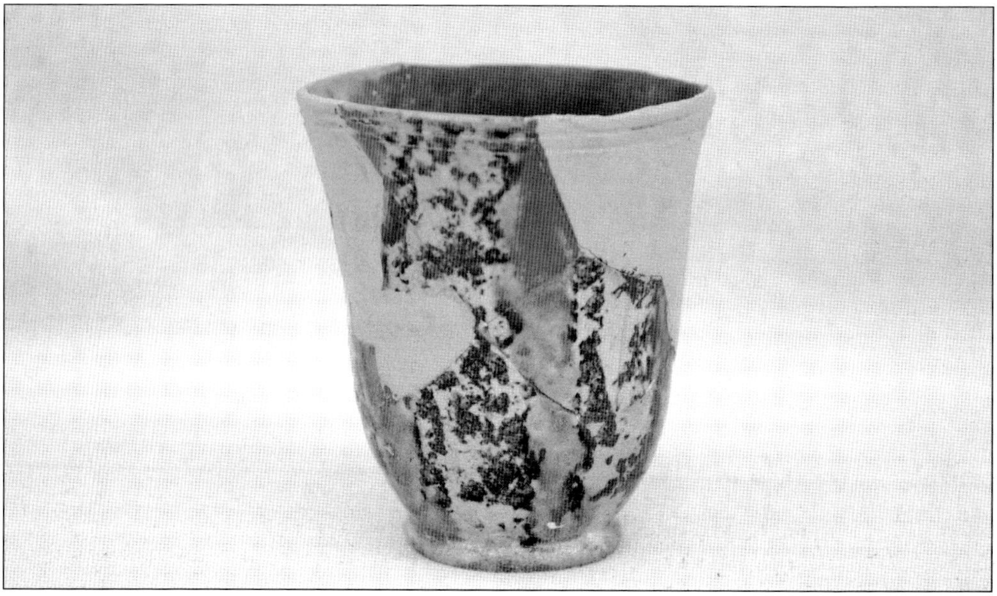

The above tortoiseshell beaker and below tortoiseshell plate were created by Rudolph Christ, who made pottery in Bethabara from 1786 to 1789. Christ first began work in Bethabara as an apprentice for Gottfried Aust. He and Aust were often at odds, but Christ continued his apprenticeship and eventually became a journeyman working in Aust's shop in Salem. According to the *Records of the Moravians in North Carolina*, a traveling potter named William Ellis came to Aust's shop while Christ worked there and offered to teach them how to make "English Queensware and Tortoise-shell, that is, a fine pottery, resembling porcelain." The Moravians offered Ellis lodging in exchange for his lessons. Christ liked this new style more than Aust and was allowed to set up his own shop in Bethabara to focus on it. (Both, courtesy of the Bethabara Collection.)

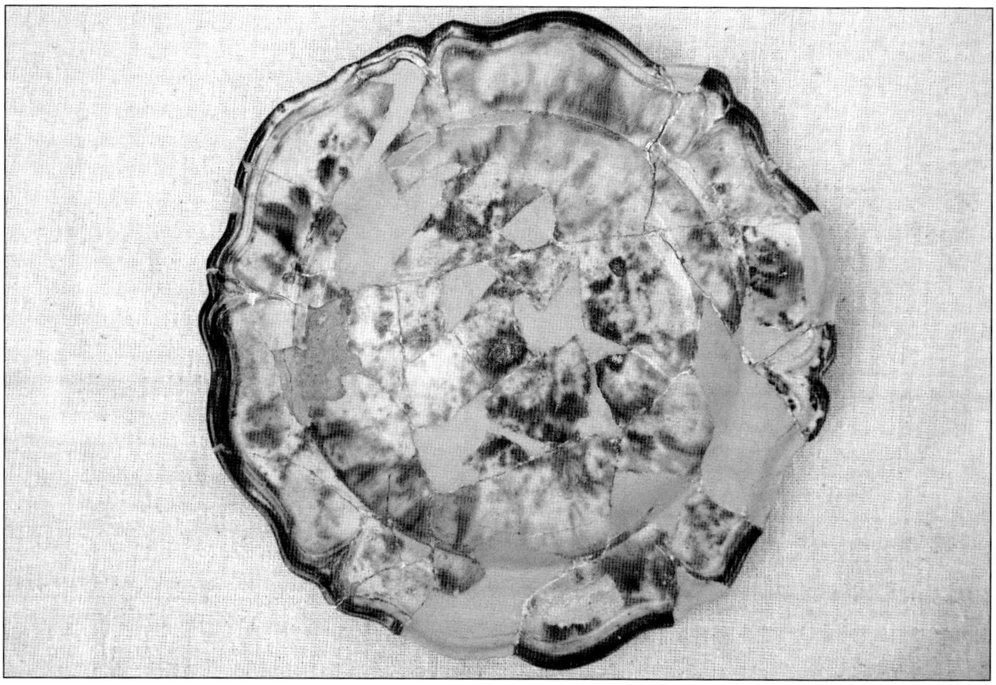

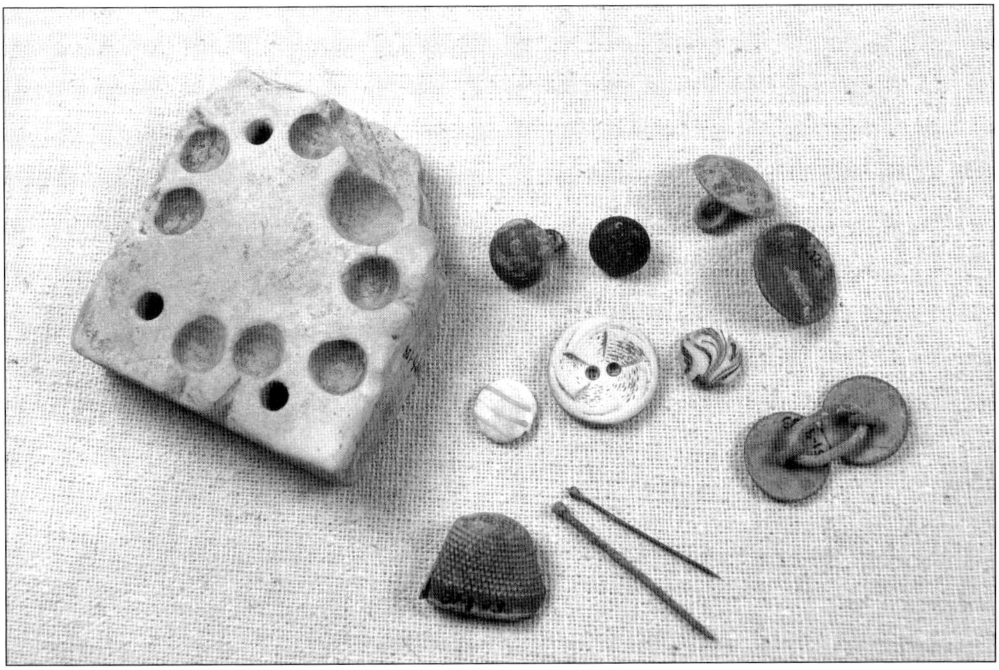

Besides pottery, a number of everyday items were discovered by Stanley South and his team. The above photograph features a bullet mold pulled out of one of the waster dumps (the one shared between the kitchen and Aust's pottery shop), straight pins and a thimble, and a variety of buttons. The paste sleeve button in the middle of the top row is a colorful blue. Portraits of Moravian women often show them wearing these types of buttons. The photograph below is a collection of post-1820 artifacts, including a child's shoe and pieces of imported china. While Stanley South's primary focus was on 18th-century artifacts, these pieces offer glimpses into what the town was like as a rural community in the 19th century. (Both, courtesy of the Bethabara Collection.)

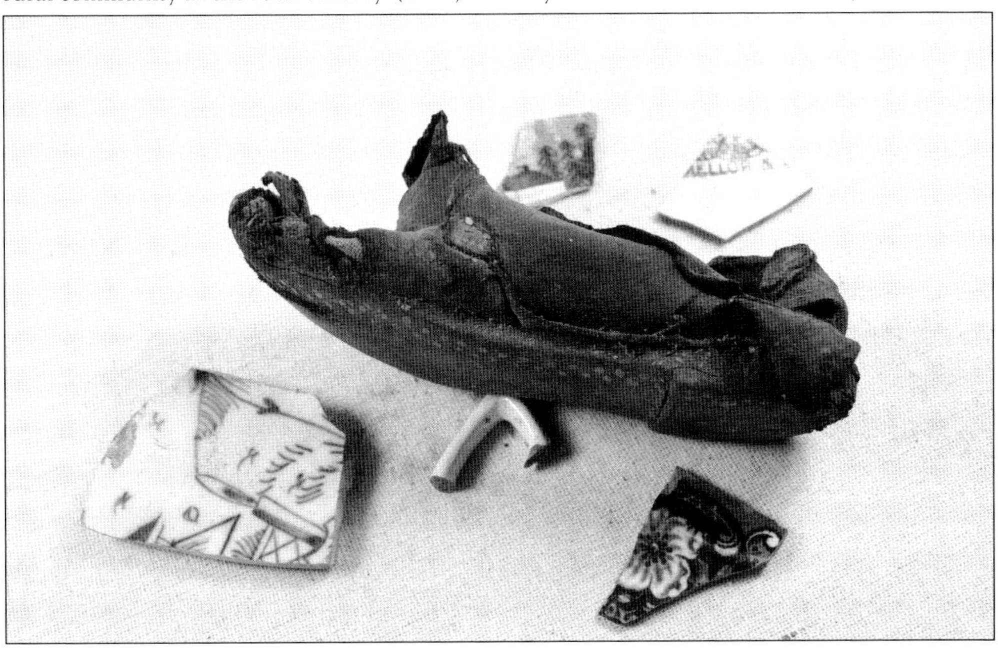

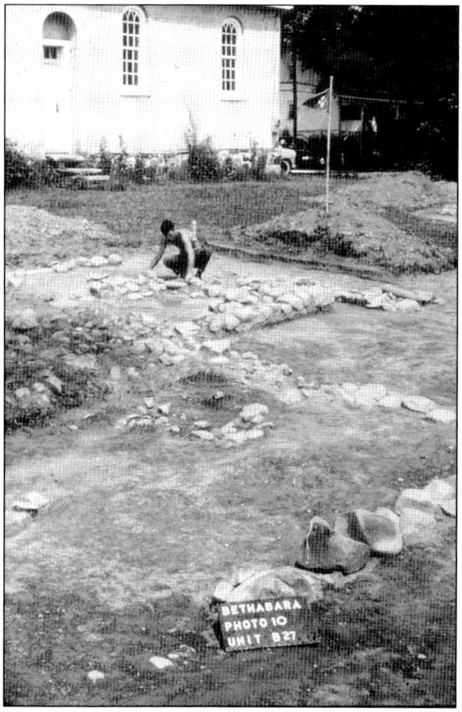

This photograph, taken in 1965, shows a crew member working on the foundation of the apothecary shop. The 1788 Gemeinhaus can be seen in the background. The apothecary shop was built in 1763 for Dr. Jacob Bonn, who moved to Salem in 1772 along with the other tradespeople. It is likely he took most of his remedies with him, as no apothecary bottles were found in the cellar of this building. (Courtesy of the Bethabara Collection.)

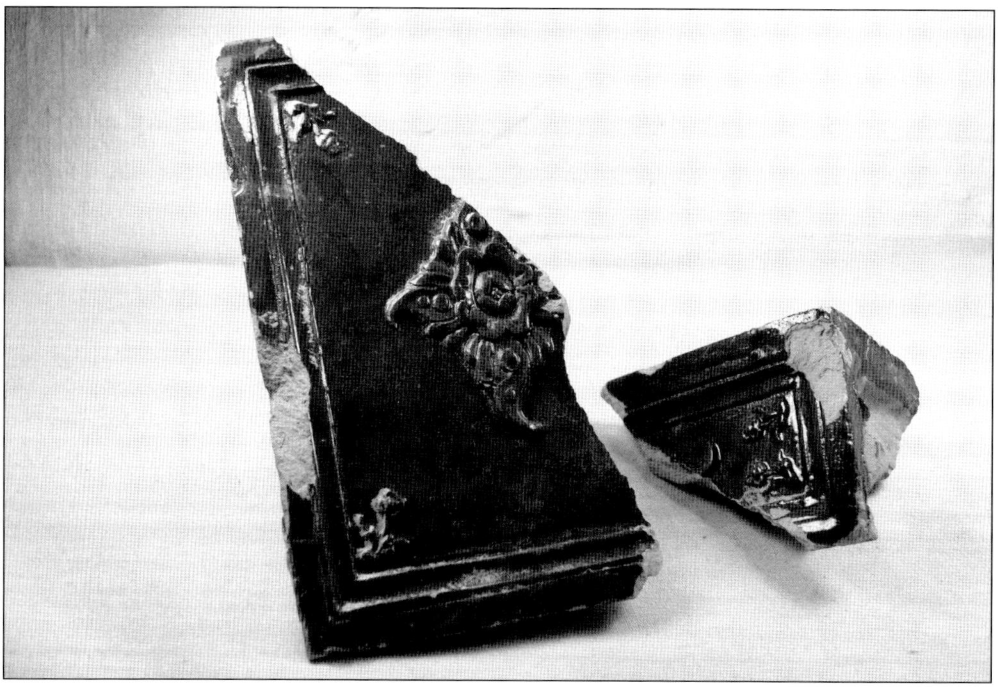

Stove tiles like this one, found in the apothecary shop cellar, were made from molds by the potters in Bethabara. Tile stoves, or *Kachelofen*, were used to efficiently heat homes in central Europe. Many buildings in Bethabara had tile stoves, including the apothecary shop. Gottfied Aust was tasked with making and assembling tile stoves in the Gemeinhaus and Single Brothers' House soon after he arrived in Bethabara. (Courtesy of the Bethabara Collection.)

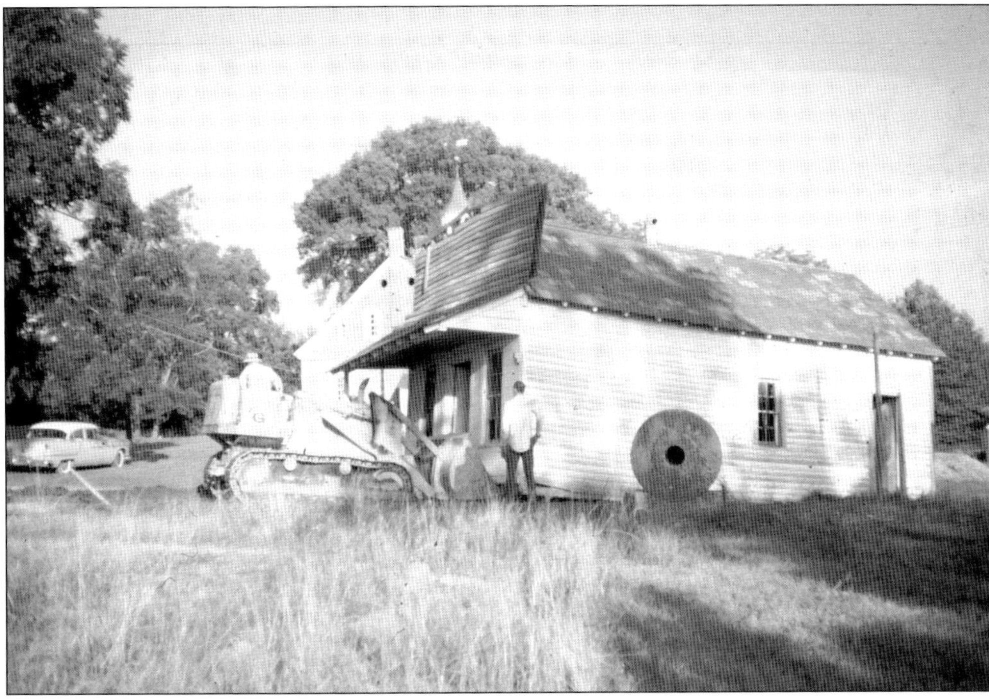

These 1965 photographs chronicle the demolition of an old store in Bethabara. Jewell South and her team used this building during the dig, but by 1965, it was no longer needed. It was torn down like other modern buildings on the property purchased by Edwin Stockton for the Moravian Church. Stanley South had recommended this to Stockton, stating that modern buildings needed to be removed for historical accuracy, although some of the oldest structures might remain as museums and places to display artifacts. (Both, courtesy of the Bethabara Collection.)

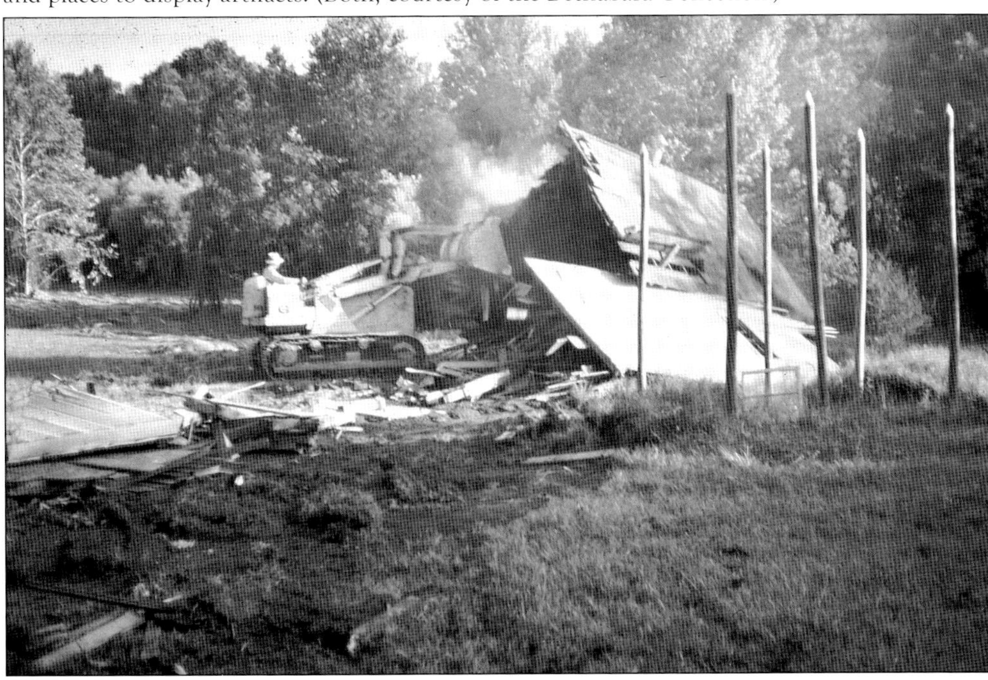

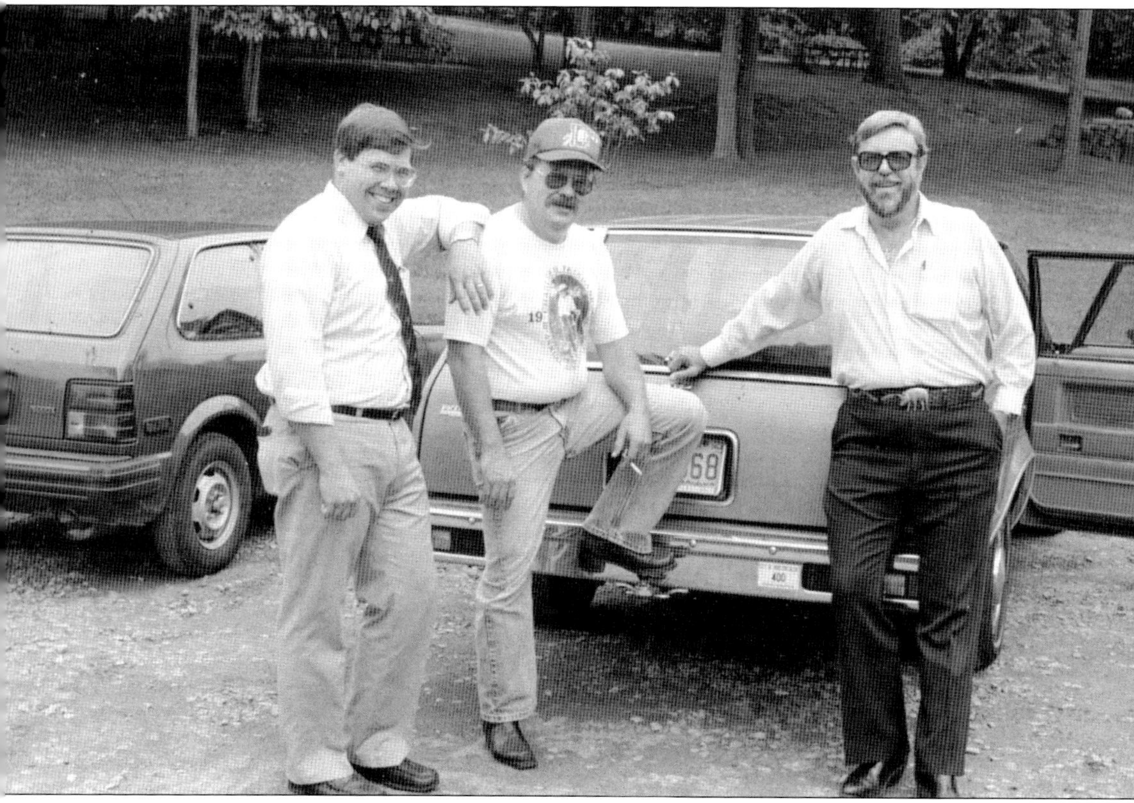

This 1980s photograph was taken in the parking lot next to the Distiller's House. William Hinman (left), Historic Bethabara Park director from 1982 to 1988, stands with John Clauser Jr. (center) and Stanley South (right). After Stanley South completed his work in the 1960s, John Clauser, who worked as an archaeologist for the North Carolina Department of Cultural Resources, conducted several digs in Bethabara in the 1970s and 1980s. He helped directors like Hinman better interpret the history of the site to the public. Clauser discovered the ruins of the Bethabara distillery in the very parking lot the three men are standing on in this photograph. Prior to that, Clauser conducted a dig behind the Potter's House, and in 1985, Hinman reached out to him to conduct an archaeological survey of the community garden site. (Courtesy of the Bethabara Collection.)

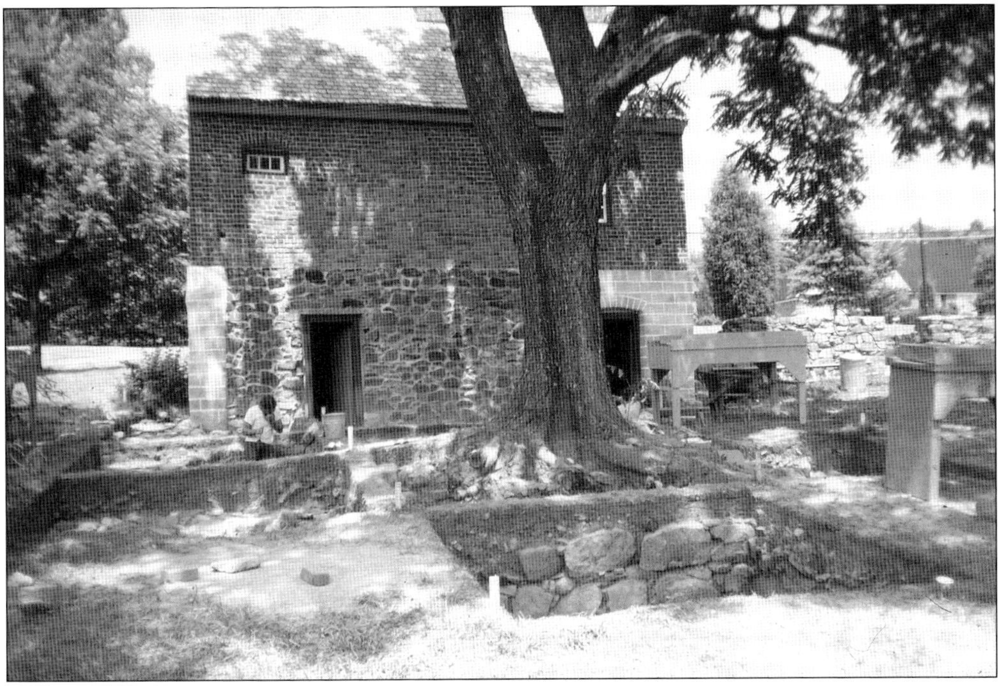

In the spring of 1974, John Clauser Jr. began an excavation of the rear wing of the Potter's House. While it was his first dig at Bethabara, Clauser had previously worked on Moravian sites in Bethlehem, Pennsylvania. Images of the Potter's House dig are seen here. While excavating to find the outline of the location, Clauser and his team came across the remains of the pottery shop's kiln. Portions can be seen in both photographs, with a large walnut tree growing through the middle of it. The kiln would have been used by John Butner and his descendants and was a major find for Clauser, as it was the first definitively identified Moravian kiln excavated in America. The kiln was documented before it was reburied for protection. (Both, courtesy of the Bethabara Collection.)

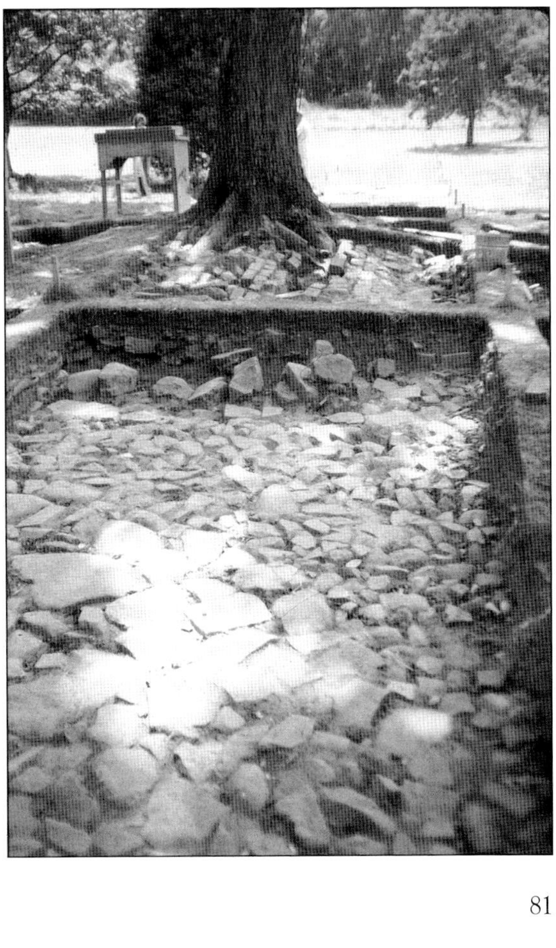

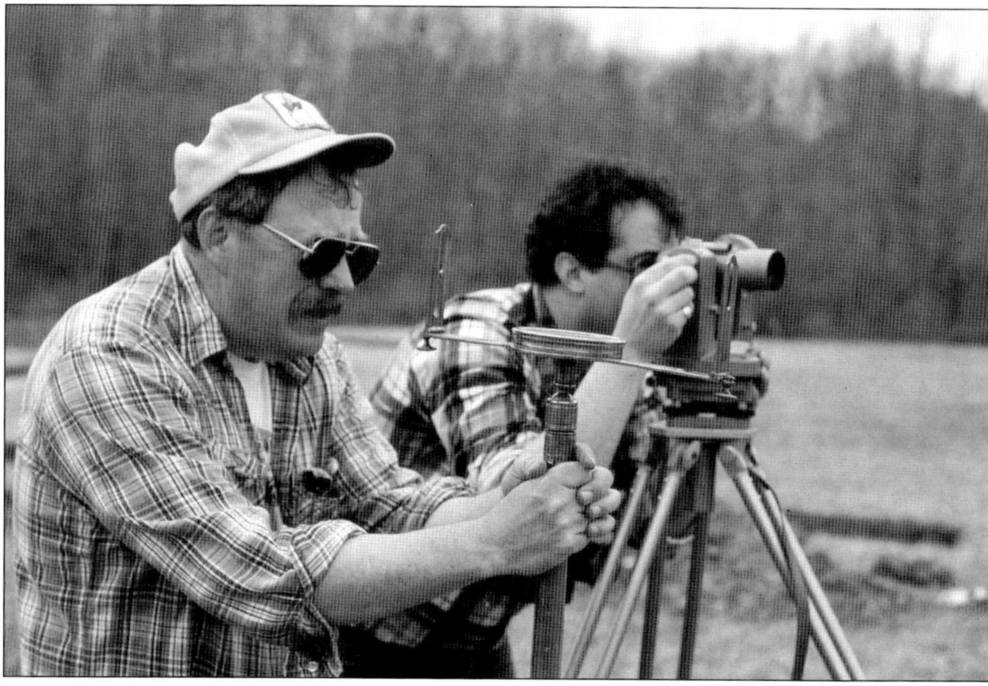

John Clauser Jr. conducted two archaeological investigations of the community garden. In 1985, he was able to determine the rough size of the garden but little about its layout. These photographs of Clauser are from the spring of 1988, when he conducted his second excavation. Above, he is using a surveying instrument called a transit. Guided by Christian Reuter's map, Clauser was able to trace out the dimensions of the garden. Below, Clauser takes a break from his work to speak with a group of visitors. By this time, Historic Bethabara Park was open to the public, and many curious onlookers made their way to the excavation site. Clauser wrote in his reports about the importance of engaging the public in archaeological work. (Both, courtesy of the Bethabara Collection.)

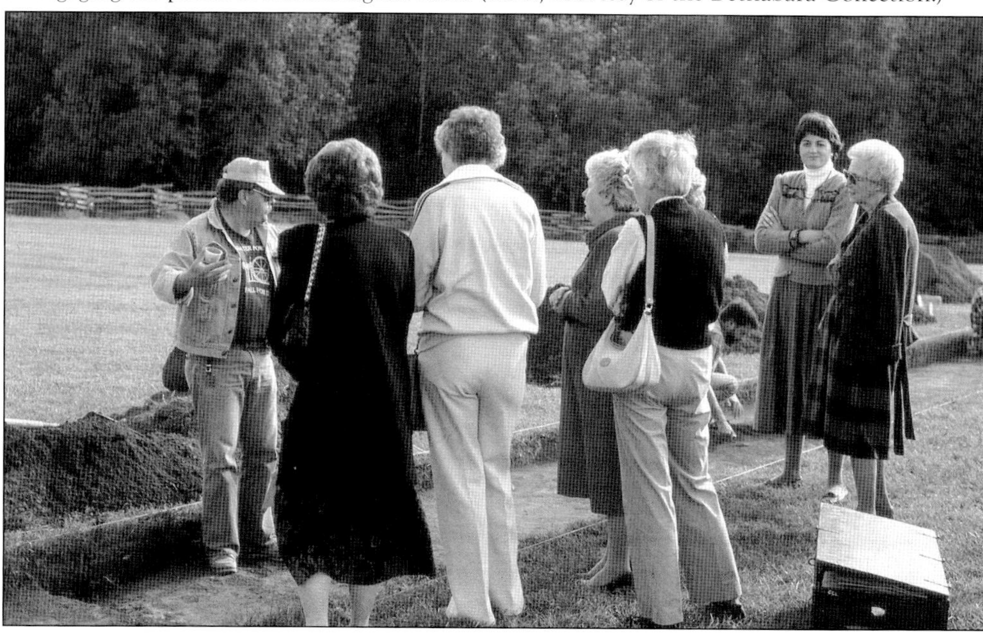

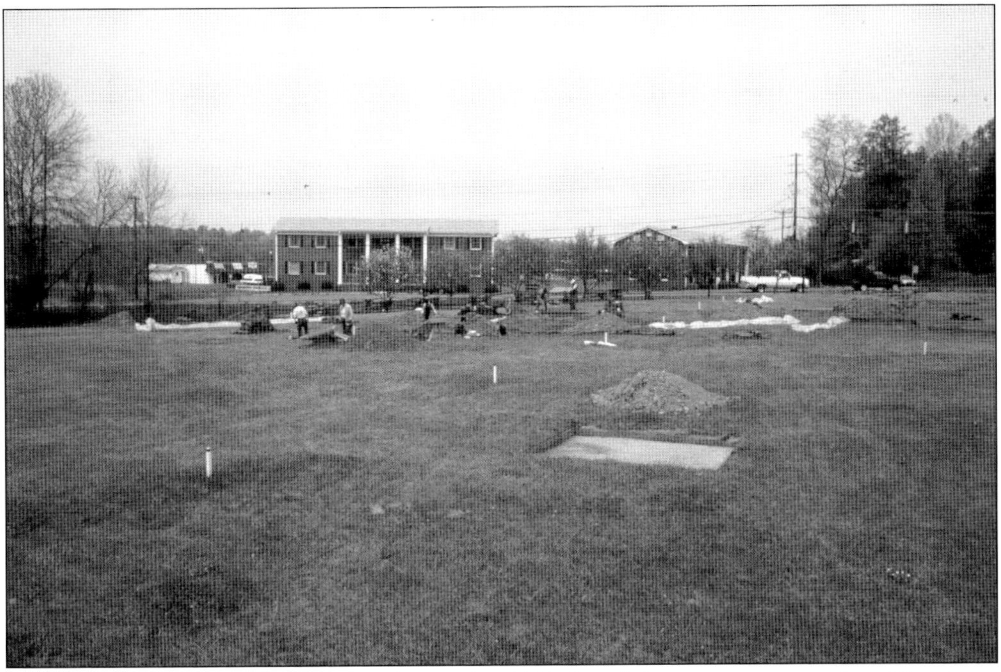

These two photographs were taken during the 1988 dig of the community garden. The above photograph shows the excavation site with apartment buildings in the background that were later removed. In the photograph below, John Clauser Jr. stands on top of a truck to get a better angle for his photograph. The 1988 dig revealed much more than the 1985 attempt, with Clauser and his team locating the grape arbor, garden paths, and three of the four fence lines and gate locations. They found portions of the smaller 1754 garden as well as the larger 1759 garden documented by Christian Reuter. (Both, courtesy of the Bethabara Collection.)

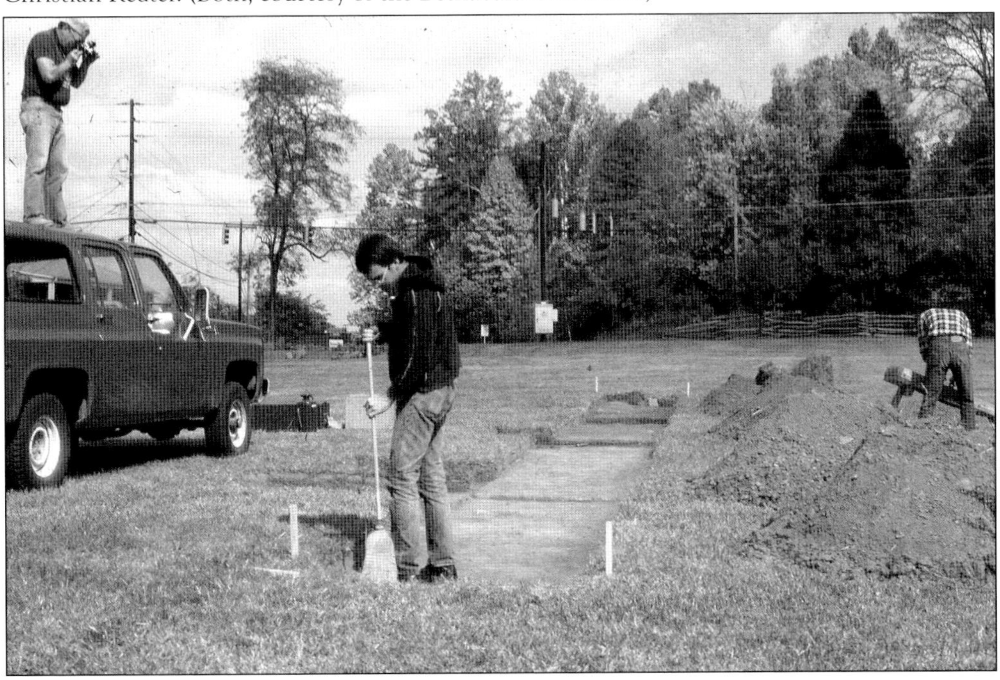

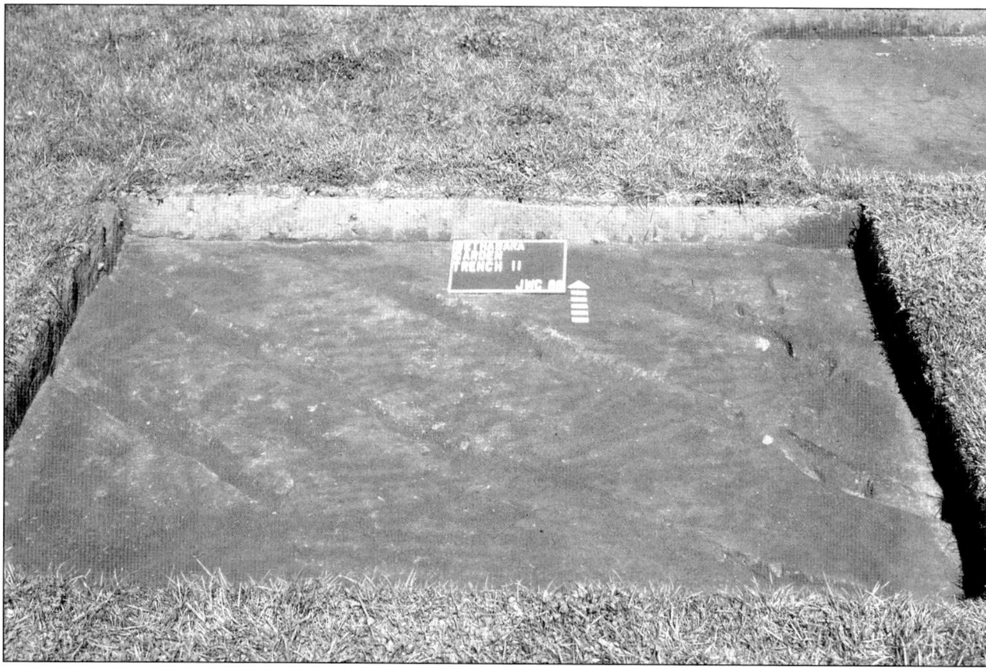

The above photograph from the 1988 dig shows a portion of the community garden with its original diagonal plow lines. The photograph below shows the postholes of the original grape arbor. After John Clauser Jr. finished his excavation of the garden, he wrote up a report in which he recommended a limited reconstruction of the 1759 garden. Using Clauser's findings, Historic Bethabara Park rebuilt the grape arbor and created garden beds like those he uncovered to give visitors an idea of what the original community garden looked like. (Both, courtesy of the Bethabara Collection.)

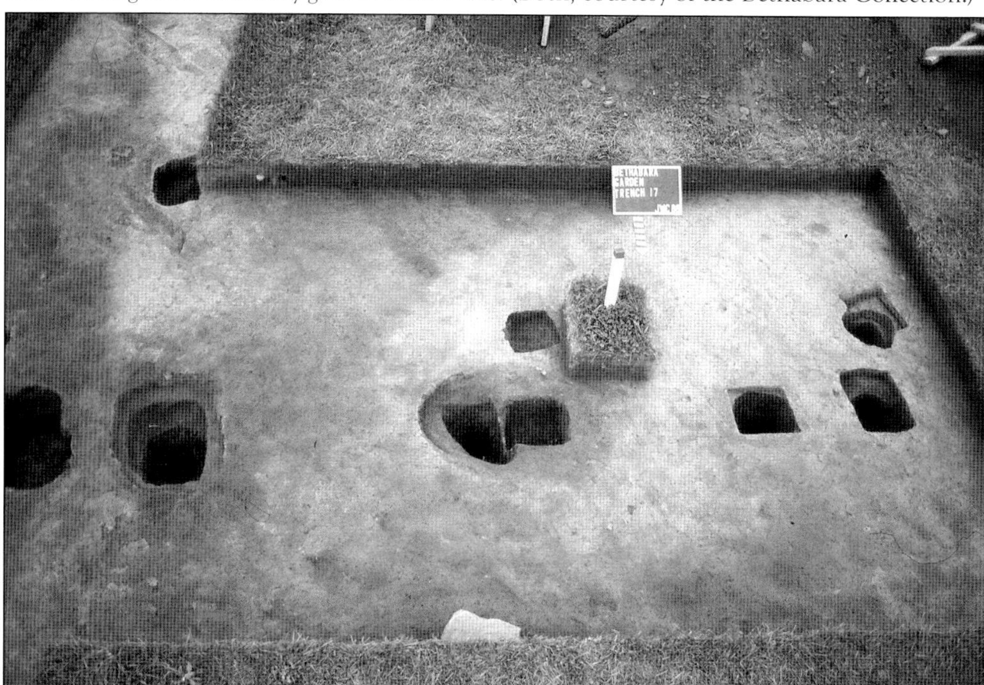

Five

Creating Historic Bethabara Park
20th-Century Restoration

When Bethabara Moravian Church's members outgrew the 1788 Gemeinhaus in the 1950s, they considered remodeling the structure to accommodate more people. Wishing to preserve the historically significant structure, Edwin L. Stockton, treasurer of the Southern Province of the Moravian Church, convinced the congregation to build an entirely new church instead.

Stockton understood the significance of Bethabara and envisioned it becoming a historic site. He enlisted philanthropist Charles H. Babcock to purchase land, including the original settlement. Babcock provided personal funds as well as grants from the Mary Reynolds Babcock Foundation, and once the purchases were made, he deeded the land to the Southern Province of the Moravian Church. Stockton and Babcock agreed that the historic site would not be a restoration or a reconstruction of the town like Old Salem was but rather an archaeological site like Jamestown, Virginia.

In 1965, W.S. Tarlton, historic site superintendent for the North Carolina Department of Archives and History, visited the site. In a letter to Stockton, Tarlton recommended restoring three historic buildings in addition to the Gemeinhaus to show the continuation of the town after the construction of Salem. Meanwhile, archaeologist Stanley South recommended the reconstruction of the palisade fort as well as stabilizing and exposing the foundations and cellars of the original settlement.

Babcock made it clear that he would provide funding to establish the historic site but not maintain it. It was hoped Old Salem might take this on, but ultimately neither it nor the State of North Carolina had the funding for the operational costs. The City of Winston-Salem did, however, and was interested in preserving the birthplace of the city while also creating a park for its citizens. The city took over running the site in 1970. That same year, Historic Bethabara Park Inc., a nonprofit organization, was also created.

While Stockton did not live to see the completion of the visitor center named after him, he did see Bethabara become a significant historic site. Today, Historic Bethabara Park is a national historic landmark and is in the National Register of Historic Places.

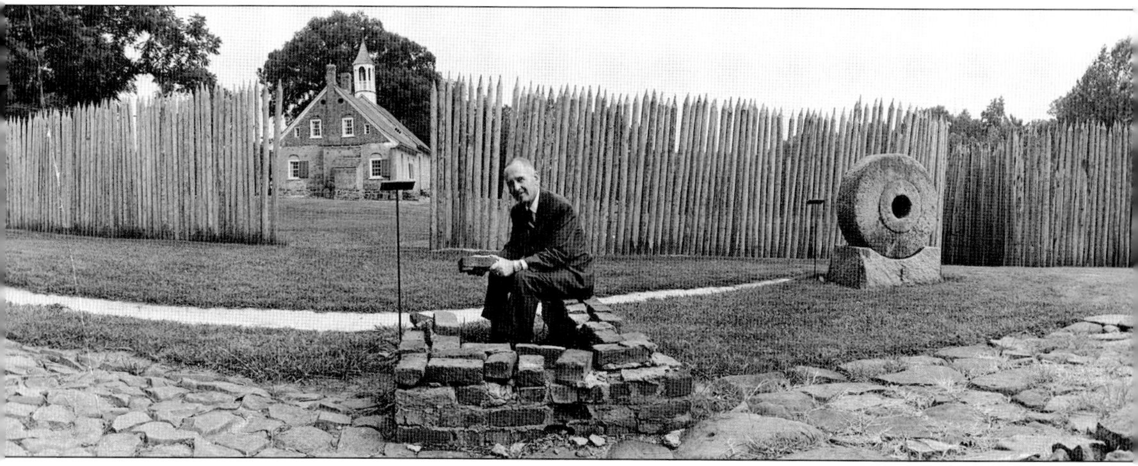

This photograph of Edwin Link Stockton was taken by Frank Jones in 1971. At this point, Stockton's dream of turning Bethabara into a historic site had become a reality, as evidenced by the stabilized foundation he sits on, with the reconstructed palisade fort and the restored 1788 Gemeinhaus behind him. Stockton was more than the visionary behind Historic Bethabara Park. A descendant of Dr. Samuel Vierling of Salem, Stockton grew up in the Moravian Church and became the secretary and treasurer of its Southern Province, a position he held from the mid-1930s until 1971. He was responsible for much of the growth of the Southern Province after World War II. While he did not live to see the completion of the Bethabara visitor center, his tireless fundraising efforts ensured the structure would be built. As reported in the *Winston-Salem Journal* in 1987, Stockton stated, "This is a culmination of 30 years of effort to save the birthplace of this community." (Courtesy of the Forsyth County Public Library Photograph Collection, Winston-Salem, North Carolina.)

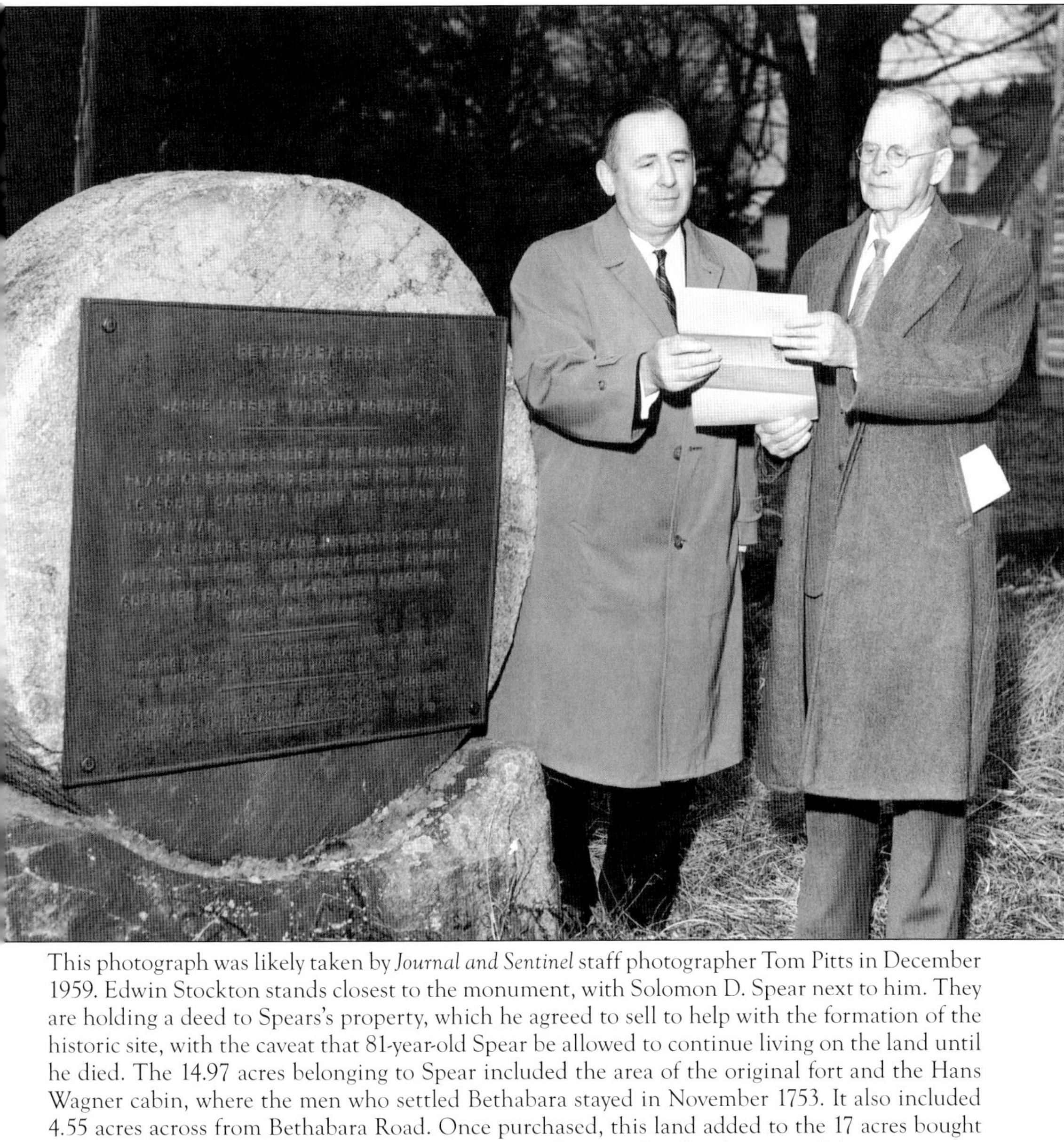

This photograph was likely taken by *Journal and Sentinel* staff photographer Tom Pitts in December 1959. Edwin Stockton stands closest to the monument, with Solomon D. Spear next to him. They are holding a deed to Spears's property, which he agreed to sell to help with the formation of the historic site, with the caveat that 81-year-old Spear be allowed to continue living on the land until he died. The 14.97 acres belonging to Spear included the area of the original fort and the Hans Wagner cabin, where the men who settled Bethabara stayed in November 1753. It also included 4.55 acres across from Bethabara Road. Once purchased, this land added to the 17 acres bought three years prior from Clyde Shore and 6 acres from the Hine family. This created the core acreage of what would become Historic Bethabara Park. (Courtesy of the Bethabara Collection.)

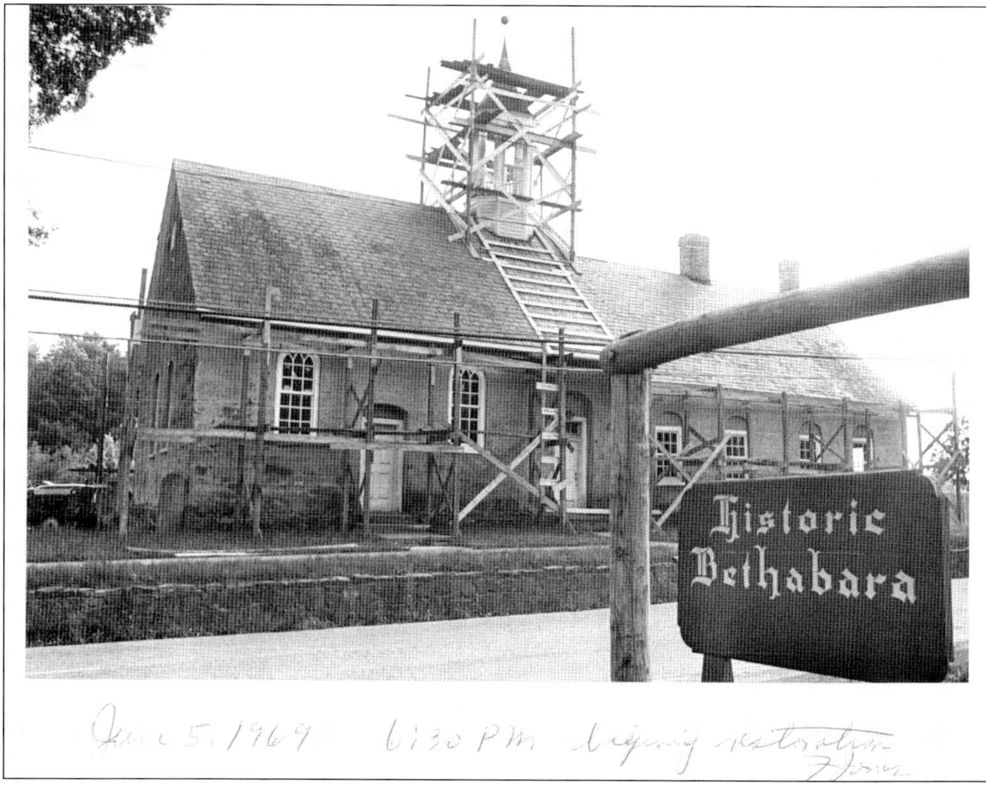

These two photographs mark the beginning of the Gemeinhaus restoration in June 1969. The image above includes a note with the time and date of when the photograph was taken. A sign for the new historic site is in the foreground. Two unidentified individuals stand on the sidewalk in the photograph below, which also features the 1903 memorial to the first Moravian settlers. A $100,000 grant for the building restoration was provided by the Mary Reynolds Babcock Foundation. Frank Horton, the director of restoration at Old Salem, wrote the restoration report for the building, which included historical information about the Gemeinhaus that informed decisions made by the restoration team, from the type of shingles to use on the roof to the best way to furnish each room. (Both, courtesy of the Forsyth County Public Library Photograph Collection, Winston-Salem, North Carolina.)

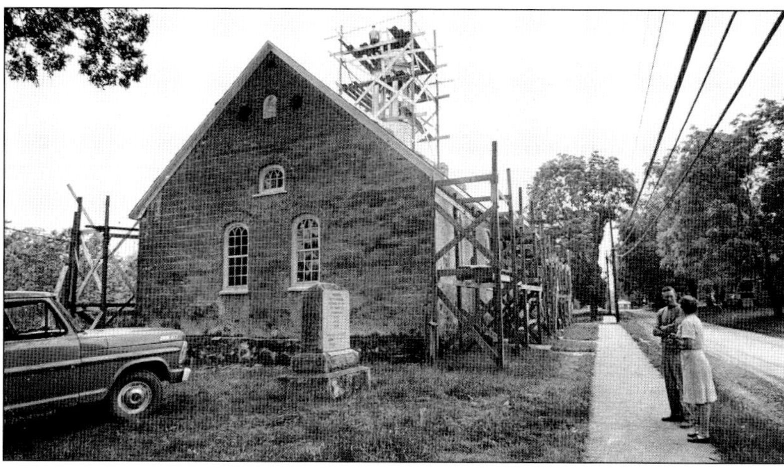

The photograph at right, taken by Frank Jones, shows a team working on the exterior windowsills of the 1788 Gemeinhaus. The image below was taken by Emory T. Welsh on July 9, 1969. Welsh labeled the photograph "Working foreman Mr. Rae Johnson with adz in hand. Skilled mechanic in building restoration." When it came to painting the exterior, the restoration team looked for clues in the building accounts and Moravian records over the years. They revealed that 50 pounds of white lead and whiting were purchased during the exterior painting of the building in 1788, which made it evident the wood trim was painted white. The same color was then used when restoring the windowsills. (Right, courtesy of the Forsyth County Public Library Photograph Collection, Winston-Salem, North Carolina; below, courtesy of the Bethabara Collection.)

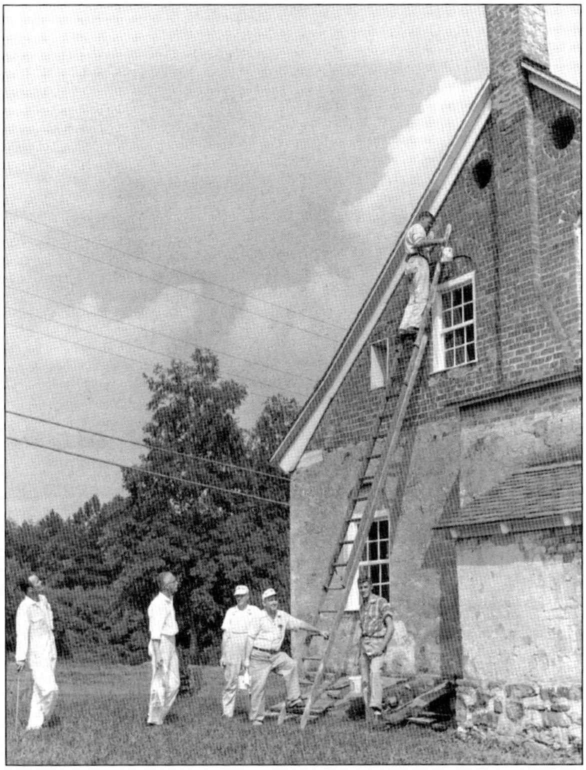

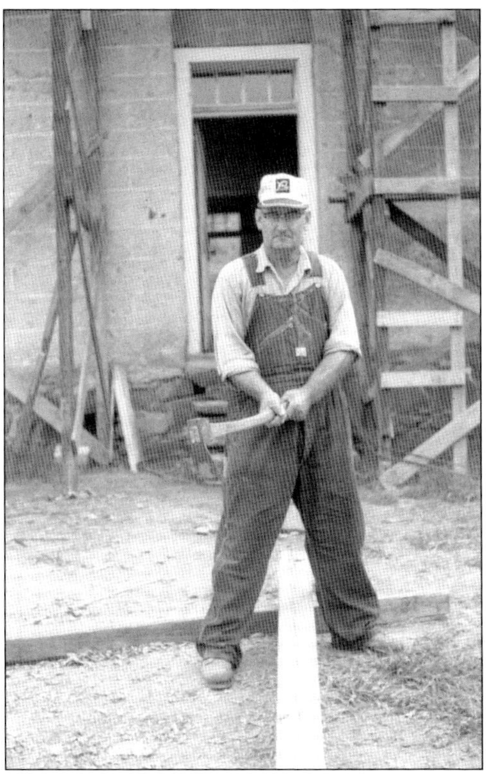

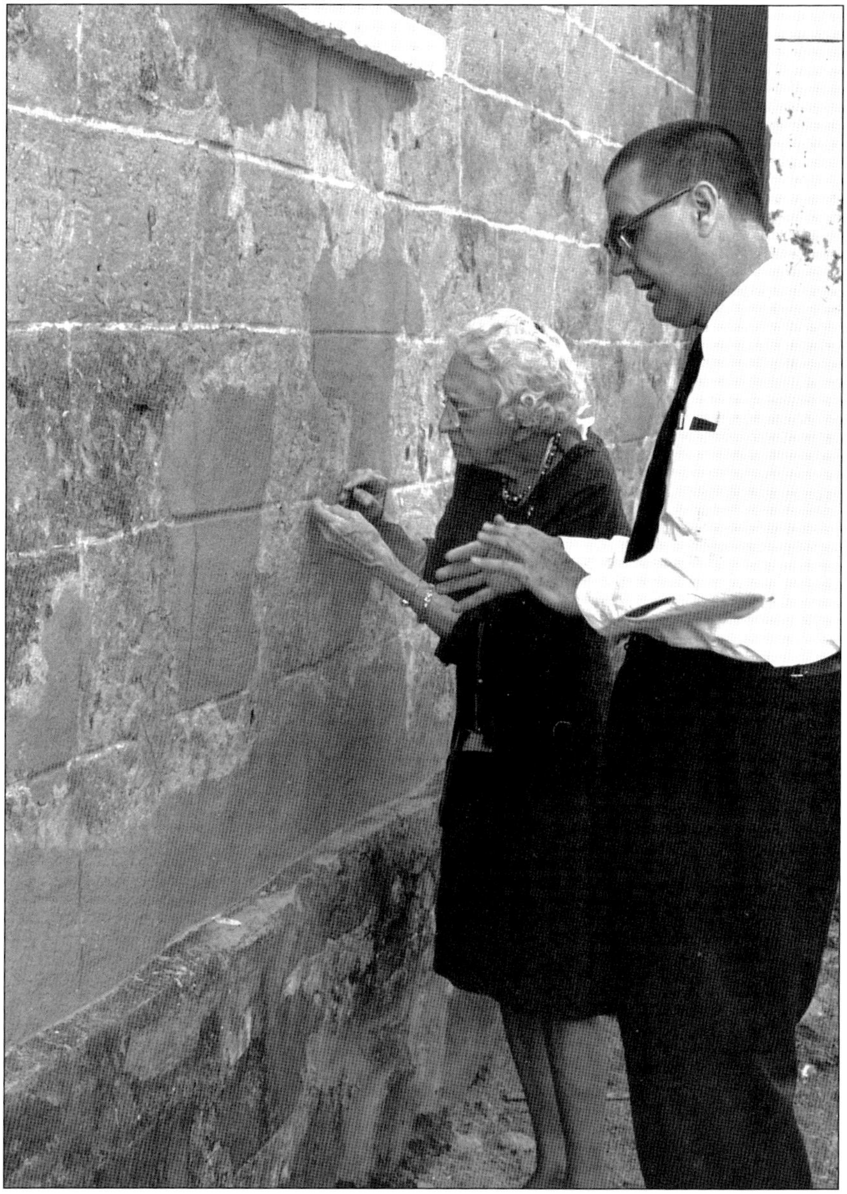

This c. 1970 photograph taken by Frances Griffin shows Ada Allen and Old Salem director of restoration Frank Horton examining the original paint on the exterior of the 1788 Gemeinhaus. As he did in Old Salem, Horton oversaw the restoration of the buildings in Bethabara. Born in 1884, Ada Allen was present for the 1903 sesquicentennial celebration at Bethabara and took photographs of the day. Her knowledge of the Gemeinhaus and its history was no doubt invaluable to Horton. The restoration team spent a good deal of time on the exterior plasterwork. Small amounts of modern gray cement plaster were removed and replaced with plaster that better matched the original. This was then painted to blend in better with the old. The plaster was originally painted a pink hue with white lines to give the plaster the appearance of cut stone. A later second painting used black lines instead, much of which had washed away by the time Horton and Allen examined the building. Where possible, the restoration team kept the surviving black lines. (Courtesy of Old Salem Museums & Gardens.)

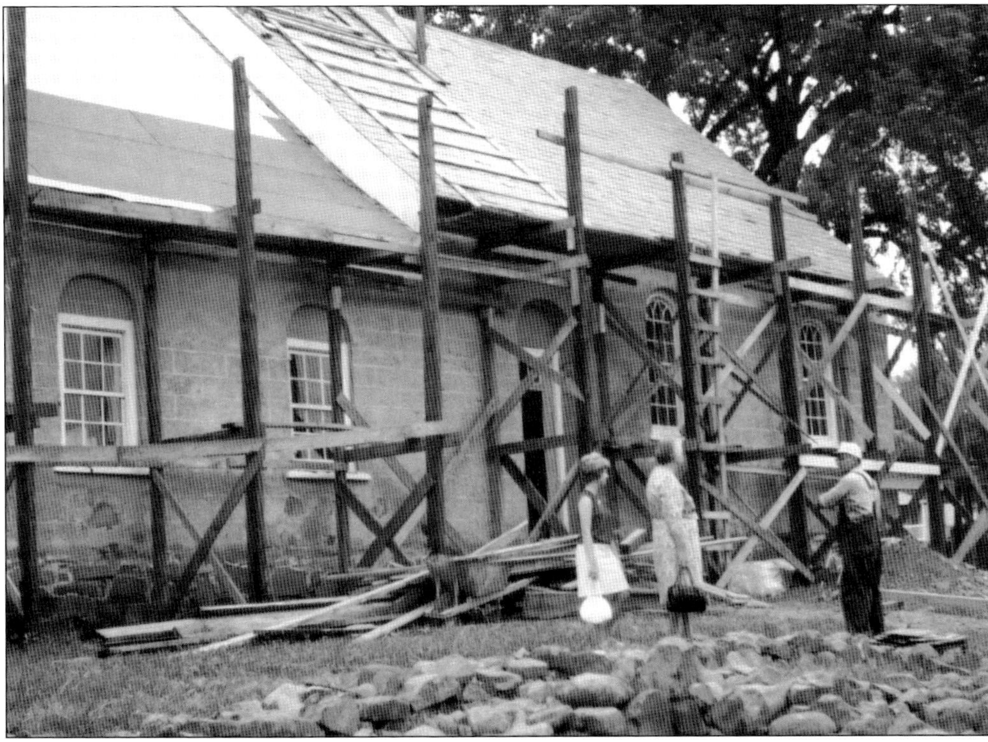

This image was taken by Emory T. Welsh during her July 9, 1969, visit to Bethabara. She labeled this photograph as "perspective back view of Gemeinhaus restoration." Rae Johnson, the foreman, can be seen talking with Welsh (left) and her companion. The restoration team replaced the 1903 slate roof with a tile roof that closely resembled the yellow poplar shingles used when the Gemeinhaus was first built. (Courtesy of the Bethabara Collection.)

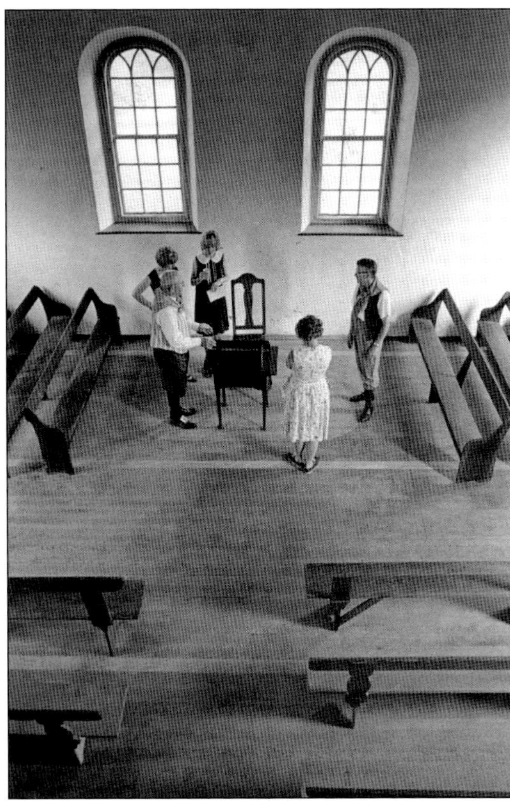

This undated photograph of the Gemeinhaus Saal was taken prior to the 1969–1970 restoration. The image shows the newer floor that was put in during the late 19th or early 20th century. The restoration team replaced the flooring and joists in this room as well as in the schoolroom, which previously had a 20th-century cement floor. (Courtesy of the Bethabara Collection.)

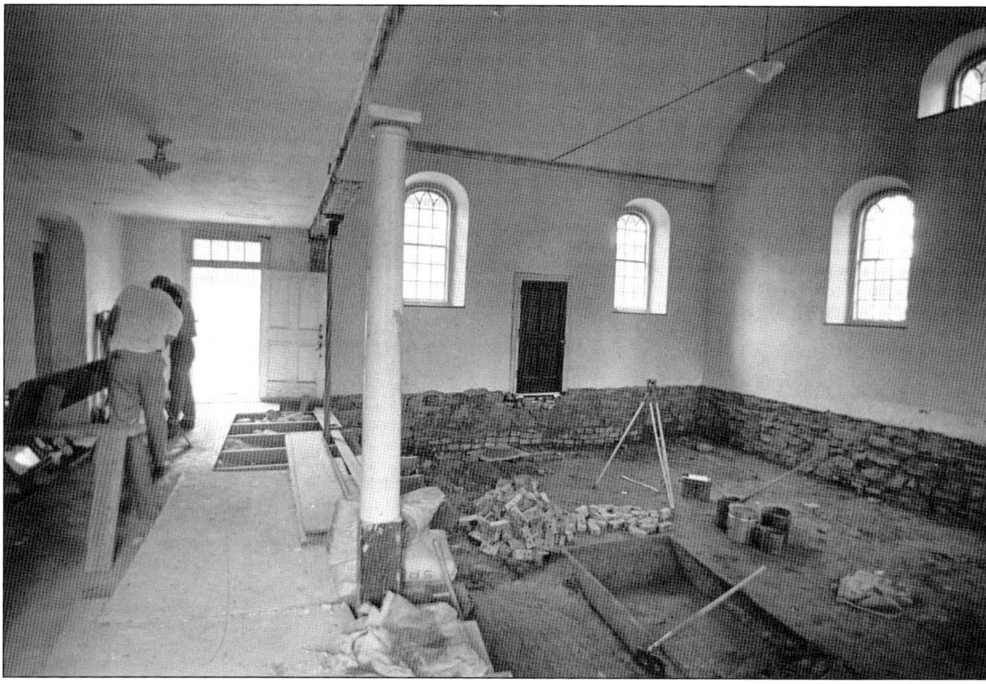

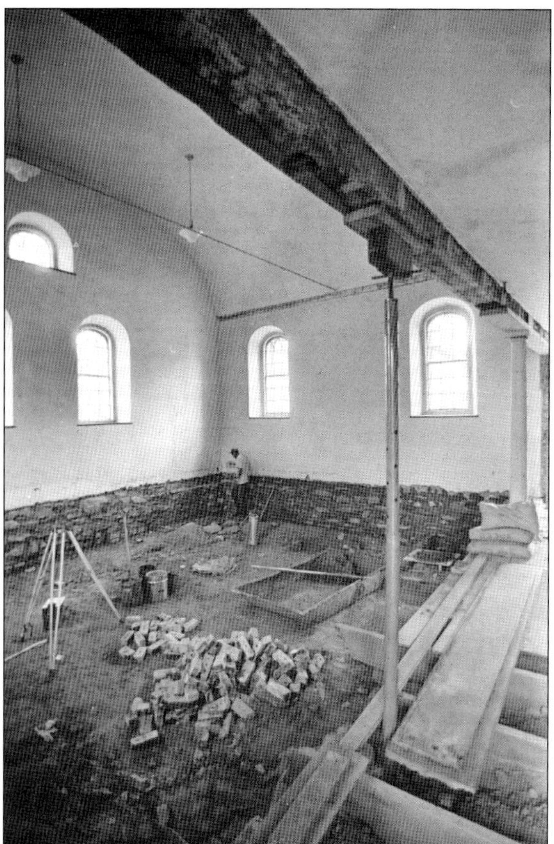

These images of the Gemeinhaus Saal were taken during the 1969–1970 restoration. The newer floor was removed and replaced with older, wider boards. In the above photograph, members of the restoration team use the vestibule area as a workstation. The wall between the Saal and vestibule was removed sometime in the late 19th or early 20th century and was put back during the restoration process. Modern lights hanging from the ceiling were also removed during the restoration. Both images show the exposed foundation, which the restoration team reinforced with modern bricks. (Both, courtesy of the Forsyth County Public Library Photograph Collection, Winston-Salem, North Carolina.)

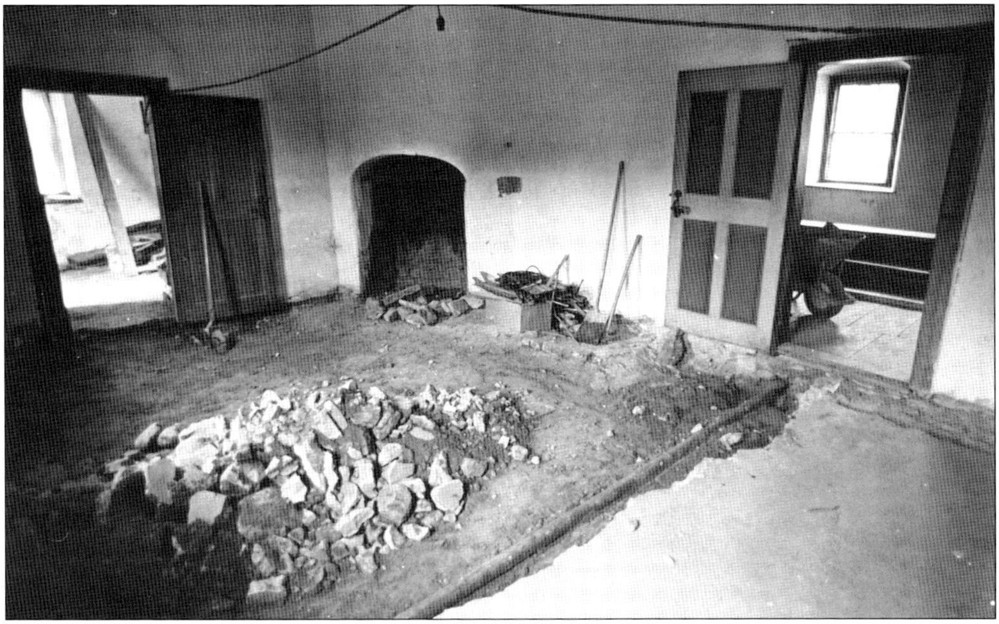

This photograph of the schoolroom was taken during the 1969–1970 restoration. The wood floor was replaced with cement during the first half of the 20th century. The process of removing that floor is documented in this image. On the far wall is the fireplace that was used to prepare coffee for Moravian lovefeasts. (Courtesy of the Forsyth County Public Library Photograph Collection, Winston-Salem, North Carolina.)

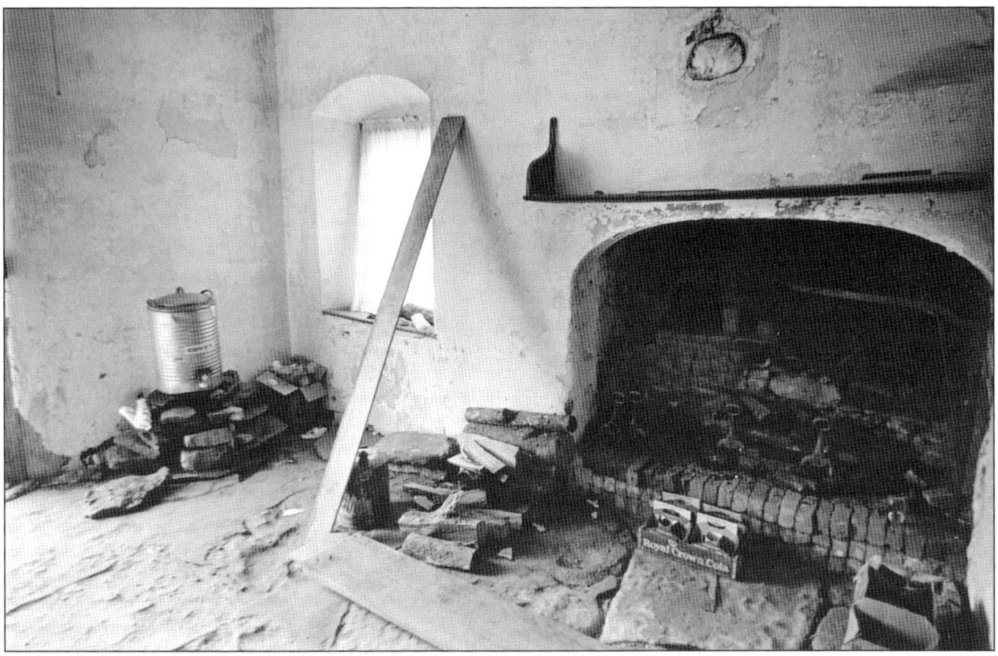

The kitchen of the Gemeinhaus was also restored. The workmen relaid parts of the stone floor and replaced the worst stones. They relaid the hearth and replaced burned-out bricks in the fireplace back. This room, like the others, was also given a fresh coat of whitewash. (Courtesy of the Forsyth County Public Library Photograph Collection, Winston-Salem, North Carolina.)

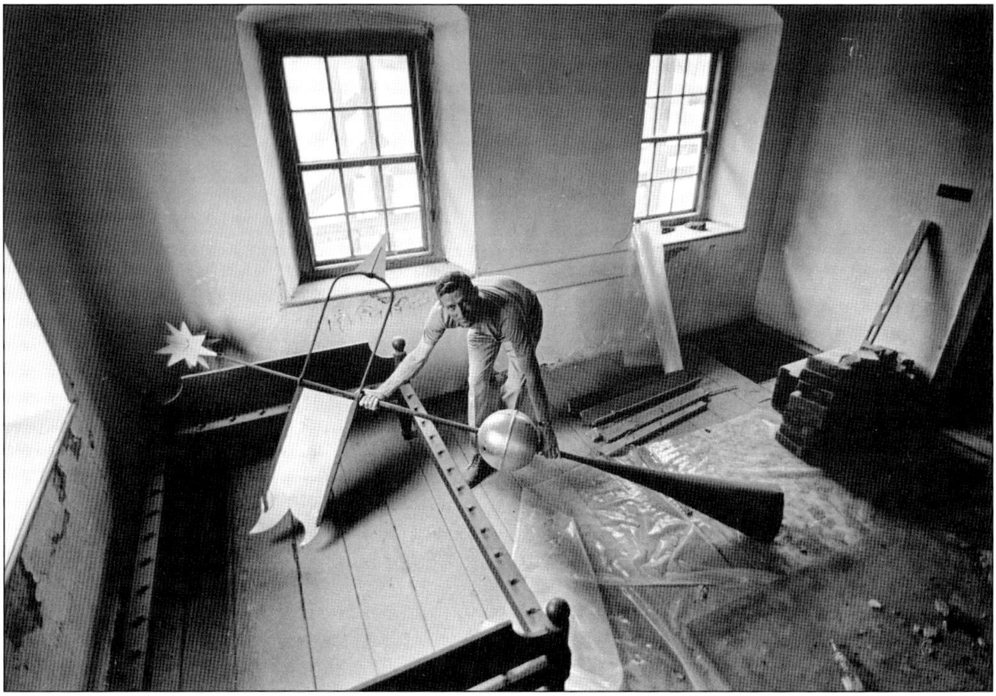

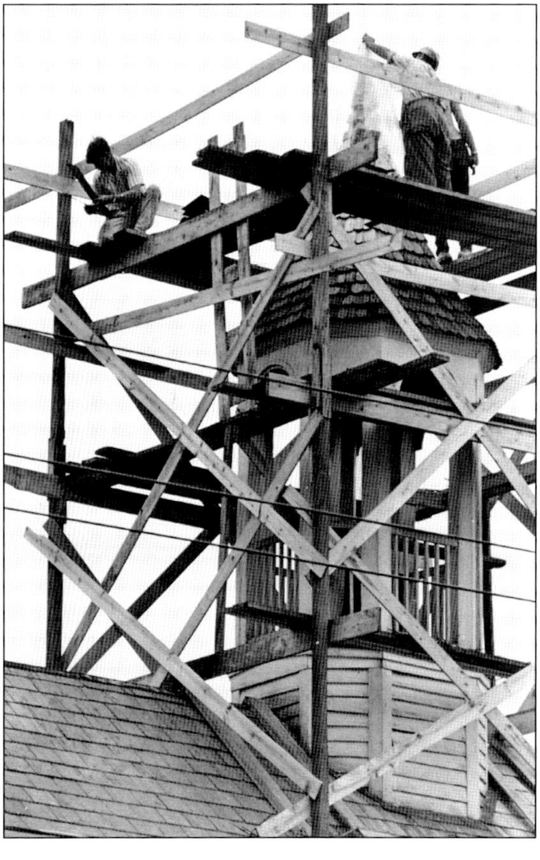

In the above image, foreman David Hunt holds the weather vane that sits atop the steeple of the bell tower, photographed at left. The original bell tower, constructed in 1788, was larger than the one seen today. It leaked, however, and a number of repairs were made between 1789 and 1805. It was noted that year that the bell tower was no longer perpendicular, but it was not seen as an immediate problem. In 1811, it was replaced with a smaller structure, which was still in place and restored in 1969–1970. A lightning rod was put on the building in 1803, and the restoration team believed it likely went on top of the weather vane. They placed it there during the restoration. (Both, courtesy of the Forsyth County Public Library Photograph Collection, Winston-Salem, North Carolina.)

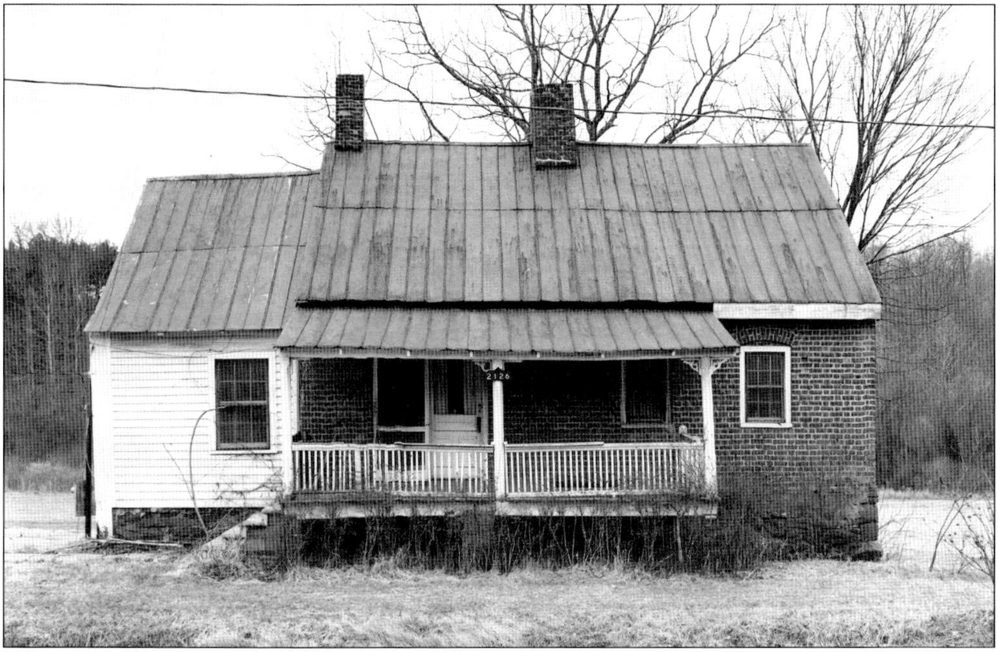

The above image, taken sometime between 1950 and 1970, captures the Potter's House prior to its restoration. The half-timbered wing that served as a potter's shop was torn down and a newer addition added. Old Salem supervised the restoration, which began in 1972. The work in progress can be seen in the photograph below, taken by Frank Jones. The Mary Reynolds Babcock Foundation provided a $45,000 grant to remove the additions to the original 1782 house, stabilize it, and restore its walls and roof. Any leftover funds were used for the interior of the building, with the hope that it could become exhibit space. (Above, courtesy of Old Salem Museums & Gardens; below, courtesy of the Forsyth County Public Library Photograph Collection, Winston-Salem, North Carolina.)

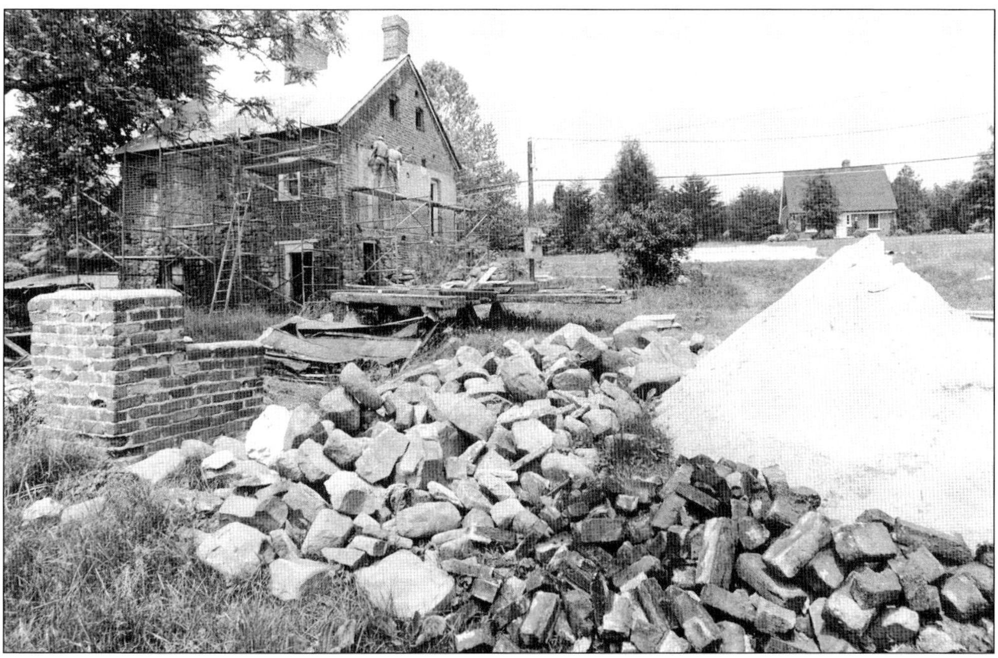

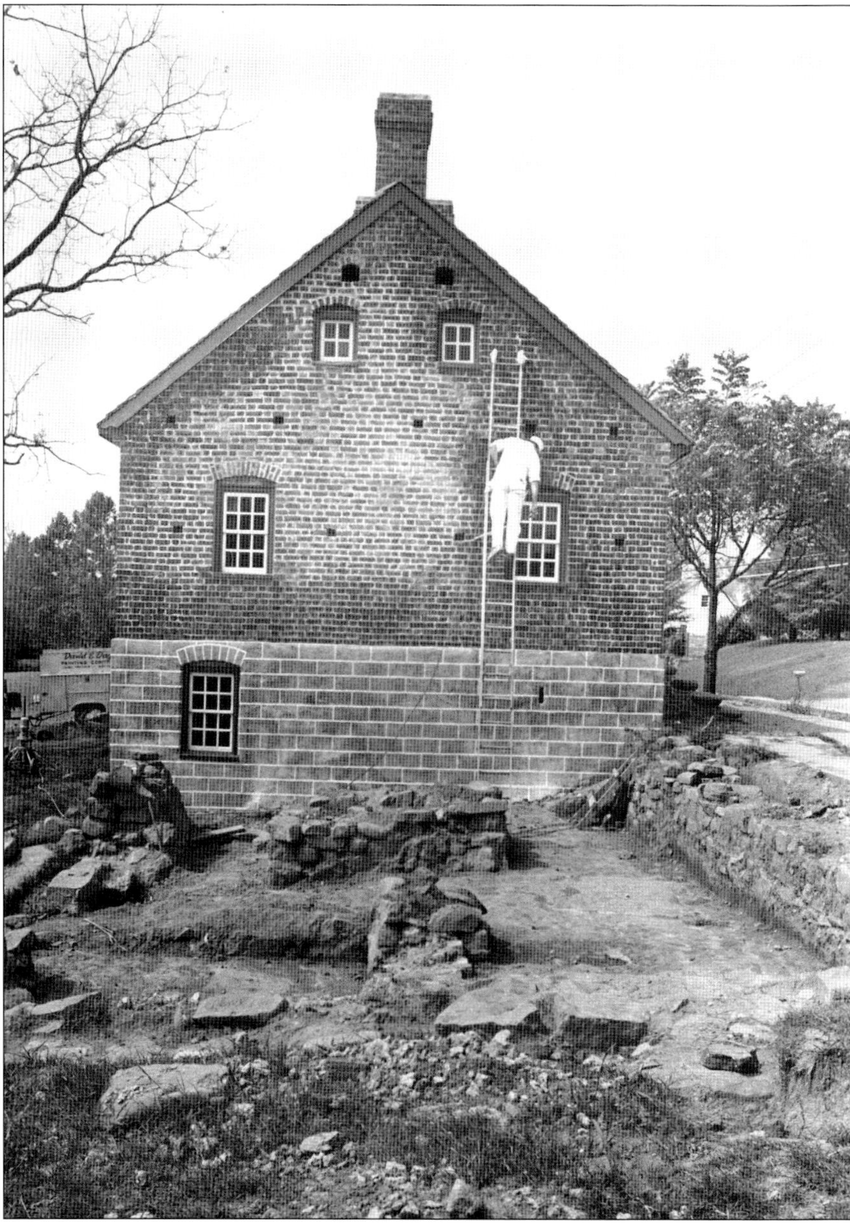

This photograph of the Potter's House restoration was taken on September 18, 1973. In the background on the left is a vehicle with "David E. Day Painting Contractor" written on the side. The foreground features the ruins of the original half-timber addition of the Potter's House. In the summer of 1973, Jacqueline Fehon of the University of Arkansas conducted a dig of the addition with the assistance of Wake Forest University students. The addition to the Potter's House had been used as a potter's shop by Gottlob Krause in the 18th century and later by the Butner family in the 19th century. Prior to the excavation, only a small portion of the foundation was visible. Fehon and her team exposed the entire foundation and in doing so found stove and roof tiles, utilitarian ware, slip-decorated ware, pottery molds, and more, all indicative of a very active pottery operation. (Courtesy of the Forsyth County Public Library Photograph Collection, Winston-Salem, North Carolina.)

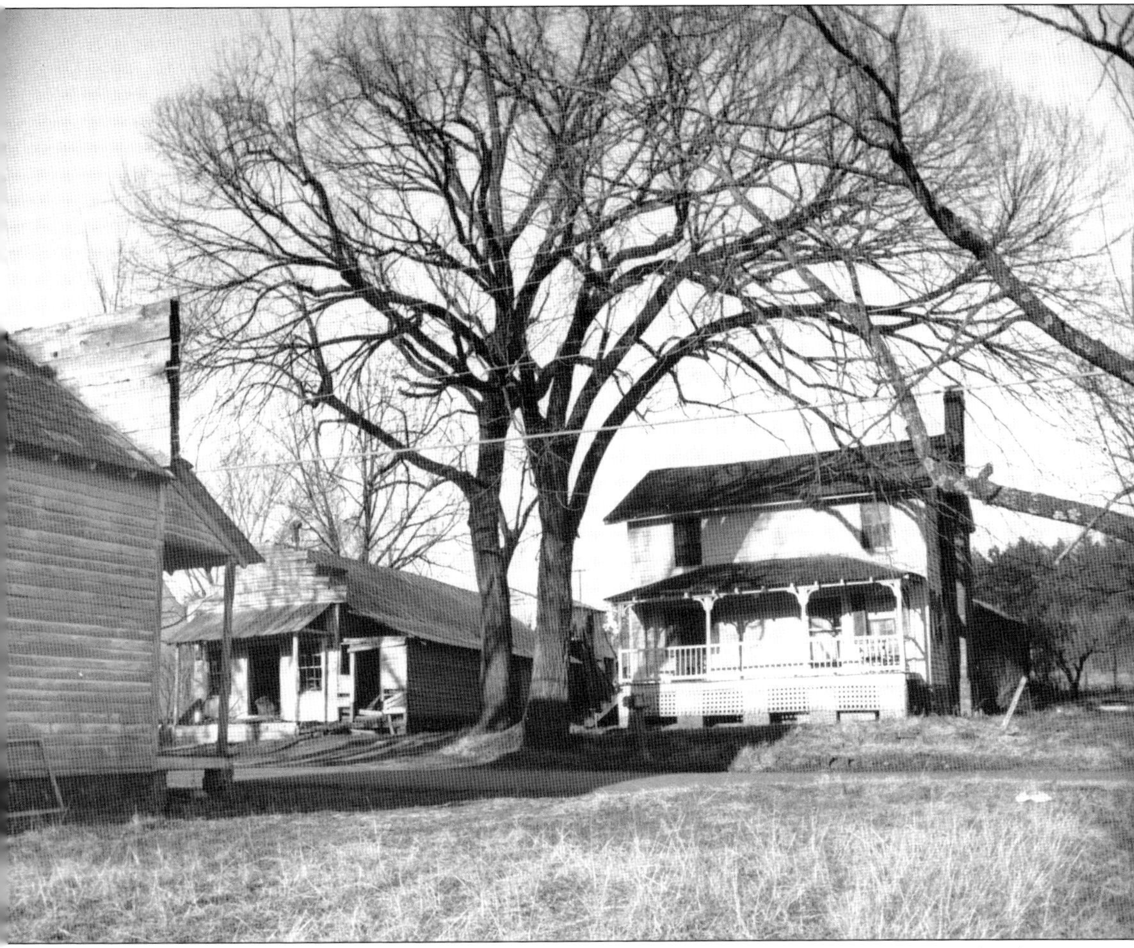

This 1959 photograph shows the main street running through Bethabara. In the foreground is the store used by Jewell South and her team to clean and catalog excavated items during the Stanley South dig of 1963–1966, which was later torn down. Across the street is the former L.M. Miller general store and post office on the left and the Pou House on the right. All the buildings were slated to be demolished; however, when the weatherboards were removed on the Pou House, a chinked log structure was revealed. It was decided the building should be saved so more could be learned about it. For a time, it was thought to be from the early 19th century, but a dendrochronology report found that the trees used for the logs were felled in late 1833. In 1975, the Bethabara Historical Society (founded in 1960) began to restore the building, believing it might make a good office for the organization. (Courtesy of the Forsyth County Public Library Photograph Collection, Winston-Salem, North Carolina.)

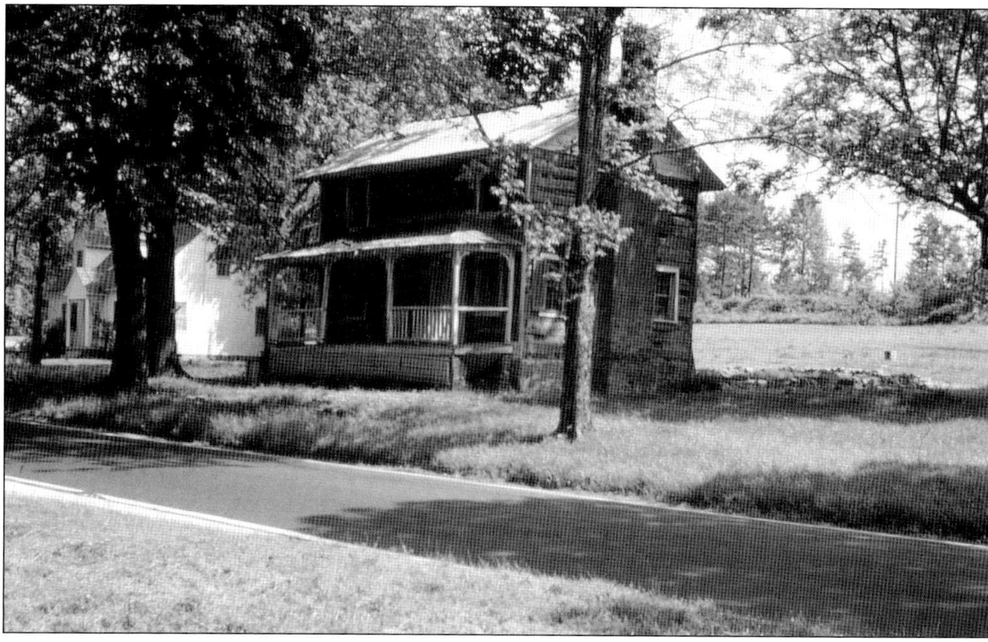

The above c. 1970–1973 photograph shows the front of the Pou House, while the below 1973 image shows the rear of the building. Both images were taken at the start of restoration. Members of the Bethabara Historical Society stabilized part of the foundation of the structure and repaired the walls along with the windows. The late-19th-century front porch and the additions to the back of the house were removed, and the metal roof was replaced with wooden shingles. This was mostly done through volunteer work and money raised through membership dues. As the years went by and membership dwindled, the Bethabara Historical Society was unable to complete the restoration. In 1986, it gave the project to Historic Bethabara Park. (Both, courtesy of the Bethabara Collection.)

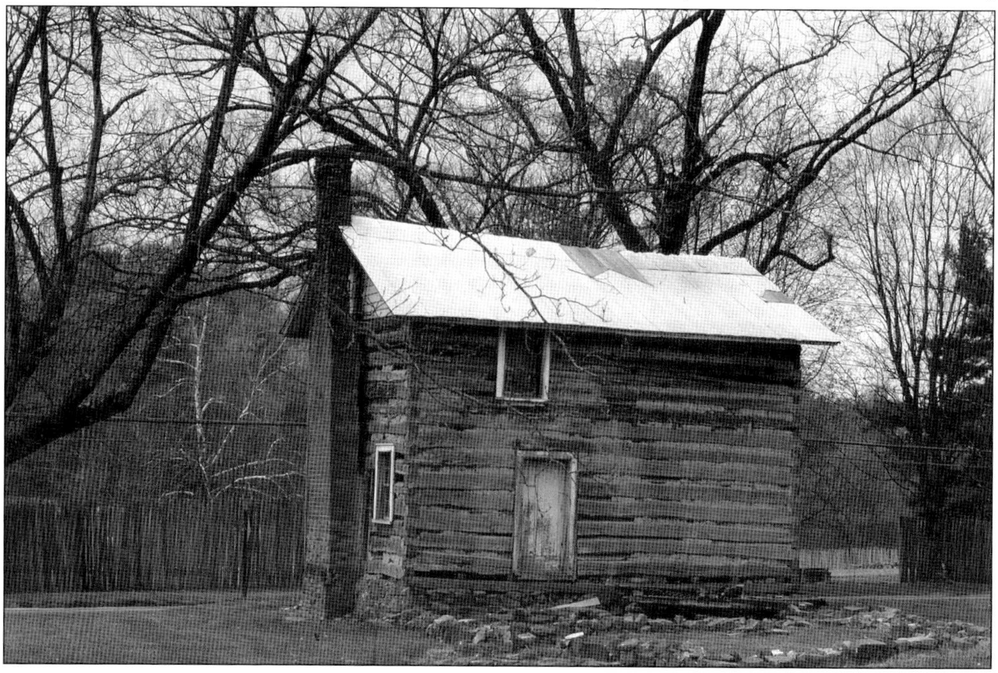

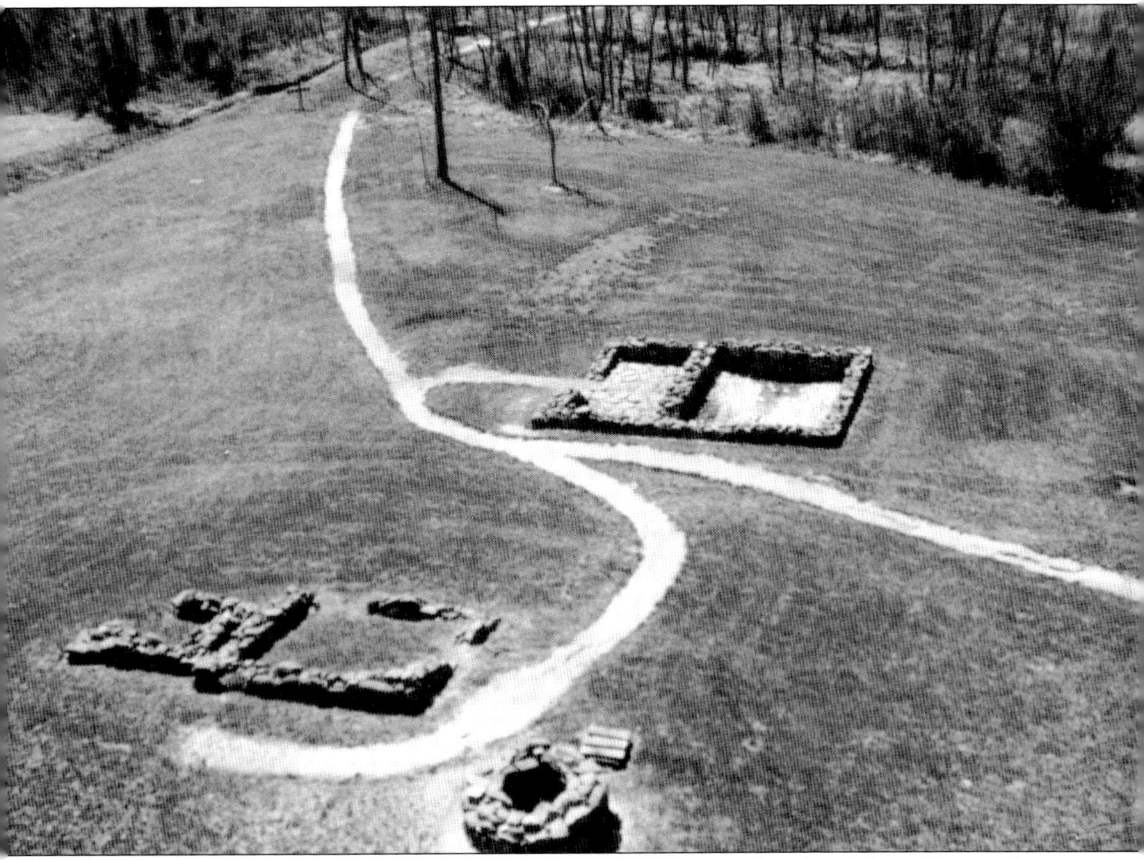

This undated image shows two of the cellars and a well uncovered and stabilized during the 1963–1966 Stanley South dig along with a sawdust trail to guide visitors through the site. The first phase of transforming Bethabara into a historic site focused on the formation of the park. Because it was the first Moravian settlement in North Carolina, Edwin Stockton looked at it as a place for Moravians to come and pay tribute to the early settlers who built Bethabara. Stanley South's work added a reconstructed palisade fort and bell tower and stabilized cellar foundations. South and his team put interpretive signs next to each foundation and cut a trail for visitors to follow. This photograph provides a glimpse of what Bethabara offered when it was first opened to the public on July 3, 1966. Along with paths among the cellars, nature trails along Monarcas Creek and up to God's Acre were laid. A visitor center with exhibit space would come a few years later. (Courtesy of the Bethabara Collection.)

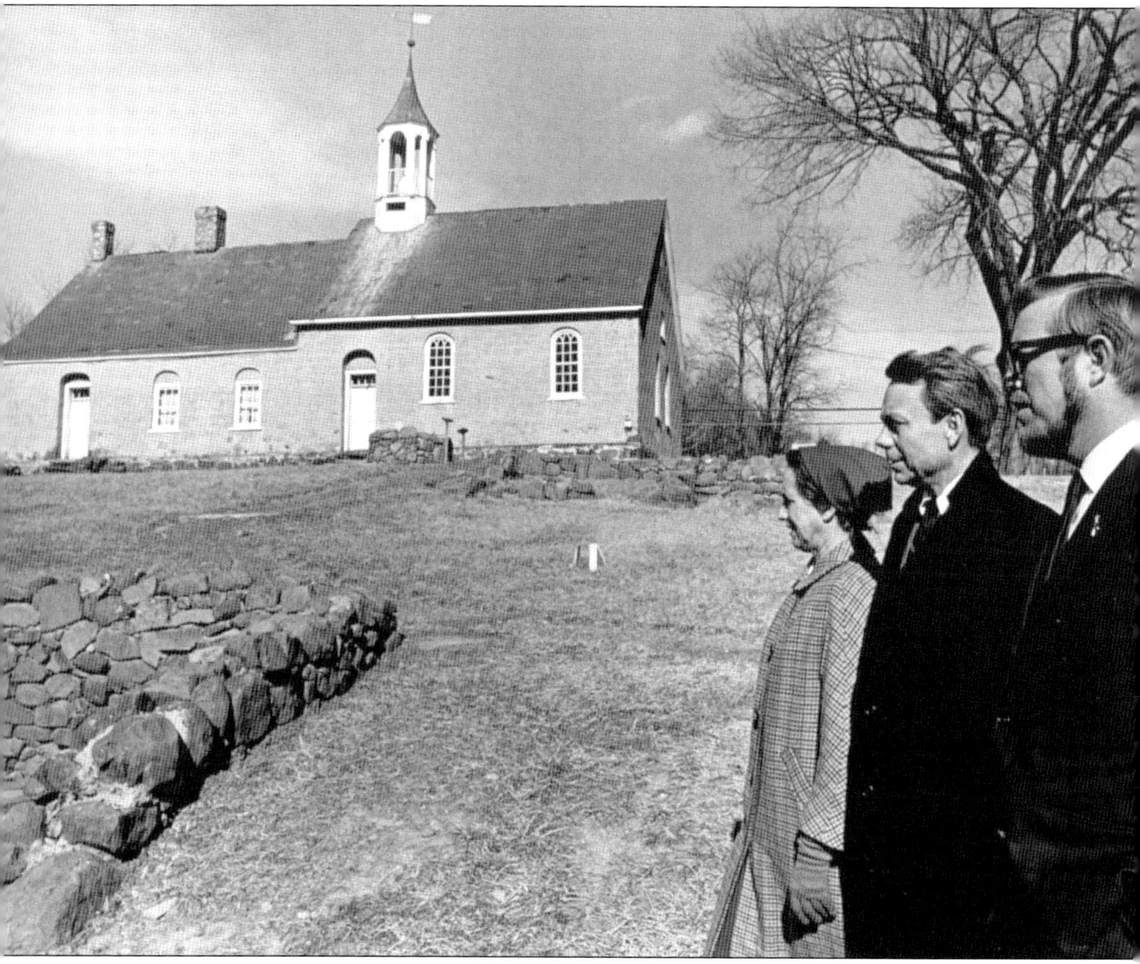

With the Gemeinhaus in the background, Mary Creech (left), W.S. Tarlton (center), and Stanley South (right) stand together in a photograph captured in 1968. Mary Creech, a Moravian herself, was hired as the first director of Historic Bethabara Park in June 1966. She was an employee of Old Salem, as it was still not known who would take the long-term responsibility of operating the site. Creech had been a staff member of the Girl Scouts of America before coming to Bethabara. She was the site's only paid staff person, and she provided tours to visitors. Her office was housed in a rented trailer. Tarlton was the historic site's superintendent for the State Department of Archives and History, and South was still the state archaeologist at the time of this photograph. It was Tarlton's idea to expand the scope of Bethabara as more than an archaeological park, suggesting that the Potter's House, Distiller's House, and Pou House be preserved so the public could see Moravian building techniques and provide a timeline of Bethabara history that spanned nearly 100 years. (Courtesy of Old Salem Museums & Gardens.)

In 1968, the former Distiller's House, which had also served as Bethabara's parsonage, was restored, becoming Historic Bethabara Park's first visitor center. Guests are greeted as they enter the ground-floor entrance in the photograph at right. Below, Emory T. Welsh poses in front of the new visitor center on July 9, 1969. Mary Creech's office was relocated there so she could easily greet guests and show them a slide presentation about the Moravians and their arrival in Bethabara. This building would serve as the site's visitor center from 1968 to 1988. (Right, courtesy of Old Salem Museums & Gardens; below, courtesy of the Bethabara Collection.)

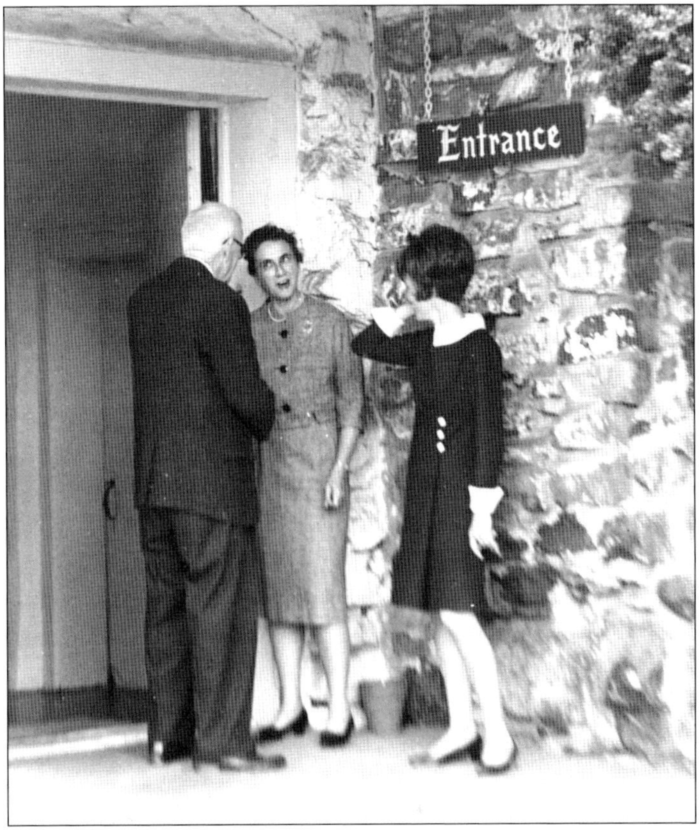

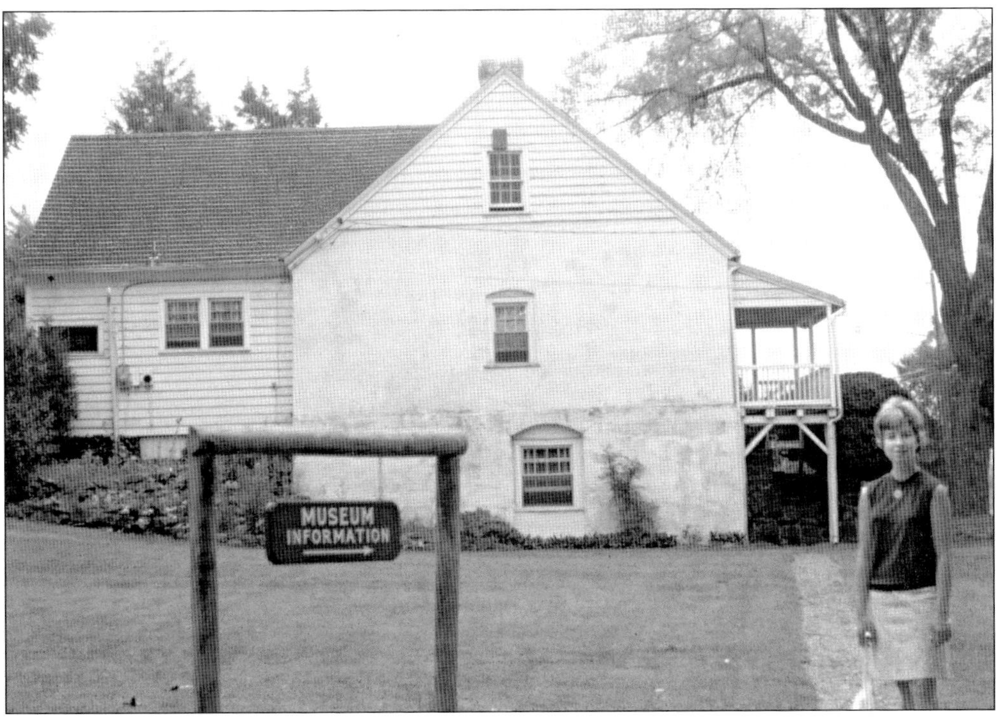

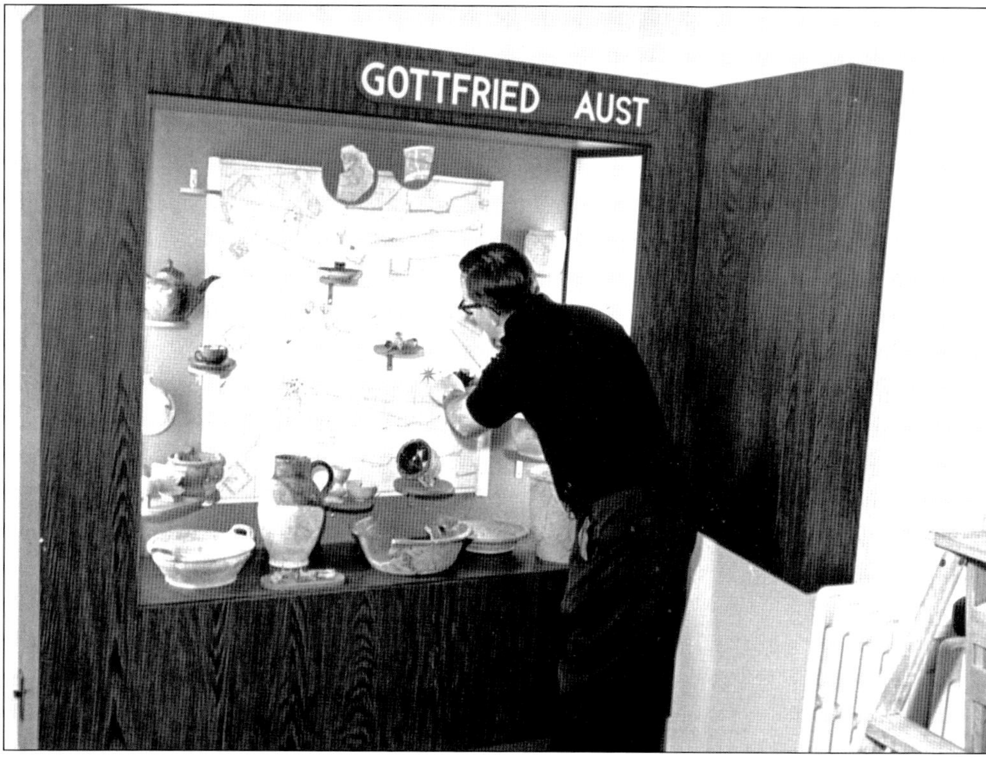

Prior to the opening of the 1968 visitor center, Henry Clay Watson of New Orleans was hired to install exhibits inside the former Distiller's House. He had prior exhibit installation experience as the first director of the New Orleans Jazz Club Museum, where he designed and curated its growing collection. Watson went to work creating displays that would showcase the pottery found during the Stanley South dig. These display cases were located on the second floor of the visitor center, while the ground floor contained maps and photographs. The Mary Reynolds Babcock Foundation provided $5,000 to pay for the exhibits. (Both, courtesy of Old Salem Museums & Gardens.)

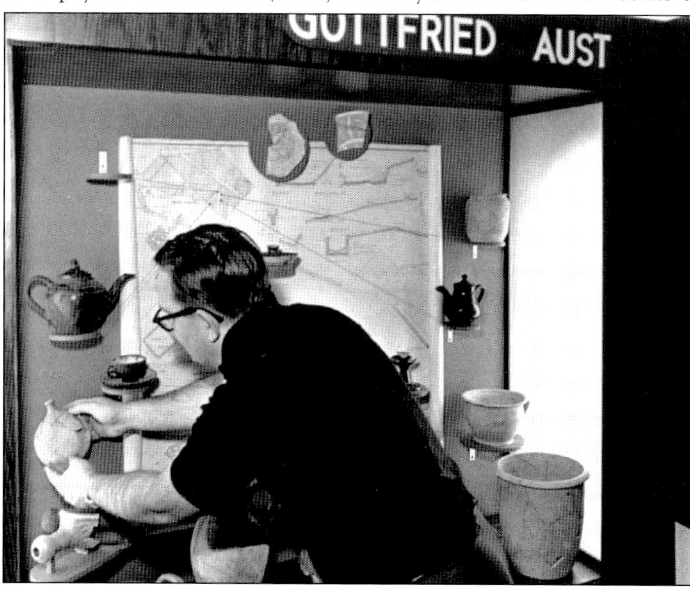

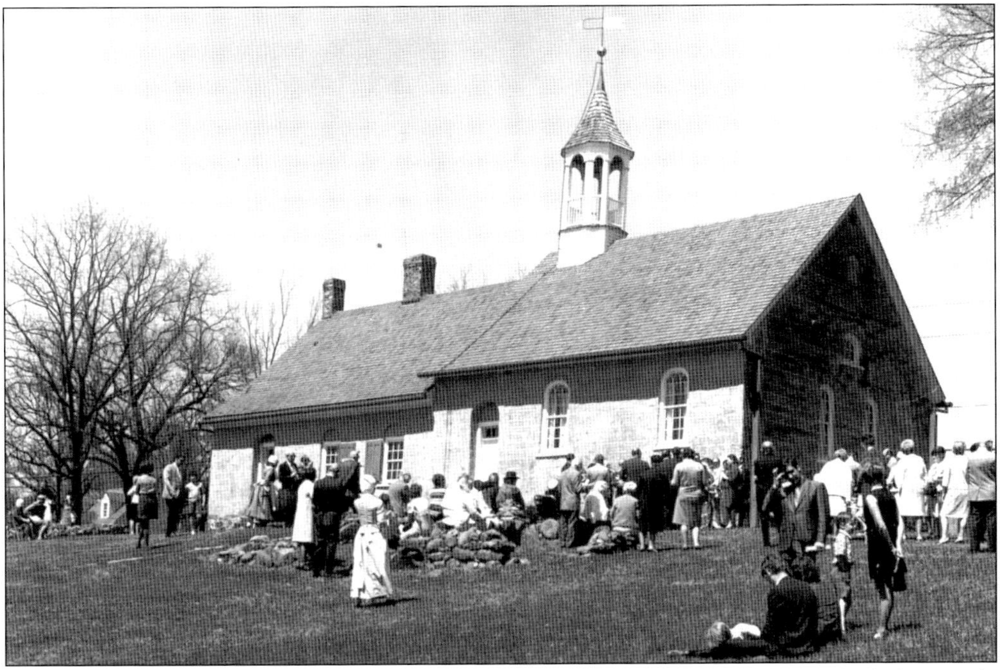

For years, it was unknown who would take up the operational costs to run Historic Bethabara Park. The state and Old Salem lacked funding, and Charles Babcock said from the outset he would help Bethabara become a historic site but would not provide operational support. In 1970, the Winston-Salem Recreation and Parks Department chose to take on the costs. Bethabara was historically significant to the city, and it wanted to protect the site. Additionally, the large amount of green space would provide a park for the area, which had recently been annexed into city limits. On April 25, 1971, the restored Gemeinhaus was dedicated and reopened. Below, Charles H. Babcock's widow, Winifred Penn Knies, gives the keys to Joe White of the Winston-Salem Recreation and Parks Department. Frances Griffin's photograph above shows the crowd at the celebration. (Both, courtesy of Old Salem Museums & Gardens.)

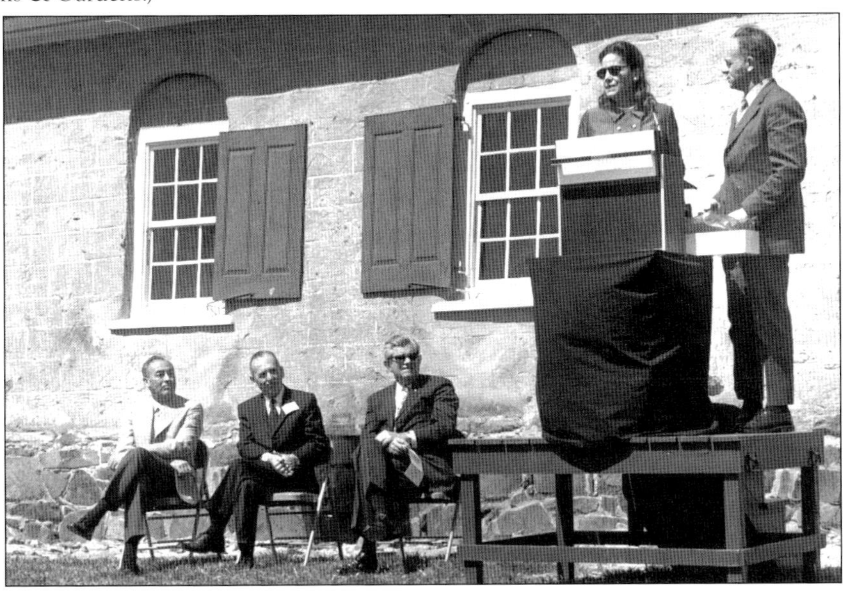

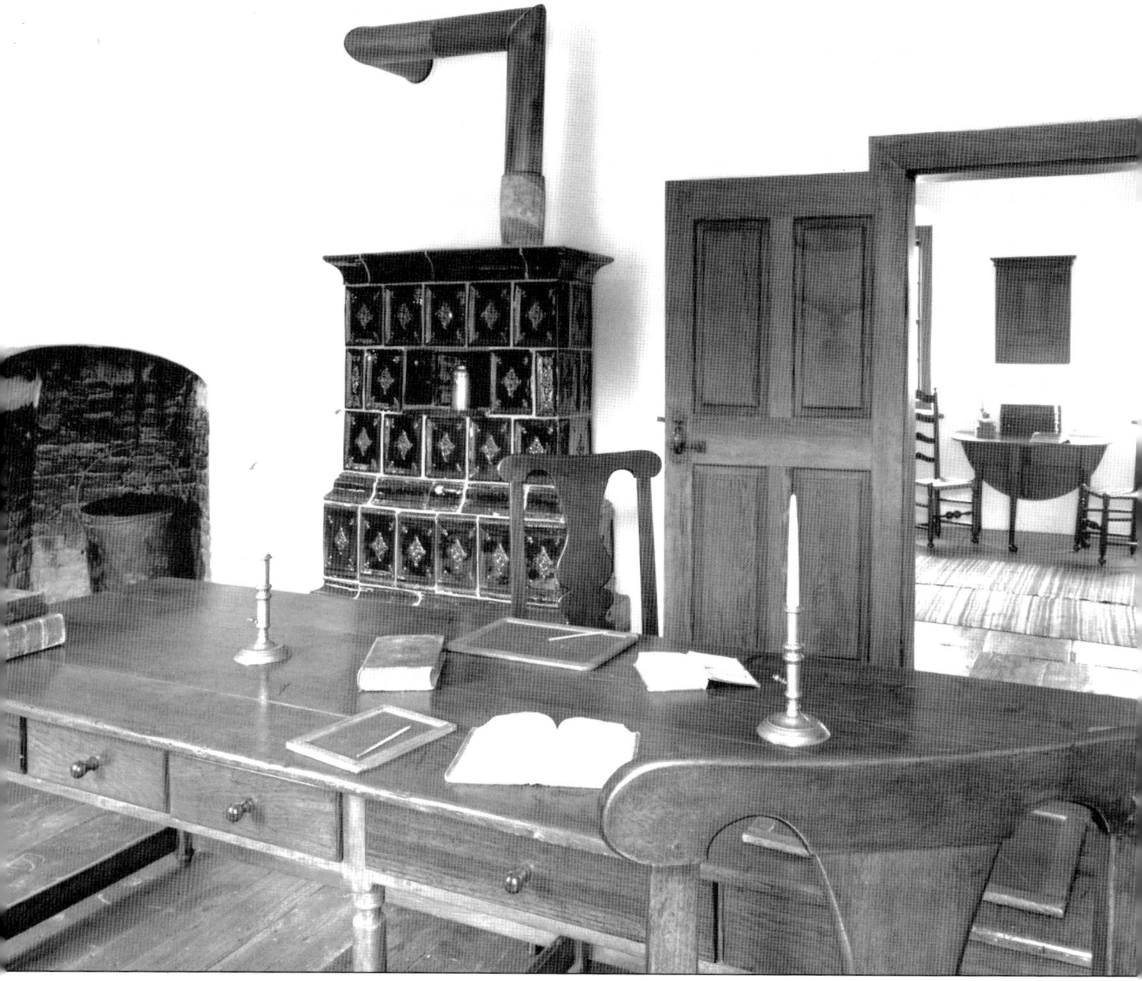

This image of the restored Gemeinhaus schoolroom was taken around 1971–1972 by Frances Griffin. The doorway leads into the minister's parlor, also restored. The cement floor was removed and replaced with a wood floor. When furnishing the rooms, Frank Horton and his team used building inventories created by the Moravians. The large copper kettle for lovefeast coffee is likely one the congregation ordered in 1817 from Christoph Reich in Salem. Through Horton's research, he learned that the room was called the schoolroom, even though it served multiple purposes. In 1805, the school was moved out of the Gemeinhaus, but the room continued to be used for meetings, lovefeast preparation, and a warm place to gather prior to services thanks to the tile stove. Horton and his team decided the back room in the Gemeinhaus was the schoolroom due to strong local tradition as well as the discovery of a stovepipe hole and a long hearth, which supported the idea of a tile stove being in that room as documented in the Moravian records. The restored stove is shown in this photograph. (Courtesy of Old Salem Museums & Gardens.)

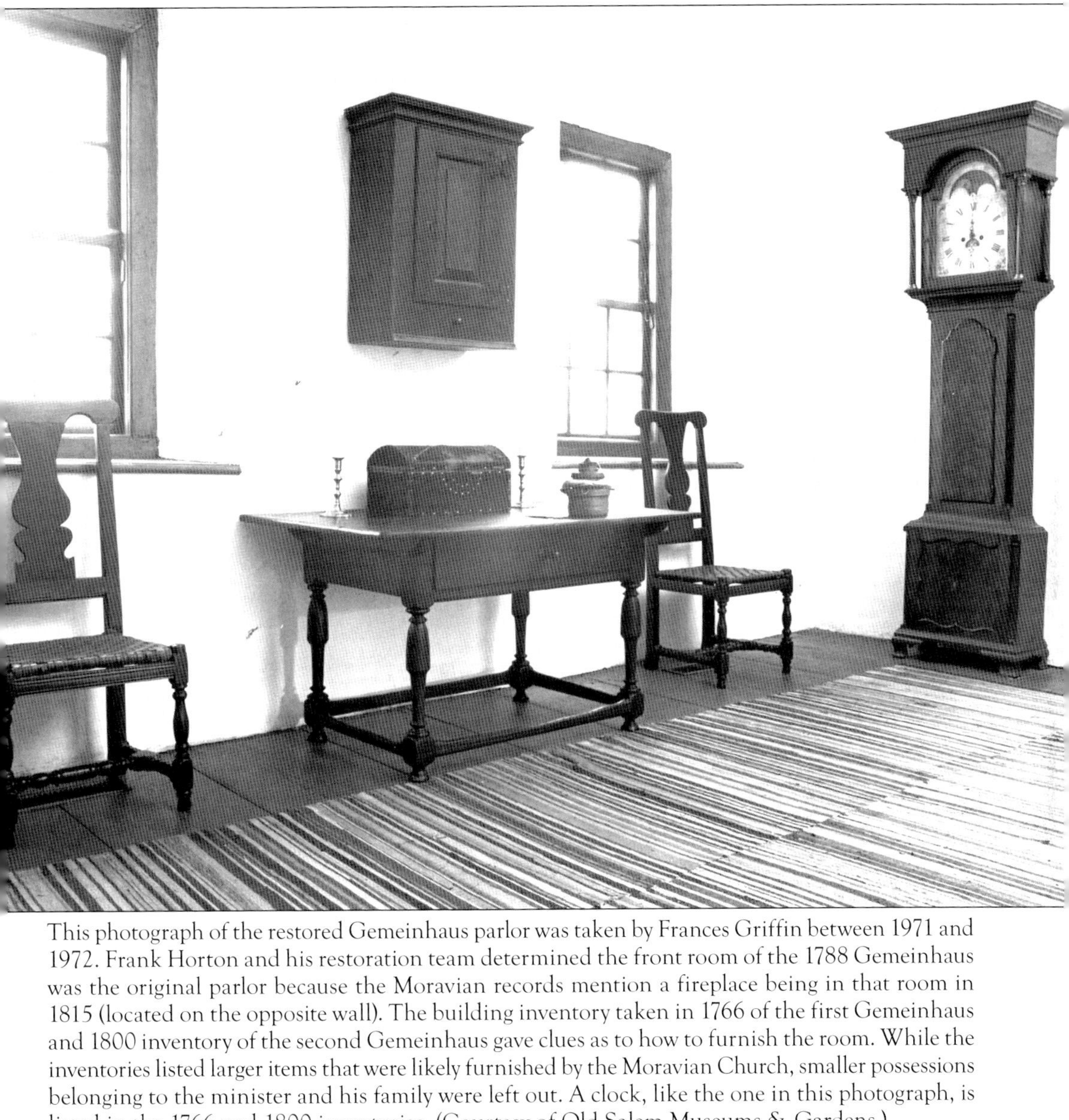

This photograph of the restored Gemeinhaus parlor was taken by Frances Griffin between 1971 and 1972. Frank Horton and his restoration team determined the front room of the 1788 Gemeinhaus was the original parlor because the Moravian records mention a fireplace being in that room in 1815 (located on the opposite wall). The building inventory taken in 1766 of the first Gemeinhaus and 1800 inventory of the second Gemeinhaus gave clues as to how to furnish the room. While the inventories listed larger items that were likely furnished by the Moravian Church, smaller possessions belonging to the minister and his family were left out. A clock, like the one in this photograph, is listed in the 1766 and 1800 inventories. (Courtesy of Old Salem Museums & Gardens.)

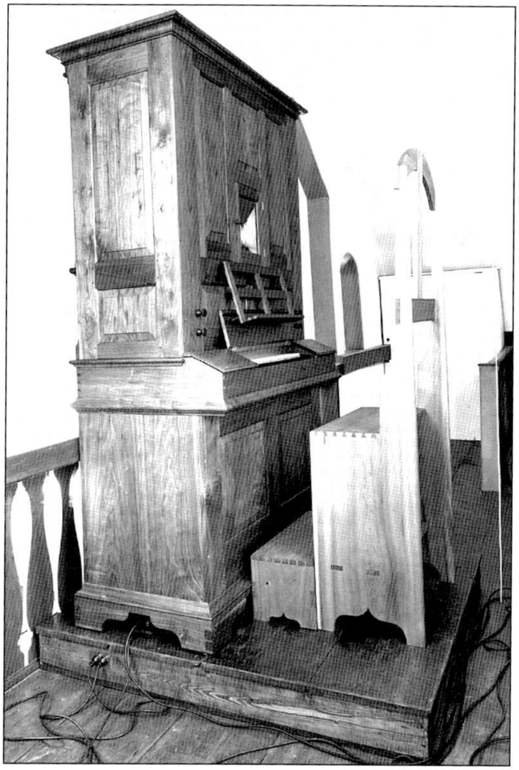

These images capture the new organ placed in the upstairs balcony of the restored Gemeinhaus. Music has always been an important part of Moravian culture and features heavily in their worship services. The first organ in Bethabara was brought from Bethlehem, Pennsylvania, in 1762. It was listed in the 1766 inventory and was the organ that moved to the new church when it was completed in 1788. When the new Tannenberg organ was built for Salem in 1798, the congregation gave its old organ, built by Joseph Bullitschek of Bethania, to Bethabara. Bethabara's organ moved to the Saal of the Single Brothers' House in Salem. It then went on to serve the congregation in Friedland, but after that, the organ seems to have disappeared. (Both, courtesy of Old Salem Museums & Gardens.)

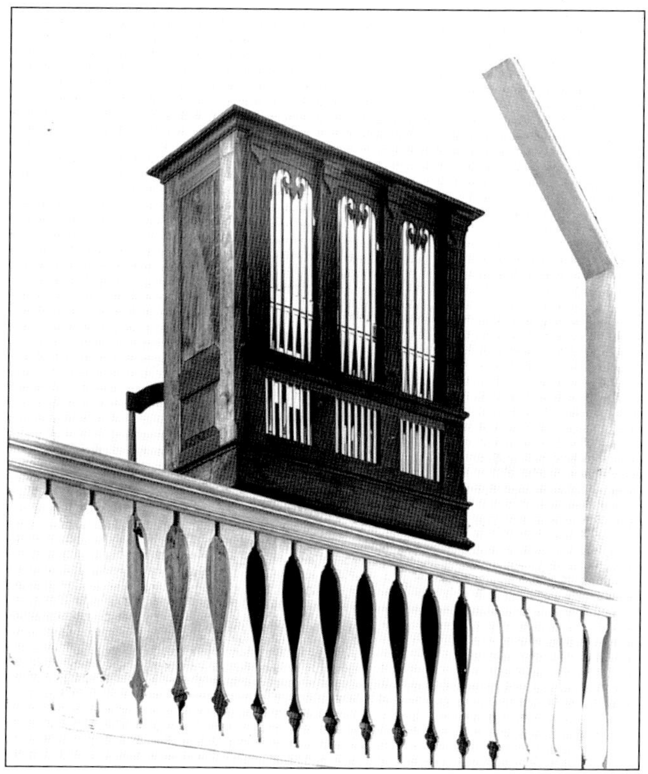

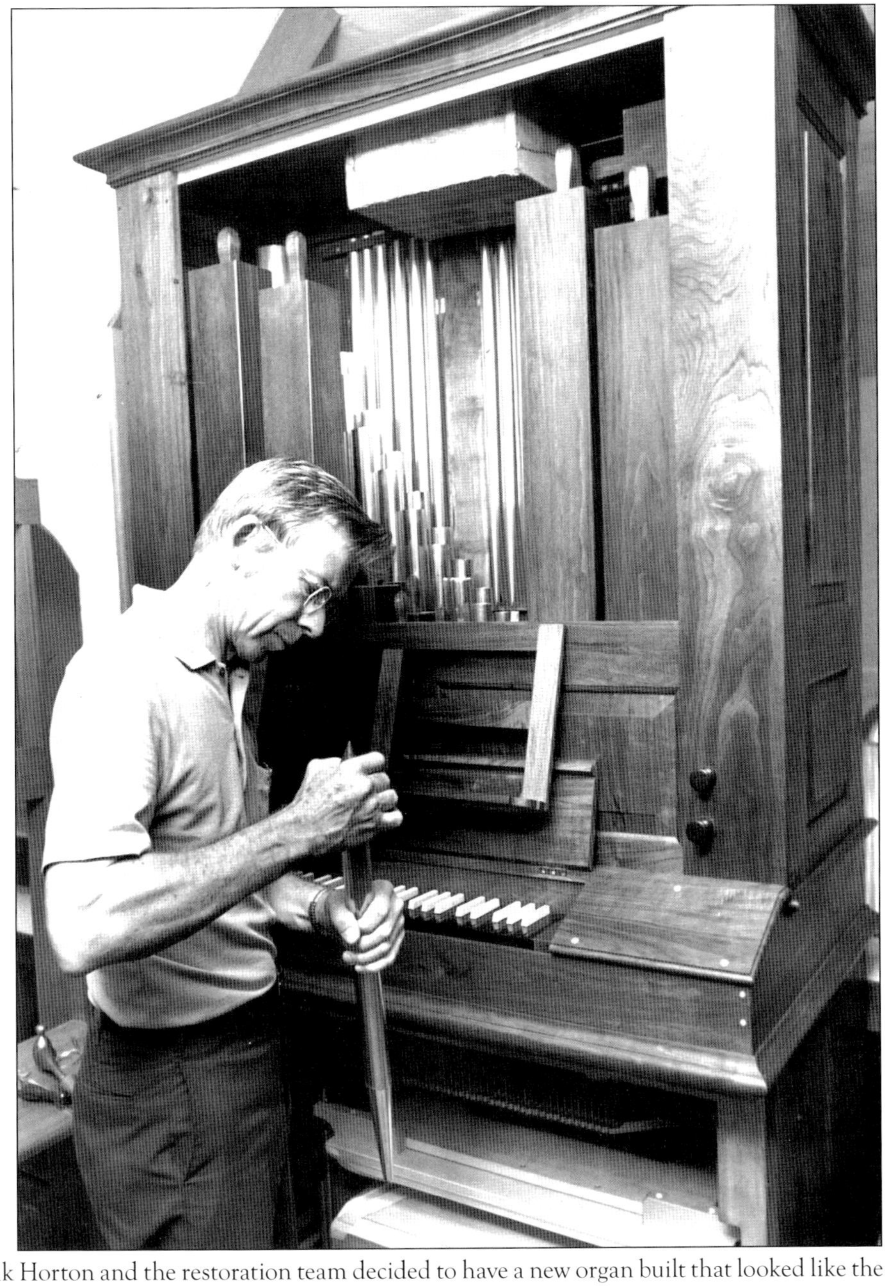

Frank Horton and the restoration team decided to have a new organ built that looked like the organ Joseph Bullitschek made for the Bethania congregation. It is thought that it looked very similar to the one he made for Bethabara, and photographic evidence of the Bethania Bullitschek organ survived. The reproduction organ case was designed by Frank P. Albright and made in the Old Salem cabinet shop by Hayden Allen. John Chrastina of Denver, Colorado, and Charles McManis of Kansas City, Kansas, made the organ works. This photograph, taken by Frances Griffin, shows Charles McManis voicing the instrument before it was officially dedicated and played on October 17, 1971. The pipes facing him are the ones that actually play music, while 18 "show" or false pipes are located on the opposite side facing the audience. The organ continues to provide music at Historic Bethabara Park today. (Courtesy of Old Salem Museums & Gardens.)

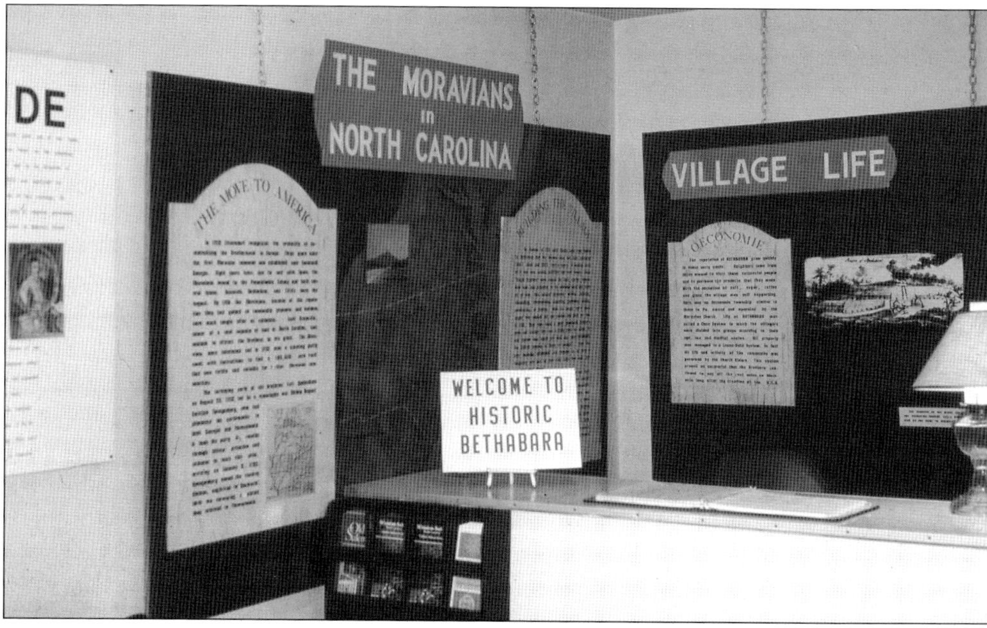

These images were taken in 1983 and show the exhibits featured in the original Bethabara visitor center. At this point, the former Distiller's House had served as the Historic Bethabara Park visitor center for 15 years, and the site was outgrowing the cramped space. The room where the slideshow was shown could only seat 25 people, and the building did not have any public restrooms. Visitation continued to grow as park directors such as Betty Pitt spoke to community groups and schools to encourage them to come out to the site. By this time, the Potter's House had also been restored, and archaeologist John Clauser Jr. installed exhibits in the two main rooms of the house. Even with this addition, the site still needed a larger space for visitors. (Both, courtesy of the Bethabara Collection.)

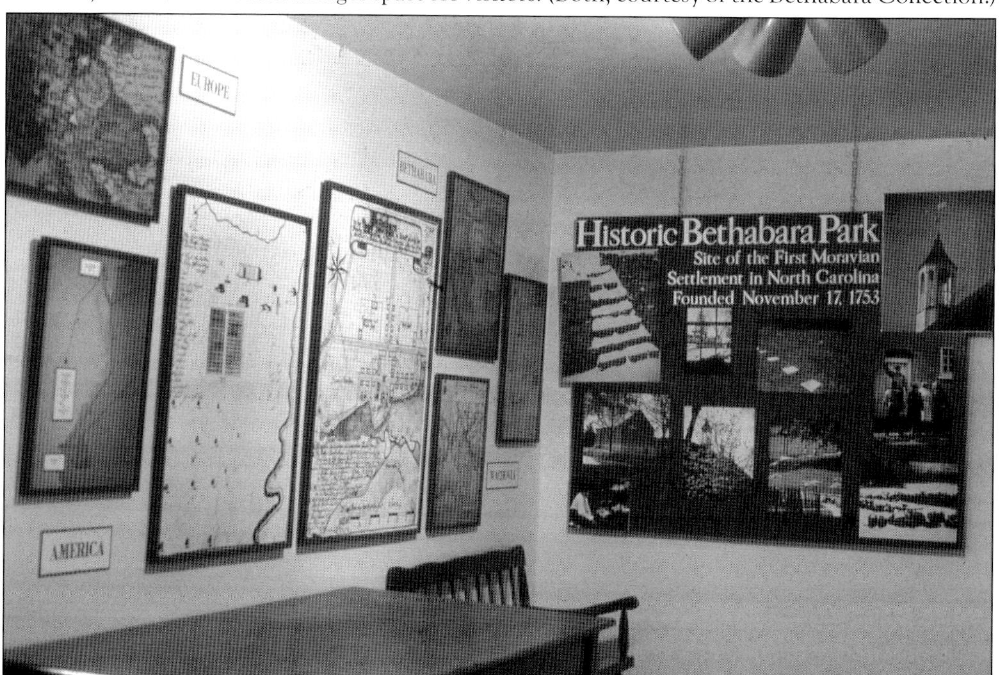

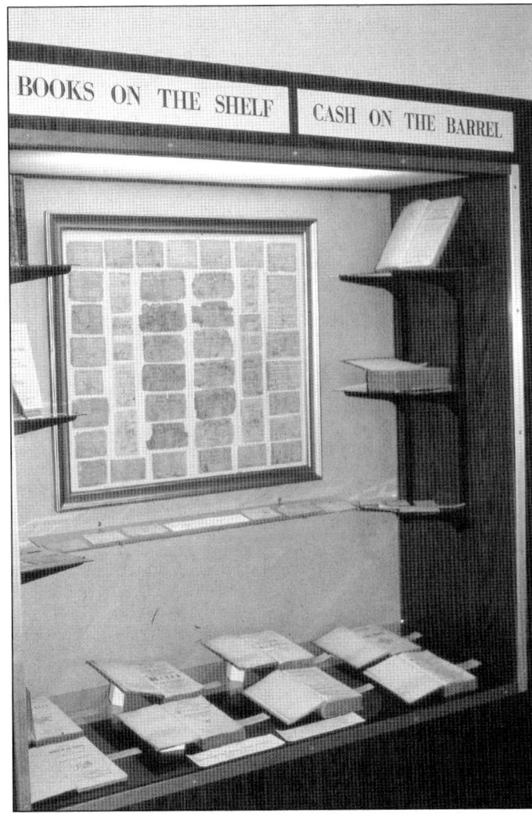

Taken in 1983, these images show exhibits were featured on the upper floor of the first visitor center. When Betty Pitt left Bethabara in 1975, she was replaced by Ann Joyner Cross, who had worked with the state's travel and promotion division. She was replaced three years later by Gwynne Taylor, who was the first director with a background in history and architecture. She stayed until 1982. During her tenure, Taylor started an annual Fourth of July event and Christmas concert to increase awareness of the site. As visitation continued to grow, Taylor hired 14 part-time guide staff to provide tours. The site was also nominated to the National Register of Historic Places during Taylor's time as director. (Both, courtesy of the Bethabara Collection.)

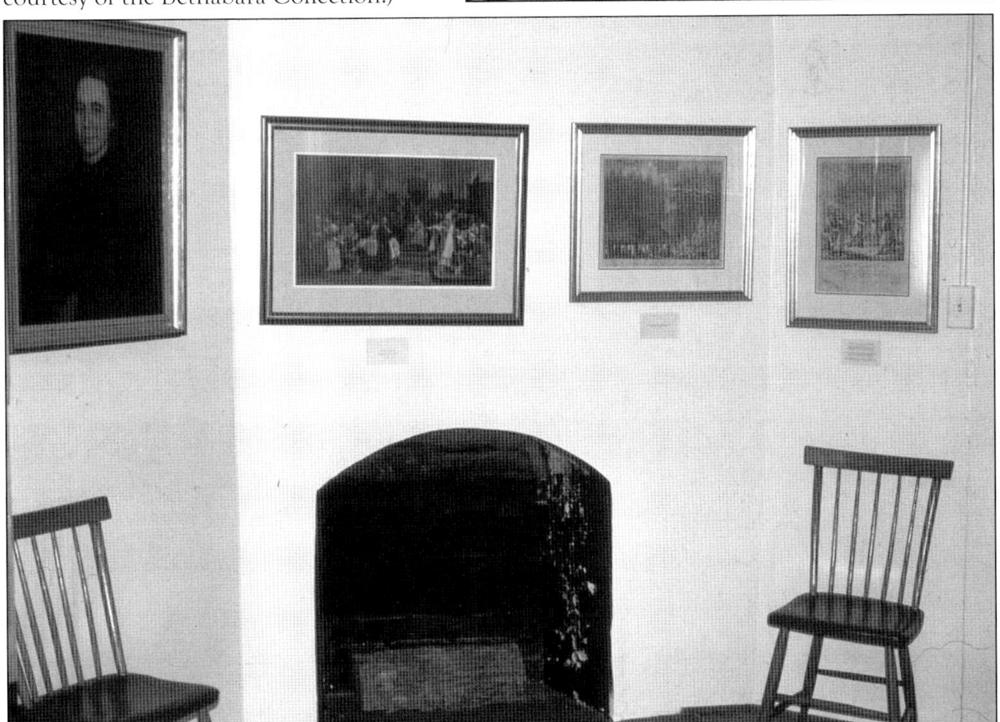

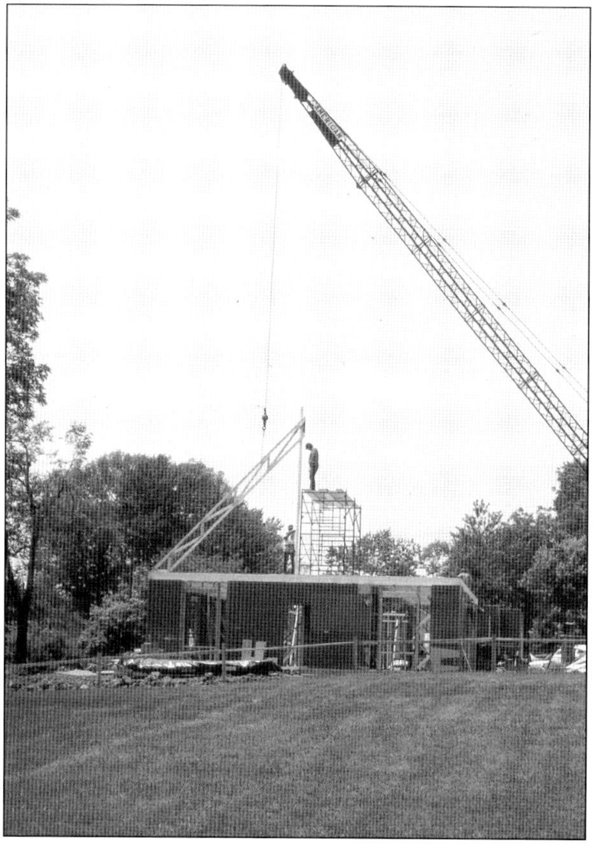

These 1987 photographs chronicle the construction of a new visitor center for Historic Bethabara Park. The Distiller's House had served as the visitor center since 1968, but the number of annual visitors had grown from 5,000 in 1971 to 20,000 in 1981. A designated visitor center had been a dream of Edwin Stockton's since 1966. Early plans for the building included a 100-seat theater, exhibit space, a classroom, much-needed restroom facilities, and offices for administrative staff. Between 1982 and 1986, director William Hinman and the board of trustees raised over $600,000 for the building. The Mary Reynolds Babcock Foundation, the City of Winston-Salem, the State of North Carolina, and Forsyth County all contributed money to the project. (Both, courtesy of the Bethabara Collection.)

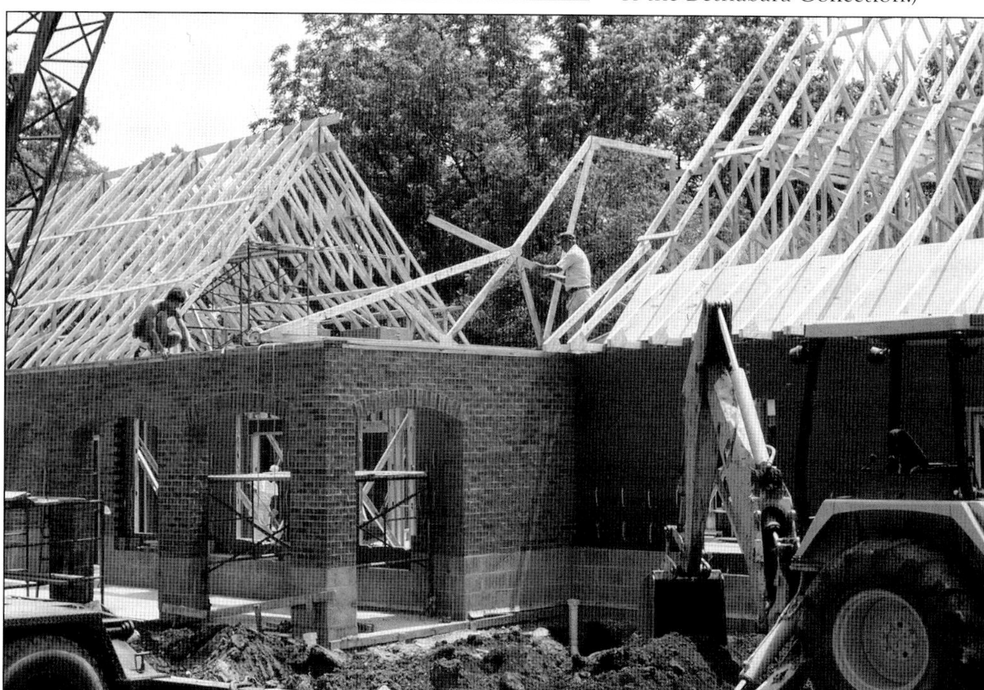

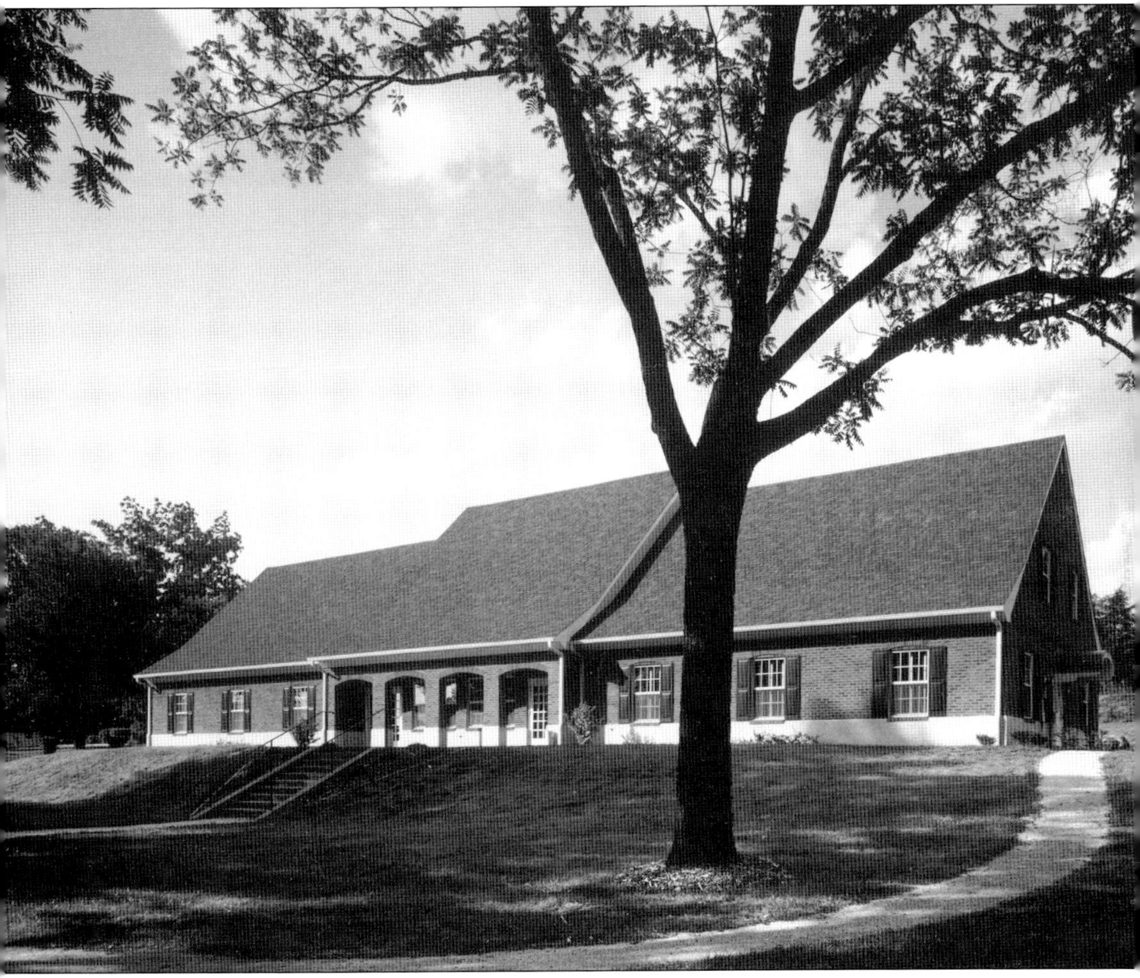

This 1988 photograph was taken shortly after the new visitor center was completed. The site of the building was chosen in an area that was not of major archaeological significance. The new structure was named the Edwin L. Stockton Sr. Visitor's Center after the man who had been the driving force behind the creation of Historic Bethabara Park. Stockton passed away before the visitor center was built, but one of his final acts as the chair of Historic Bethabara Park Inc. was to authorize the start of construction. It took nearly a year to complete the building. Still used today, it houses a large room for visitors to watch an introductory video, a classroom space, an exhibit and gift shop space, and offices for staff. (Courtesy of the Bethabara Collection.)

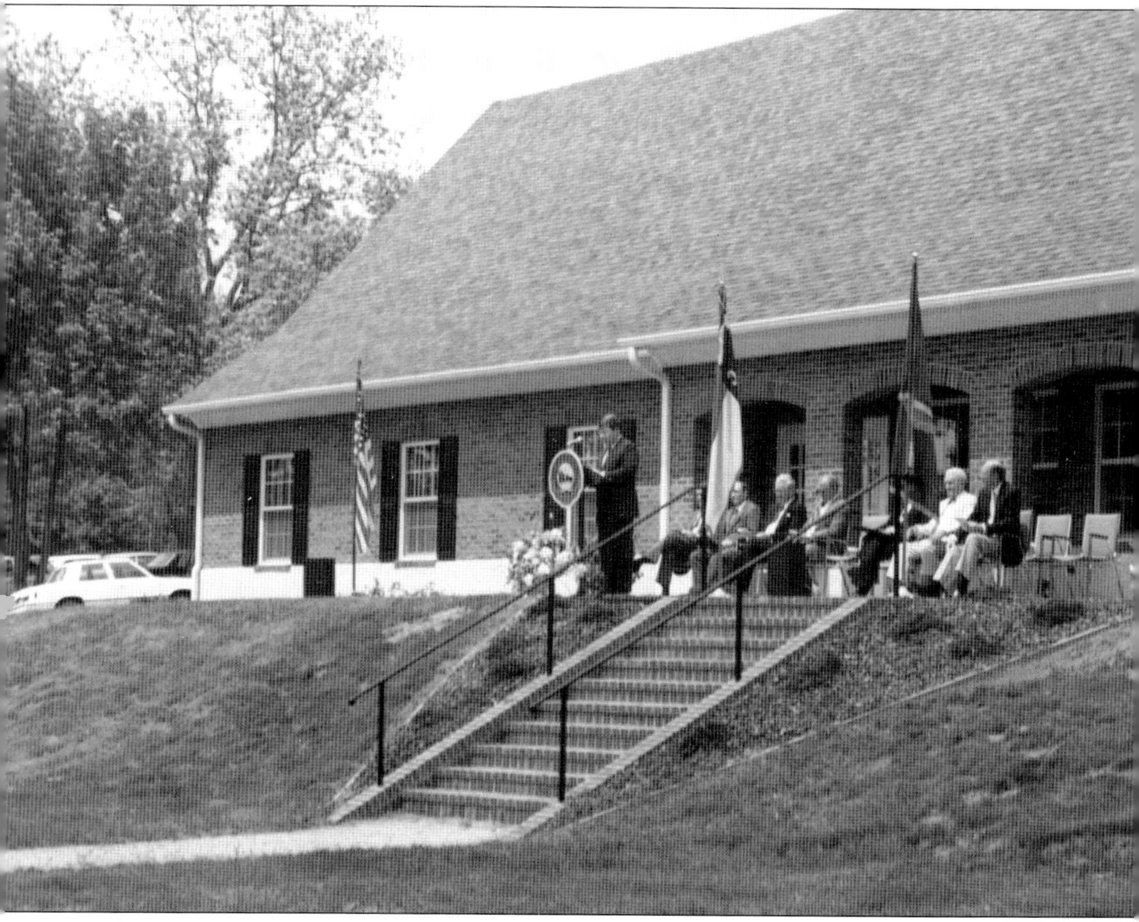

The dedication of the new visitor center took place on Sunday, May 15, 1988. At 2:00 p.m., attendees enjoyed Moravian cookies and lemonade as they listened to a concert by the Bethabara band. Speakers included Mayor Wayne A. Corpening, Edwin Stockton Jr., and James N. Ziglar Jr., who was the chairman of the Forsyth County commissioners. Former director William Hinman, photographed here, was instrumental in raising the funds for the building. J. Rodney Meyer, the new director, spoke to a newspaper reporter from the *Winston-Salem Journal* about the new facility. "We're suddenly highly visible," Meyer stated. Visitation doubled from 2,000 to 4,000 visitors for the month of April alone. He also remarked on the visitor center's unusual roof. "The pitch of the roof is very Moravian, or really mid-German. It has a little kick to it, to shed snow." The new visitor center allowed park staff to do things they had never been able to before, like seating 125 people at one time to watch the introductory video about Bethabara. (Courtesy of the Bethabara Collection.)

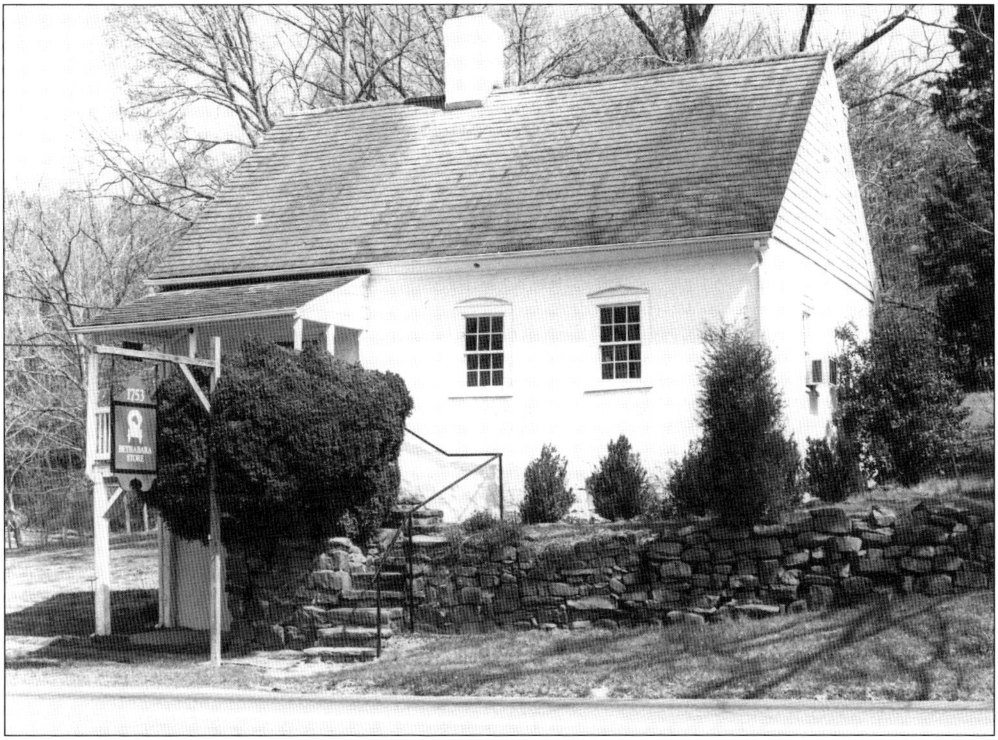

After the new visitor center was completed, the Distiller's House needed a new purpose. As seen in these photographs, it was used as a gift shop for some period. Eventually, the gift shop moved into the new visitor center. Archaeologist John Clauser Jr. used the Distiller's House as temporary lodgings while completing the excavation of the community garden. By the early 2000s, the Distiller's House had been repurposed as a meeting space. It is hoped that in the future it will be used as an archaeology resource center. (Both, courtesy of the Bethabara Collection.)

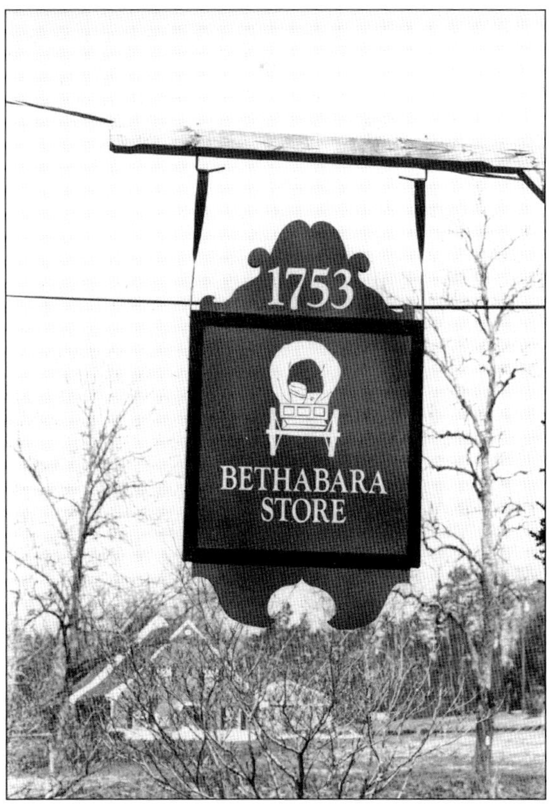

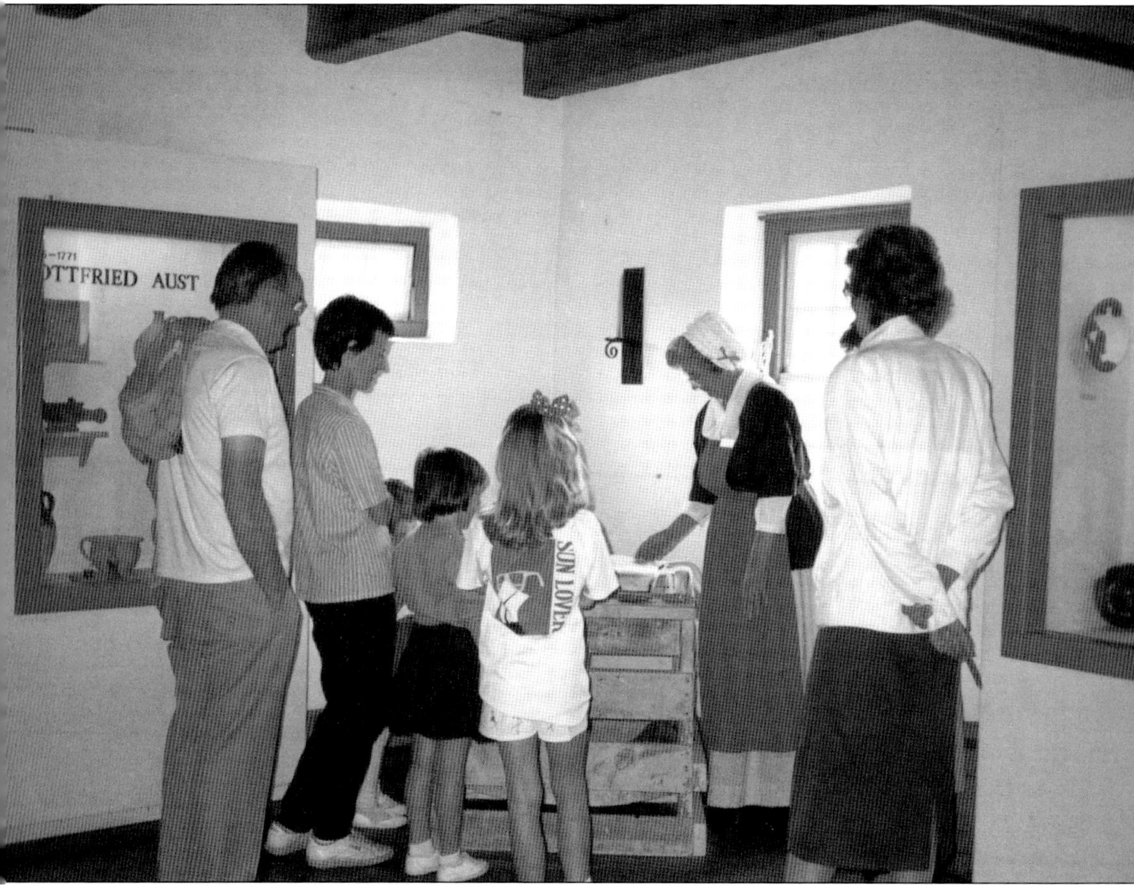

In this photograph, tour guide Margaret Gabriel speaks to a group of visitors on the main floor of the Potter's House. The exhibits highlighting each of the four main potters can be seen on either side. These were created by archaeologist John Clauser Jr. and focused on each potter's style. Gabriel stands next to a potter's wheel, which was installed in the Potter's House for demonstration purposes. Historic Bethabara Park tour guides, both past and present, have the important job of teaching visitors about the history of the Moravians who settled the site in 1753. They complete a rigorous training course to learn the history of the site. They then use that knowledge to give informative tours of the site to walk-in visitors and groups. Schools from Winston-Salem and the surrounding areas also visit to learn about what life was like for the Moravians in Bethabara. (Courtesy of the Bethabara Collection.)

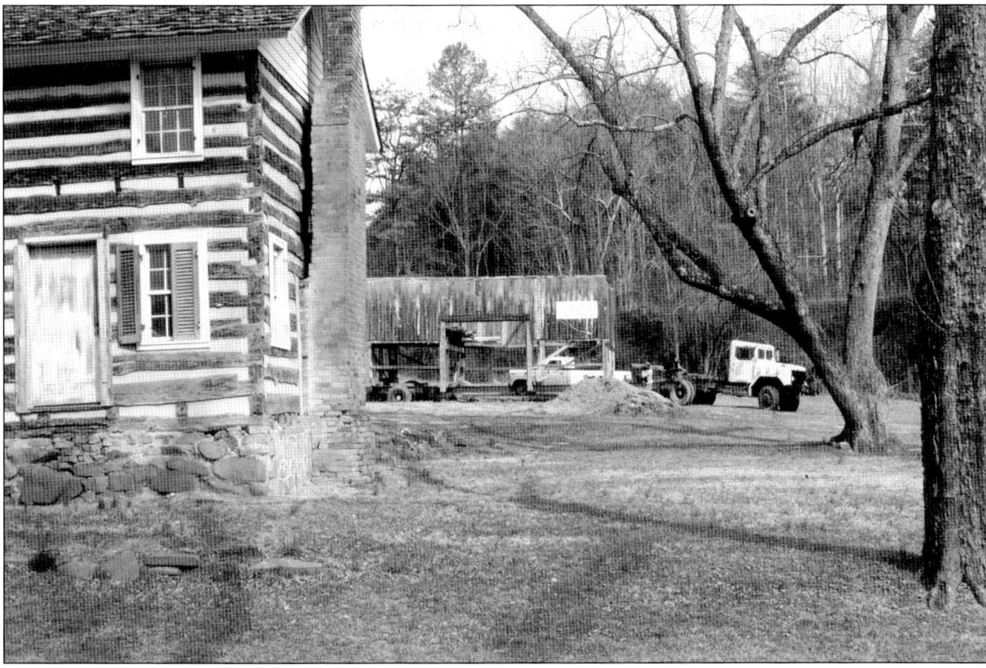

Over the course of 1992 and 1993, director J. Rodney Meyer organized the relocation of a c. 1790s–1820s barn from a farm on Indiana Avenue to Historic Bethabara Park. The barn was owned by Rex and Helen Baker, who donated it to the site. The roof was lifted off with a crane and placed on a truck, which took the barn down Indiana Avenue, North Point Boulevard, and Bethabara Road. The barn was placed in the location of former Moravian calf and cow barns. Meyer obtained the barn to showcase the site's collection of antique farming equipment and its Conestoga wagon. (Both, courtesy of the Bethabara Collection.)

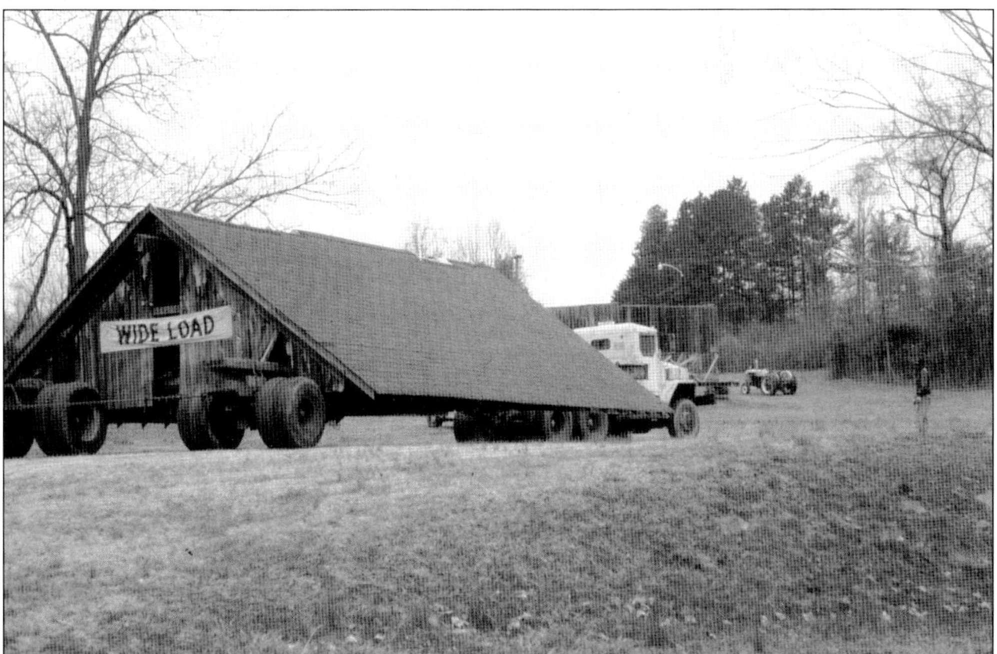

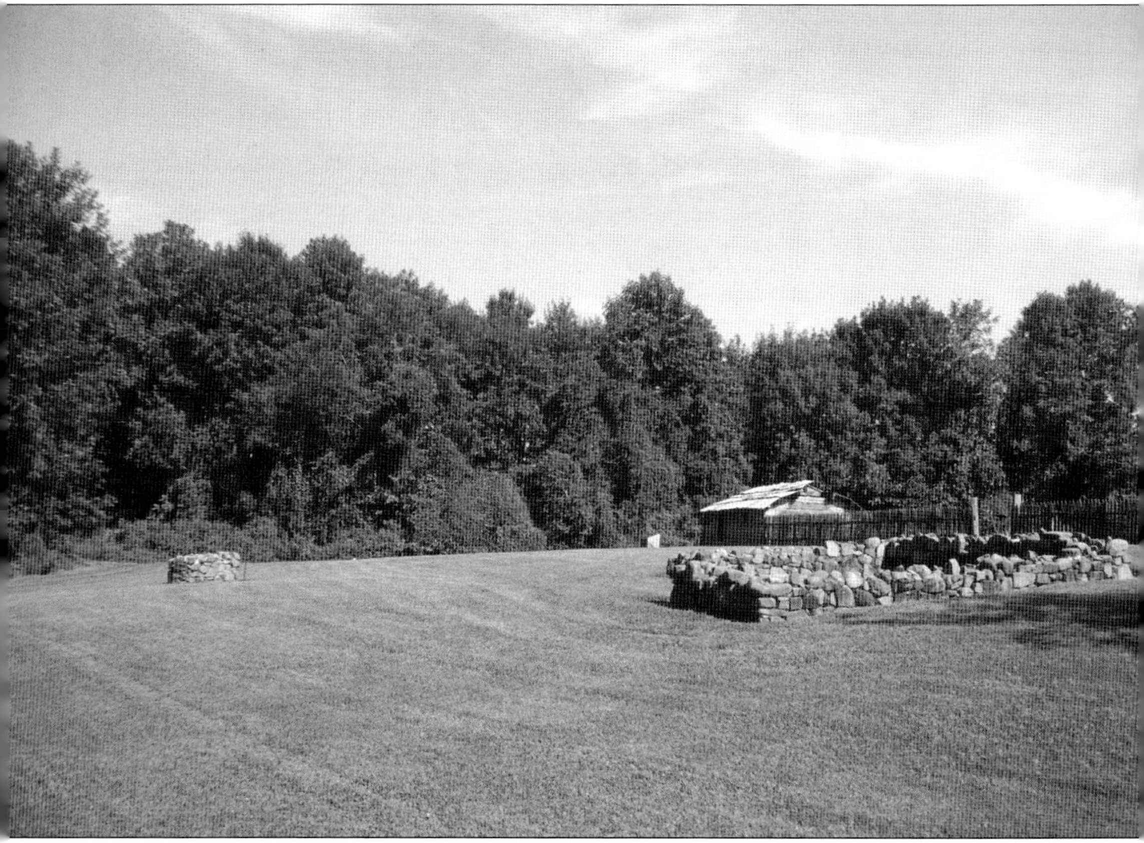

This undated photograph captures the area of the original 1754 settlement. Shown here are a reconstruction of the Hans Wagner cabin and the 1903 marker, with the stabilized 1757 tavern cellar in the foreground. By the 1990s, reconstructions of original structures began taking shape at the site. In 1990, director J. Rodney Meyer used archaeological research to rebuild the grape arbor in the community garden, and in 1991, he rebuilt the Hans Wagner cabin. In 1996, Wake Forest University anthropology professor Ned Woodall, along with graduate students, found what they believed was the foundation of the original sleeping hall. These structures were harder to identify because they were not meant to be permanent like the buildings Stanley South uncovered during his 1963–1966 dig. Along with the sleeping quarters, Meyer oversaw the reconstruction of the cowhouse, the washhouse, the bake oven, and the dogtrot that housed both a storage building and lodging for non-Moravians. (Courtesy of the City-County Planning Division.)

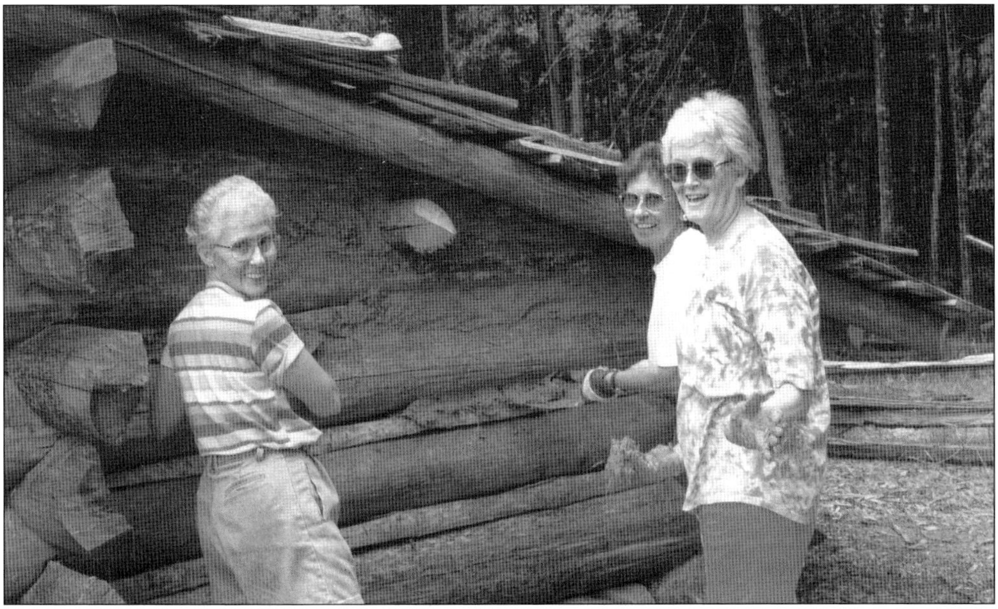

These c. 1996–1997 images capture members of the Beroth family working on the reconstruction of the 1754 village. Above, Mallie Beroth Graham is featured on the far right; below, from left to right are Allen Beroth, Charles Beroth, and Vernice Beroth Jr. The Beroth family's ancestor was one of the original settlers who came to Bethabara. Director J. Rodney Meyer approached the family about becoming involved in the reconstruction. In a *Winston-Salem Journal* article, Vernice V. Beroth Sr. stated, "I said I would have to talk to some of the relatives about it. We had a meeting, and they started saying things they would give—logs and rails and labor." The Beroth family held several workdays at the site as well as a family reunion, where Beroths from all over the country came to help with the project. (Both, courtesy of the Bethabara Collection.)

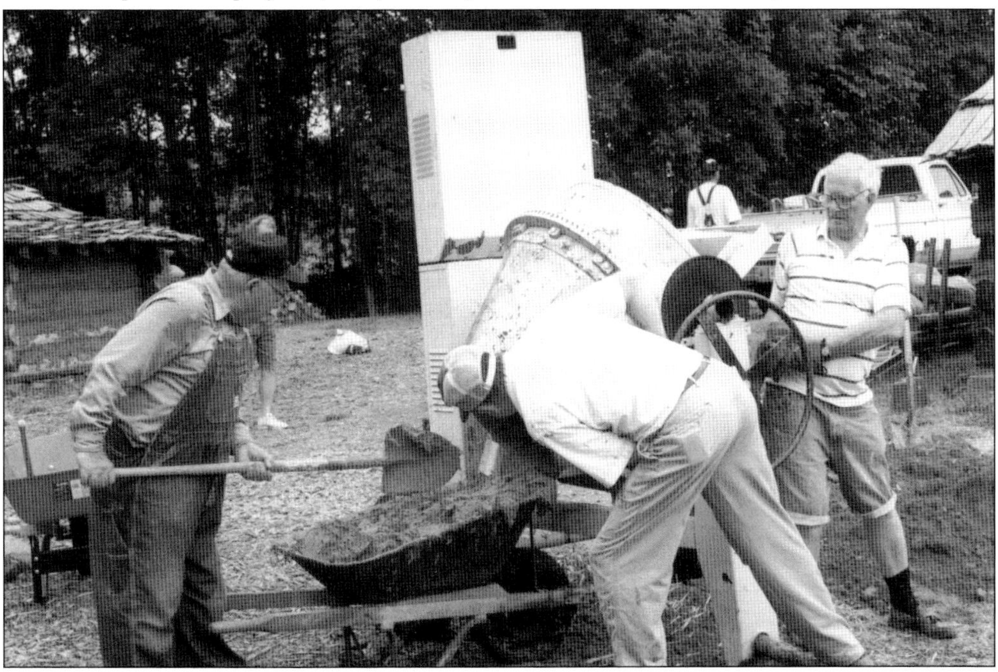

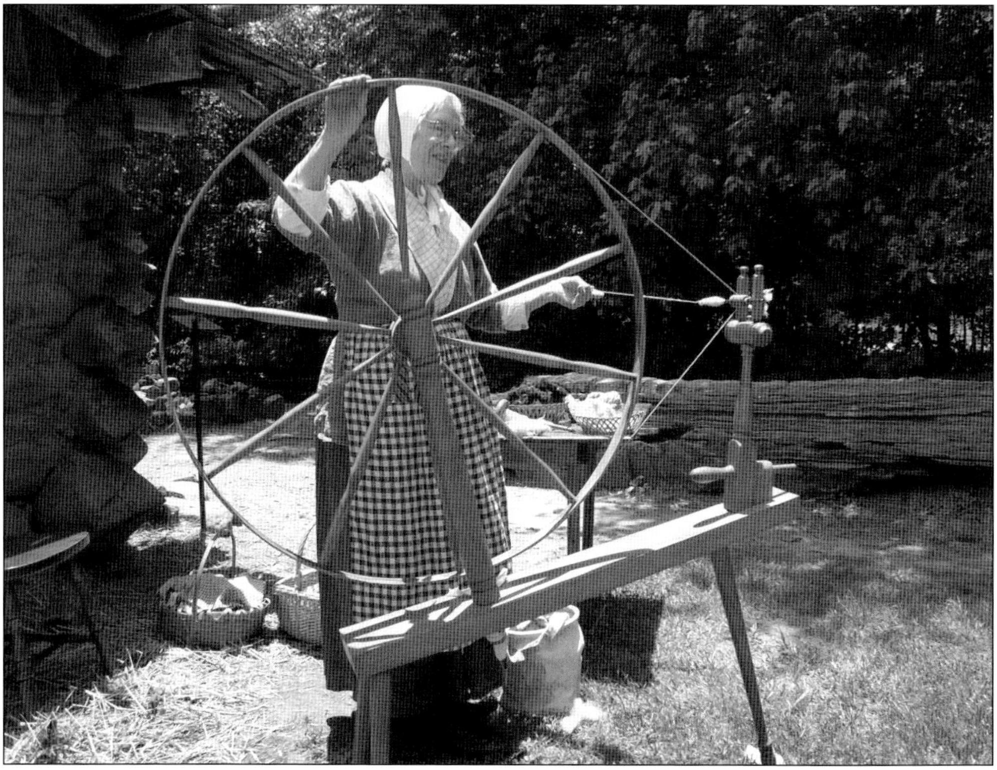

Once the reconstructed village was complete, it was used for school tours as well as special events. These two photographs were taken during a French and Indian War encampment event in the summer of 2011. Above, tour guide Linda Frey demonstrates spinning wool next to the cowhouse. Below, tour guide Vince McHenry shows how to use a draw knife on a shave horse he built. Visitors stopped by throughout the day to learn more about the Moravians and their daily lives. (Both, courtesy of the Bethabara Collection.)

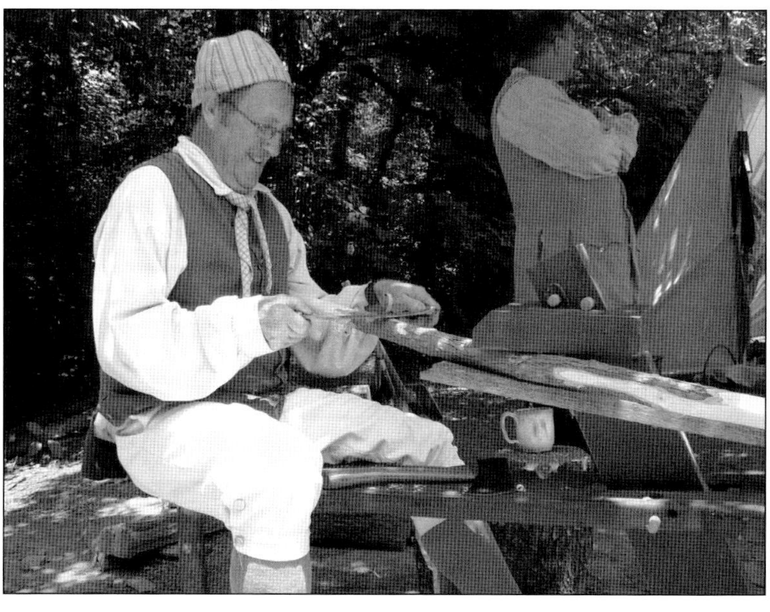

The photograph at right was taken during the 2009 French and Indian War encampment event. The garrison from Fort Dobbs State Historic Site in Statesville came to Historic Bethabara Park to discuss their site's role in the conflict as well as their interactions with the Moravians. Fort Dobbs site manager Scott Douglas (left) speaks to visitors while the other soldiers, including Patrick Morton (right), prepare to fire their weapons. The French and Indian War played a major role in the development of Bethabara and delayed the construction of Salem. The photograph below was taken during the 2019 British Occupation of Wachovia event, which chronicled Gen. Charles Cornwallis's army's visit to Bethabara. (Both, courtesy of the Bethabara Collection.)

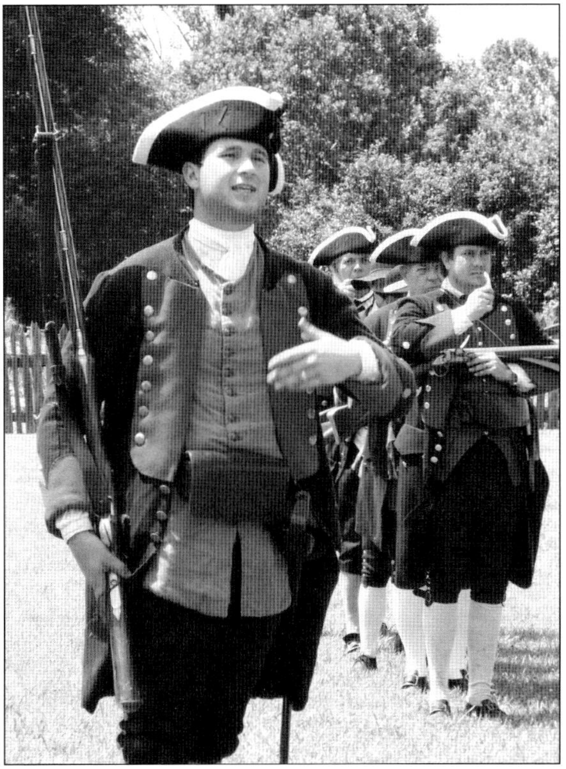

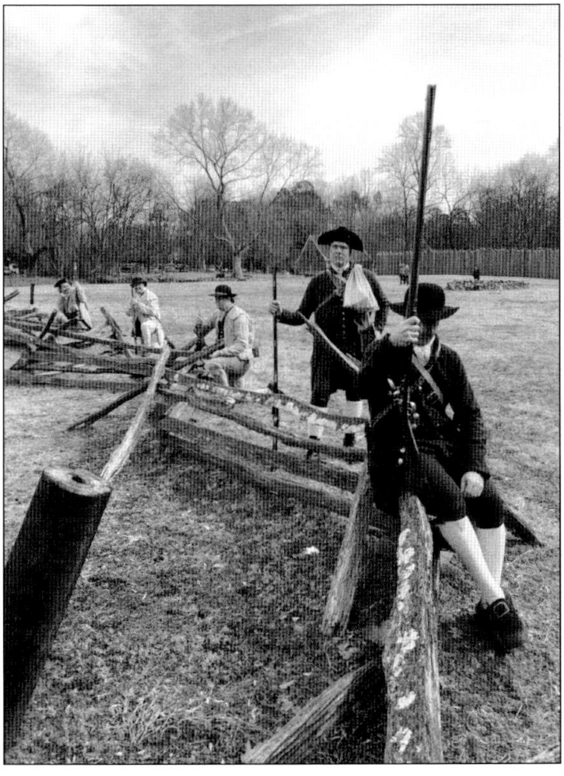

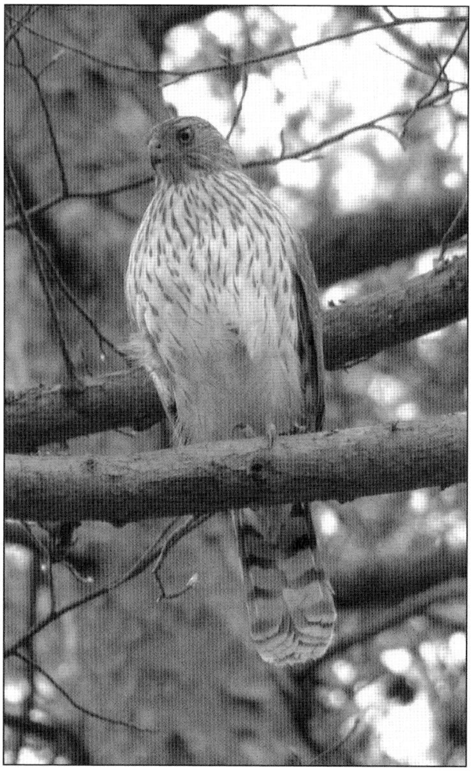

In addition to its history, Historic Bethabara Park also draws visitors to its nature trails. These trails were first cut by archaeologist Stanley South's team in the 1960s. Bird watchers, including members of the Audubon Society, come to Bethabara to see a wide variety of bird species, including the Cooper's hawk featured in the photograph at left, taken by Katherine Thorington. Historic Bethabara Park has offered a children's summer birding program for many years, which can be seen in the 2008 image below. Participants learn about birds they can spot in their own backyards before going on a birding expedition around the park with tour guides. (Both, courtesy of the Bethabara Collection.)

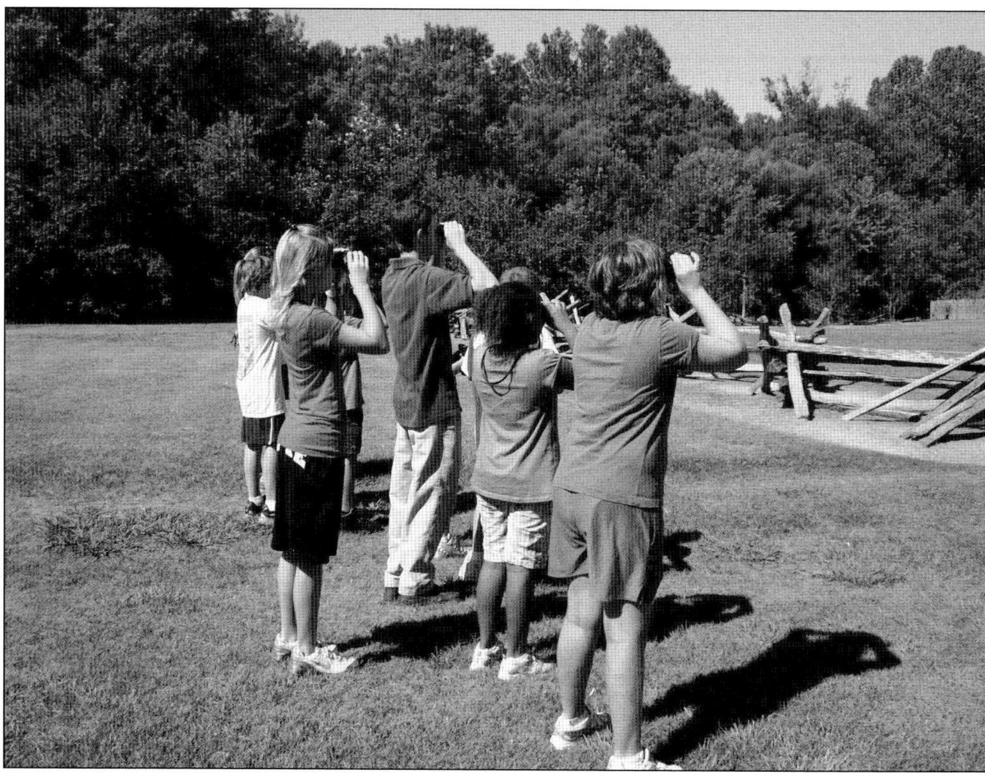

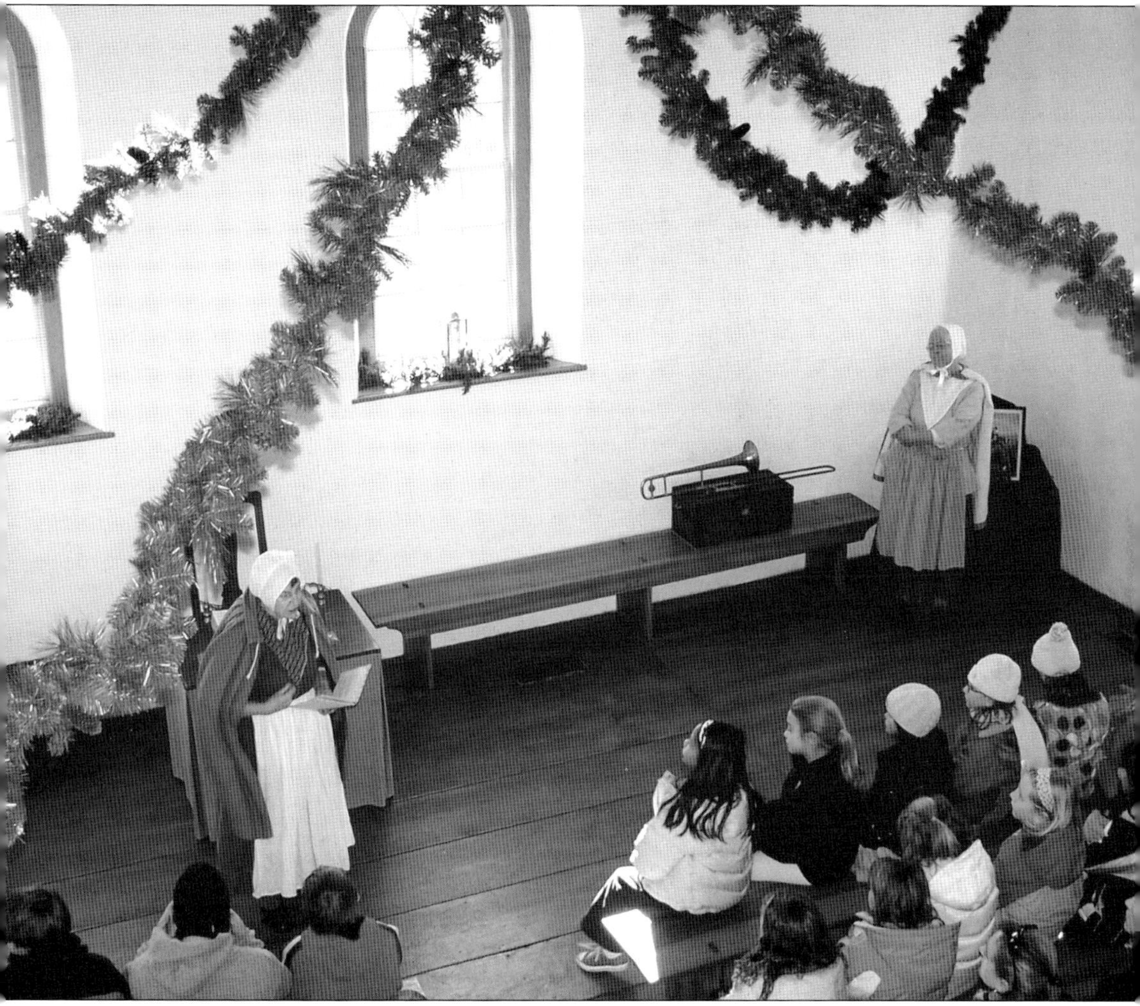

This 2010 image, taken from the balcony of the Saal in the Gemeinhaus, shows tour guides Barbara Giesler (left) and Henrietta Church (right) conducting a Christmas tour for a school group. The students begin their tour in the Saal and hear a Christmas story complete with a trombone prop. Other school tours given throughout the year include lower elementary tours, which are about everyday life in Bethabara and include colonial games, counting in German, and trying on 18th-century clothes. Upper elementary tours take place in the reconstructed 1754 village. Students learn what it took to create a town in the backcountry of North Carolina through hands-on activities like plowing, shingling a roof, and working with tools. (Courtesy of the Bethabara Collection.)

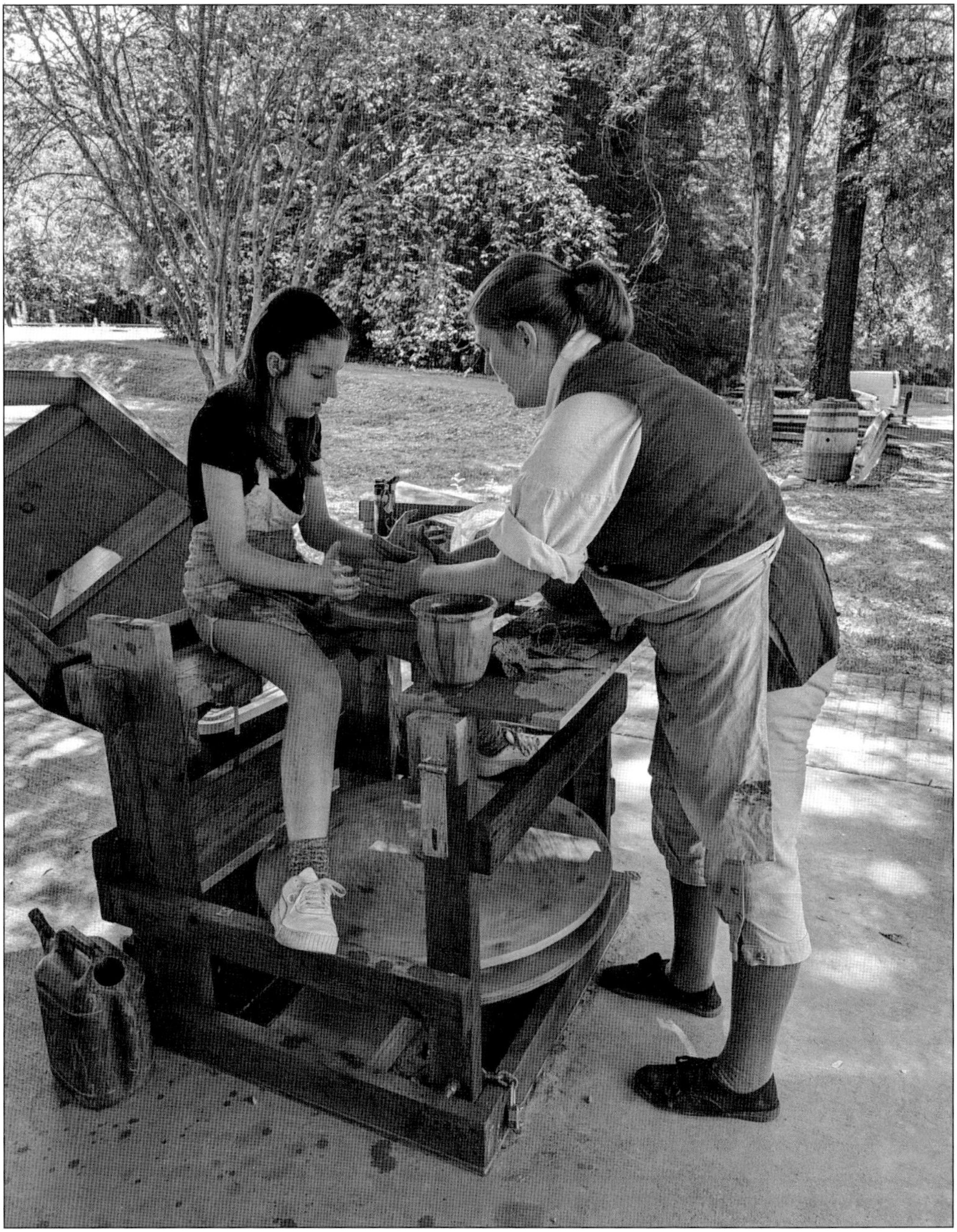

Historic Bethabara Park's Young Apprentices Program began in 2021. A weeklong camp for 12- to 15-year-olds, the Young Apprentices Program gives participants the opportunity to connect with history in a hands-on way. The program expanded on Historic Bethabara Park's mission to provide "hands-on-history" opportunities to the public. During the week, participants get a chance to learn from tour guides who are skilled at trades such as woodworking, blacksmithing, and pottery. Tour guide Hannah Browning teaches an apprentice how to throw and center clay on a kick wheel in this image taken during the 2024 Young Apprentices camp. At the end of the week, participants help a tour guide prepare an 18th-century meal to celebrate their achievements. (Courtesy of the Bethabara Collection.)

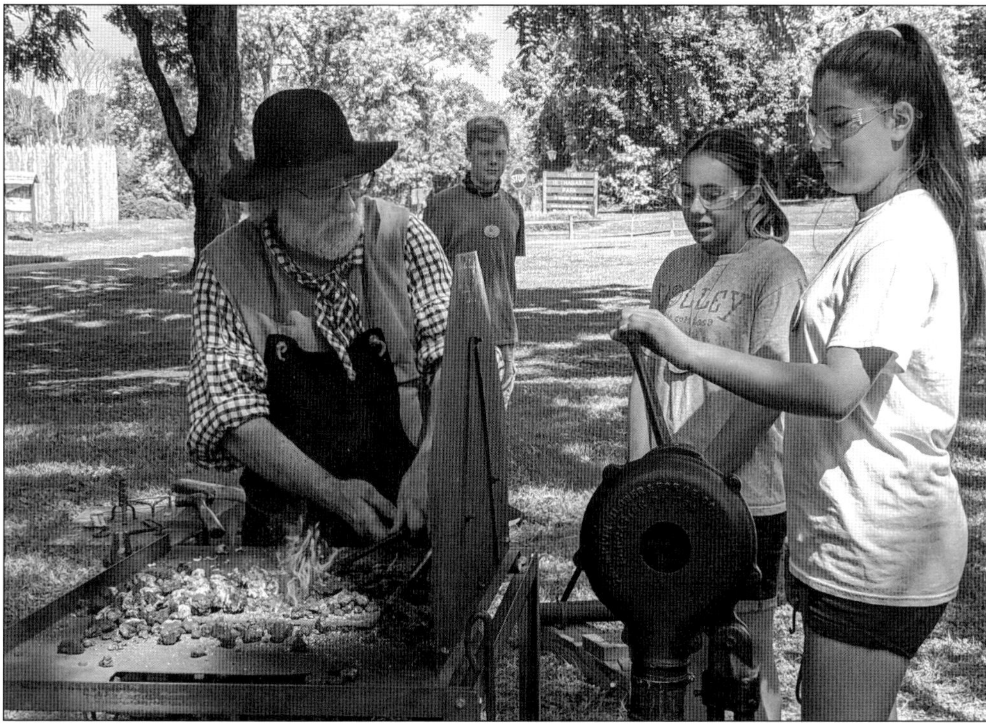

This photograph was captured during the first Young Apprentices Program in the summer of 2021. Bethabara blacksmith Keith Roberts teaches two apprentices how to make a decorative S-hook. Apprentices had to keep air blowing on the coals to maintain the appropriate temperature that makes metal malleable. Each apprentice got to take their creation home with them. (Courtesy of the Bethabara Collection.)

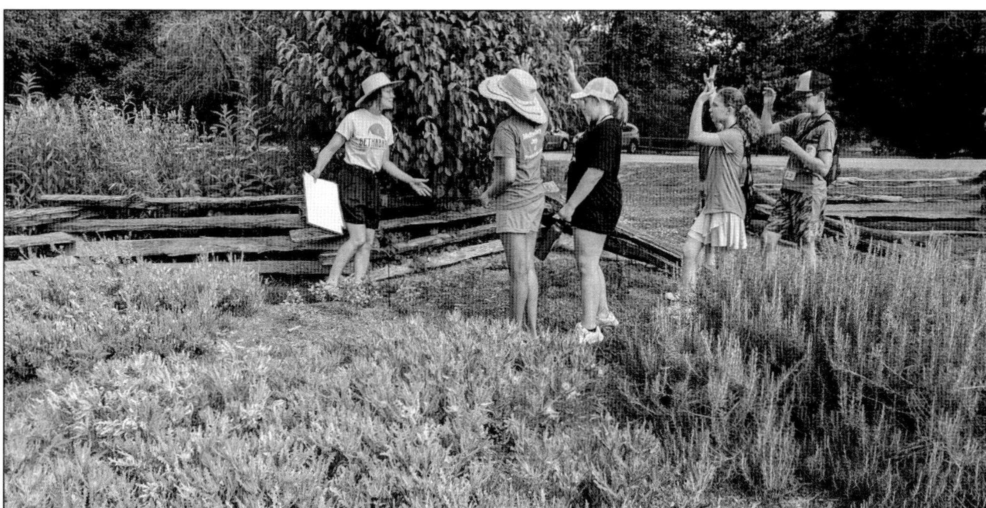

In 2024, the Young Apprentices Program introduced a new experience. Apprentices got to spend a morning in the reconstructed 1761 medicinal garden. They learned about plants and their medicinal uses from tour guide Amanda Lindsey, photographed here with a group of apprentices. Each participant received a book to write and sketch their observations about each plant. (Courtesy of the Bethabara Collection.)

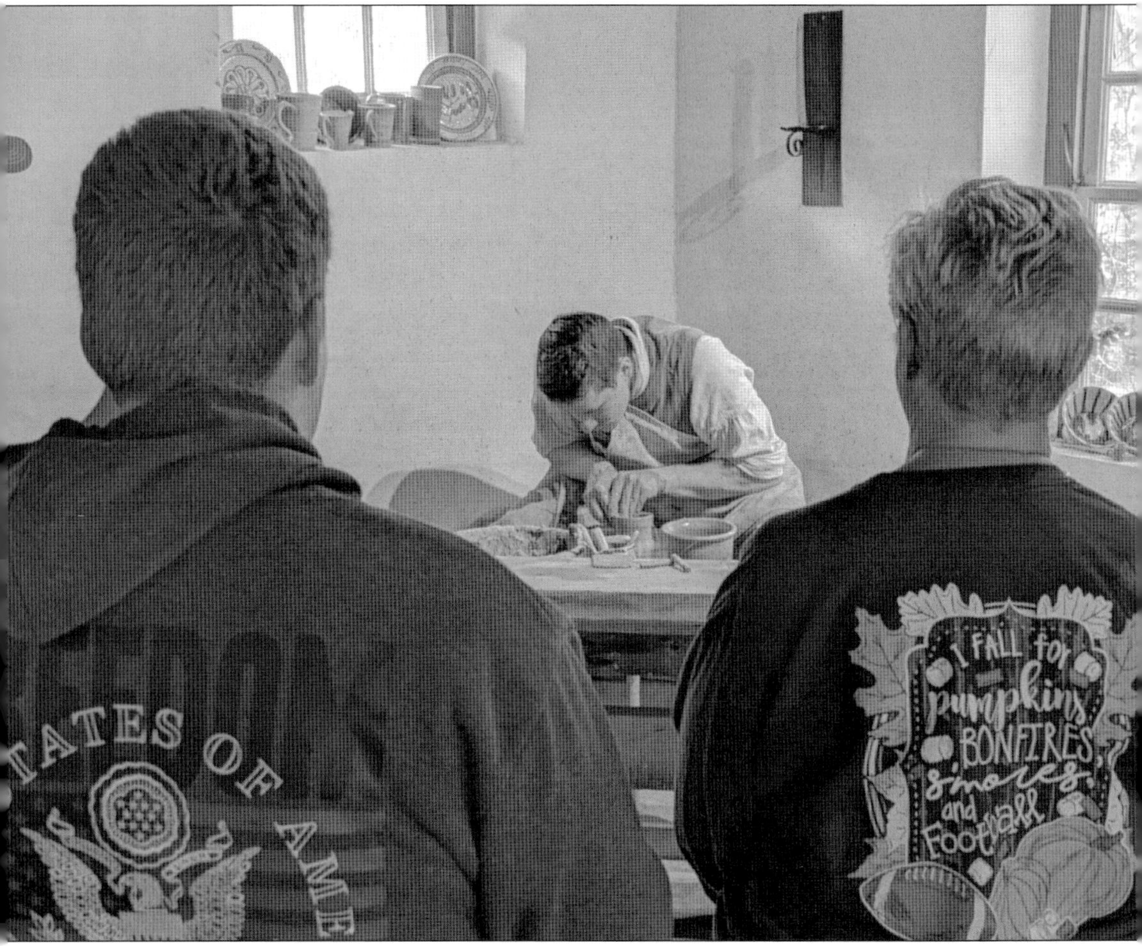

Historic Bethabara Park hosts several events throughout the season, including Apple Fest, where this photograph was taken in 2022. Bethabara events always feature historical elements, including demonstrations from tour guide staff. In this photograph, tour guide Stuart Marshall works on a piece of pottery while talking with visitors. In the 2010s, Marshall created a pottery program at the site so that visitors could watch tour guides throw pottery on a weekly basis. He studied the forms made by Gottfried Aust and Rudolph Christ and duplicated them on Historic Bethabara Park's two kick wheels. Marshall even dug clay in the same spot Aust did. Pottery was an integral part of Bethabara's economy, and demonstrating the art to the public teaches them how much work and skill was involved. A kiln was purchased so that items could be fired on-site and sold in the gift shop, just as the original potters sold their items in Bethabara's community store. (Courtesy of the Bethabara Collection.)

This 2023 photograph features tour guide Hannah Browning demonstrating candle making outside the visitor center. Since 2021, Historic Bethabara Park has held regular hands-on history demonstrations outside for the public. These free demonstrations give visitors the opportunity to experience skills that are no longer widely used and to see how they were practiced by the Moravians living in 18th-century Bethabara. Browning researched and created Bethabara's candle-making demonstration. (Courtesy of the Bethabara Collection.)

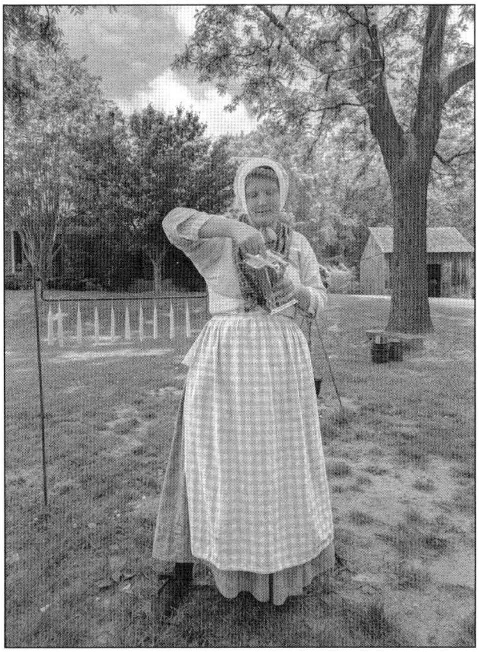

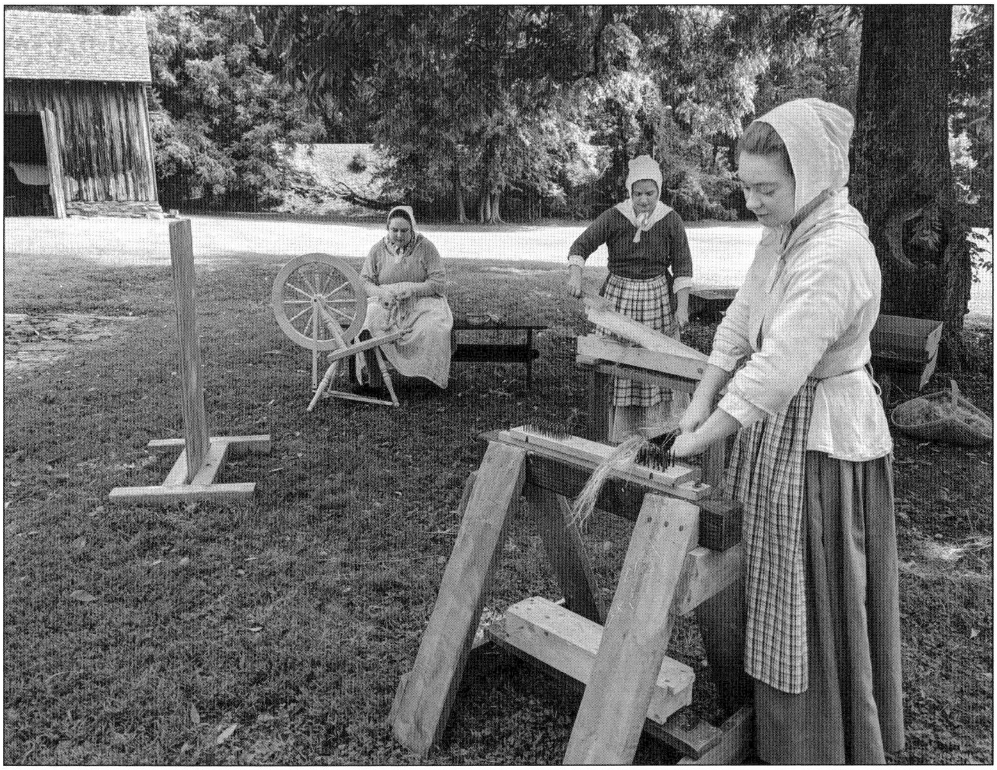

This photograph, taken in 2021, shows the process of breaking flax so that it can be made into linen thread. From left to right are tour guides Kait Dodd, Christina Wheeler, and DeLayne Jolly. Dodd spins flax while Wheeler uses a flax brake to crush the husk of the plant. Jolly uses hackles or combs to process the flax into fiber that is ready for spinning. (Courtesy of the Bethabara Collection.)

Bibliography

Chapman, Sarah Bahnson. *Bright and Gloomy Days: The Civil War Correspondence of Captain Charles Frederic Bahnson, a Moravian Confederate*. Knoxville: University of Tennessee Press, 2003.

Compton, Stephen C. *North Carolina's Moravian Potters: The Art and Mystery of Pottery-Making in Wachovia*. Mount Pleasant, SC: History Press, 2019.

Crews, C. Daniel, and Lisa D. Bailey. *Records of the Moravians in North Carolina*. Vols. 12 and 13. Raleigh: Office of Archives and History, North Carolina Department of Cultural Resources, 2000–2006.

Fries, Adelaide L. *Records of the Moravians in North Carolina*. Vols. 1–7. Raleigh: State Department of Archives and History, 1922–1947.

Hamilton, Kenneth G. *Records of the Moravians in North Carolina*. Vol. 10 and 11. Raleigh: State Department of Archives and History, 1966–1969.

Journal and Sentinel (Winston-Salem)

Morris, David R. *Permanence of the House of Passage: The Establishment of Historic Bethabara Park, Winston-Salem, North Carolina*. Winston-Salem: Wake Forest University, 1994.

Rights, Douglas L. *Records of the Moravians in North Carolina*. Vol. 8. Raleigh: State Department of Archives and History, 1954.

Sensbach, Jon F. *A Separate Canaan: The Making of an Afro-Moravian World in North Carolina, 1763–1840*. Williamsburg, Chapel Hill: Omohundro Institute of Early American History and the University of North Carolina Press, 1998.

Smith, Minnie J. *Records of the Moravians in North Carolina*. Vol. 9. Raleigh: State Department of Archives and History, 1964.

South, Stanley. *Historical Archaeology in Wachovia: Excavating Eighteenth-Century Bethabara and Moravian Pottery*. New York: Kluwer Academic/Plenum Publishers, 1999.

Thorp, Daniel B. *The Moravian Community in Colonial North Carolina: Pluralism on the Southern Frontier*. Knoxville: University of Tennessee Press, 1989.

Union Republican (Winston-Salem)

Wachovia Moravian

Winston-Salem Journal

About Historic Bethabara Park

Since 1970, Historic Bethabara Park has been operated by the City of Winston-Salem with the support of the nonprofit group Historic Bethabara Park Inc. The site sits on 183 acres of land that encompasses the original settlement of Bethabara. Two trails run through the park, which is certified by the National Wildlife Federation as a refuge for unique birds, animals, reptiles, and plants. Historic Bethabara Park is in the National Register of Historic Places and is a national historic landmark. The historic district consists of four restored historic buildings ranging from 1782 to 1834, a reconstructed palisade fort, stabilized cellar ruins of the original town, a reconstructed 1754 village, and reconstructed community and medicinal gardens. Visitors can enjoy hands-on history trades demonstrations and tours of the site throughout the year. During Historic Bethabara Park's main season from April to December, special events, including Hands on History Day, Apple Fest, and Christmas at Bethabara, are held. Thousands of schoolchildren visit the site each year to experience what life was like in 18th-century Bethabara. To learn more about Historic Bethabara Park and what the site has to offer, visit historicbethabara.org.

Consistent with our mission to preserve history on a local level, this book was printed in South Carolina on American-made paper and manufactured entirely in the United States. Products carrying the accredited Forest Stewardship Council (FSC) label are printed on 100 percent FSC-certified paper.

MADE IN THE USA